*Utopianism and Radicalism
in a Reforming America*

**Recent Titles in
Contributions in American History**

Utopianism and Radicalism in a Reforming America

1888–1918

FRANCIS ROBERT SHOR

Contributions in American History, Number 178

Greenwood Press
Westport, Connecticut • London

Library of Congress Cataloging-in-Publication Data

Shor, Francis Robert.
    Utopianism and radicalism in a reforming America : 1888–1918 /
Francis Robert Shor.
        p. cm. — (Contributions in American history, ISSN 0084–9219
; no. 178)
    Includes bibliographical references (p.) and index.
    ISBN 0–313–30379–7 (alk. paper)
    1. Socialism—United States—History. 2. Utopias—United States—
History. 3. Radicalism—United States—History. 4. Social
problems—United States—History. 5. Social action—United States—
History. 6. United States—Social conditions. 7. United States—
Economic conditions. I. Title. II. Series.
HX83.S56   1997
335′.00973—dc21   97–9380

British Library Cataloguing in Publication Data is available.

Library of Congress Catalog Card Number: 97–9380
ISBN: 0–313–30379–7
ISSN: 0084–9219

First published in 1997

Greenwood Press, 88 Post Road West, Westport, CT 06881
An imprint of Greenwood Publishing Group, Inc.

Printed in the United States of America

The paper used in this book complies with the
Permanent Paper Standard issued by the National
Information Standards Organization (Z39.48–1984).

10 9 8 7 6 5 4 3 2 1

Copyright Acknowledgments

The author and the publisher are grateful to the following for granting permission to reprint from their materials:

Excerpts from Francis Shor, "The Ideological Matrix of Reform in Late Nineteenth Century America and New Zealand: Reading Bellamy's *Looking Backward*," *Prospects* 17 (1992): 29–58, reprinted with the permission of Cambridge University Press.

Excerpts reprinted in part from "Power, Gender, and Ideological Discourse in *The Iron Heel*," by Francis Shor, from *Rereading Jack London*, edited by Leonard Cassuto and Jeanne Campbell Reesman, with the permission of the publishers, Stanford University Press. © 1996 by the Board of Trustees of the Leland Stanford Junior University.

Excerpts from Francis Shor, "*The Iron Heel*'s Marginal(ized) Utopia," *Extrapolation* 35 (Fall 1994): 211–29, reprinted with permission of The Kent State University Press.

Excerpts from Francis Shor, "Contradictory Tendencies in the Emergence of American Socialism and the Utopian Ruskin Colony of Tennessee," *Journal of American Culture* 12 (Winter 1989): 21–27, appear courtesy of the *Journal of American Culture*.

To my parents and grandparents,
who kept hope alive in the past.

To my wife and daughters,
who keep hope alive in the present
and for the future.

Contents

Part II Utopianism and Radicalism in Political and Communal Projects

Acknowledgments

Because of its long gestation and the help of numerous midwives, the birthing of this book has many to thank:

For help in securing sabbatical time in the winter of 1995 and grants from the Humanities Center and the Research and Sponsored Program Office in order to pursue research, thanks to Wayne State University.

For assistance with that research, thanks to the staff at the Huntington Library and at the Purdy Library and Walter Reuther Archives at Wayne State University.

For suggestions, materials, and commentary about the various subjects covered in the book, thanks to Paul Buhle, Carol Kolmerten, Kathryne Lindberg, Jeanne Campbell Reesman, Lyman Tower Sargent, Gary Scharnhorst, and Csaba Toth.

For aid in the preparation of the text, including the typing and transferring of disks from one computer to another, thanks to LaJoyce Jones, Crystal Lomax, Tom Moeller, David Nelson, and especially to Gail Ryder, who brought everything together with tremendous skill and perseverance.

For help in securing the book contract with Greenwood and assistance along the way, thanks to John Dan Eades and Karen D. Treat.

For copyediting the manuscript, thanks to Ouida Taylor.

And finally, for everything else that sustained me, my special loving thanks to my wife, Barbara.

Introduction: "A Better World's in Birth"

Arise, ye prisoners of starvation!
Arise, ye wretched of the earth!
For Justice thunders condemnation.
A better world's in birth.
—*Internationale*

The whole world is coming.
A nation is coming, a nation is coming.
The Eagle has brought the message to the tribe.
—*Sioux Ghost Dance*

On the eve of the meeting of the Second International in Paris in 1889, delegates were very likely singing the stirring verses of the *Internationale*. Instilled with a critique of the present and a utopian vision of the future that offered a better life for workers everywhere, the words articulated the hopes of a rising power in the industrial world. While the vision would inspire the delegates to the Second International and become an anthem of the international left, the badly splintered radical forces would find it difficult to cohere as a movement of international solidarity. In that same year, thousands of miles away on the plains of North America, in response to what appeared to be an inexorable march of "civilization" and the extermination of native peoples, members of the Sioux nation gathered to await the return of the buffalo and the disappearance of their white antagonists. Instead, a year later thousands of U.S. troops were dispatched into Sioux country to eliminate the threat of the Ghost Dancers. The vision that had led a desperate people to attempt a utopian project of cultural revitalization met the same predictable murderous response that had massacred the buffalo and their proud protagonists.[1] Between Paris and the plains of North America there resonated a belief that, in the midst of turmoil and suffering, a new world might emerge that would provide a refuge for the oppressed.

Certainly, the conflicts evident in Europe and the United States in the 1880s did give birth to ideas and movements that promised a better life in the future.[2] Among those ideas and movements that took root in the United States was the eight-hour day. In a short span of three days at the beginning of May 1886, workers and police in Chicago clashed as a consequence of agitation over the eight-hour day, resulting in deaths on both sides and a national panic over the "Haymarket Riot."[3] To the east, in Chicopee Falls, Massachusetts, Edward Bellamy, fearful of the fury unleashed at Haymarket, started writing a novel about an American future that would transcend the violent conflict of contending forces. When *Looking Backward* was published in 1888, it became a lightning rod for the revival of utopian hopes, generating a thirty-year period (from 1888 to 1918) of reform and radical change.

Reform and radical change have been fundamental components of the political and cultural environment in America. As one study has suggested, reform in America is "the continuing frontier," with one critical element of that reform being the desire to effectuate a radical alteration of society.[4] This effort to reconstruct one's environment is, in turn, fundamental to the utopian element in American life. In his introduction to an anthology of utopias in America, Robert Fogarty avows: "The belief that men (and women) could remake their institutions by 'reasoned choice' has been central to American ideology."[5] The ideological underpinnings of utopianism in America are also embedded in the sense that the nation from its inception had a "special destiny."[6] As one historian has noted: "Guilty Calvinism and innocent utopianism mixed strangely together in virtually every American radical reform movement from the seventeenth century."[7]

While the thread of this utopian impulse and radical reform has run throughout American history, one cannot neglect how historical factors have shaped the emergence of utopianism in specific periods. Historical dislocations caused by the long wave of economic crises, as well as political and social conflicts rooted in increasing urbanization and industrial modernization, have created a broad epistemic context within which utopian aspirations have resonated.[8] When economic crises and social conflicts have engendered questions about the legitimacy of the dominant moral and political universe, as in the period from 1888 to 1918, utopianism and radicalism have gained prominence. Encompassing the aftermath of the Haymarket Affair, the emergence of labor struggles, the women's movement, ethnic and racial clashes, and wars, various utopian and radical ideas and movements contended for political allegiance.

Locating those ideas and movements within a shifting and contested political and cultural terrain where class, race, and gender come into play provides a framework for examining the specific articulations of utopianism and radicalism encountered during this period. It is the purpose of the essays in this book to analyze how political formations (socialism, feminism, black nationalism, anarchism, and syndicalism) and discursive practices (liberty and equality for women, blacks, and workers) reflected and refracted the multiple forms of utopianism and radicalism in a reforming America. The book is divided into two sections representing the three major forms of utopianism: (1) literary expressions; and (2) political and communal projects. In Part I, "Utopianism and Radicalism in Literary Expressions," both well-known and little-known texts and their interpretive communities will be examined in order to determine how a utopian discourse informed radical and reform ideas and practices during the period 1888–1918. In Part II, "Utopianism and Radicalism in Political and Communal Projects," movements encompassing communal experiments and cultural/political projects will be explored in order to determine their impact on those involved and the larger community. Taken as a whole, these essays attempt to probe how significant utopianism and radicalism were in the reforming of America.

One crucial formulation in determining the role of utopianism and radicalism during this period is an understanding of the fashioning of the hegemonic field where discursive practices and political formations develop. Thus, instead of seeing utopianism as "incongruous with the state of reality within which it occurs," an interpretive framework is needed which distinguishes how the context influences conflicting norms and values that constitute those discursive practices and political formations.[9] Central to identifying that context is the conceptualization of hegemony advanced by the Italian Marxist Antonio Gramsci and interpolated by British literary and social historian Raymond Williams, especially in the development of the distinction between alternative and oppositional formations.[10] (Further discussion of Gramsci and Williams on hegemony will be found throughout, but especially in Chapters 1 and 6.) The emphasis on alternative and oppositional politics and culture not only provides an understanding of the dialectical tension between reality and utopianism, but also offers an interpretive framework for analyzing the interpenetration of utopianism and radicalism during any particular historical period.

It is generally agreed that the period from 1888 to 1918 was a period of intense reform in America. For some historians those reforms were contained within political movements intended to restore order and economic rationalization.[11] However, this overdetermined political reading of the period diminishes our understanding of how the period represented a strategic conflict over norms and values where utopian and radical discourse could find a hearing, albeit one filled with various contradictions.[12] As we will see with the examples of utopianism and radicalism that follow, the construction of oppositional and alternative discursive practices, political formations, and cultural movements during the period from 1888 to 1918 interacted with hegemonic power in ways that led to reform and reformulation of that power. Thus, utopianism, as a critique of dominant values and norms and as a longing for a society based on harmony, invested radicalism during this time with a desire and hope for social redemption and political renewal. It was a time when many believed—in the words of the *Internationale*—"*a better world's in birth.*"

NOTES

1. For a concise view of the Ghost Dance, see Frederick Turner, *Beyond Geography: The Western Spirit Against the Wilderness* (New York: Viking, 1980), pp. 289–95.

2. For an overview of those ideas and movements for social change in Europe and the United States, see E. J. Hobsbawm, *The Age of Empire, 1875–1914* (New York: Vintage, 1989), esp. pp. 84–141 and 192–218; also see James T. Kloppenberg, *Uncertain Victory: Social Democracy and Progressivism in European and American Thought, 1870–1920* (New York: Oxford University Press, 1986).

3. For a concise overview of the eight-hour agitation and the May Days in Chicago, see Jeremy Brecher, *Strike* (San Francisco: Straight Arrow Press, 1972), pp. 36–50. The most complete discussion of the Haymarket Riot can be found in Paul Avrich, *The Haymarket Tragedy* (Princeton: Princeton University Press, 1984).

4. Robert H. Walker, *Reform in America: The Continuing Frontier* (Lexington: University Press of Kentucky, 1985); on the radical alteration of society, see pp. 152–53.

5. *American Utopianism*, ed. Robert S. Fogarty (Itasca, Ill.: E. F. Peacock, 1972), ix.

6. Krishan Kumar, *Utopia and Anti-Utopia in Modern Times* (New York: Basil Blackwell, 1987), p. 81. Also see Ernest L. Tuveson, *Redeemer Nation: The Idea of America's Millennial Role* (Chicago: University of Chicago Press, 1968).

7. Paul Buhle, *Marxism in the United States: Remapping the History of the American Left* (London: Verso, 1987), p. 59.

8. For an intriguing, albeit overdetermined, application of economic analysis to the historical waves of utopian thought and communal experiments in America, see Michael Barkun, "Communal Societies and Cyclical Phenomena," *Communal Societies* 4 (1984): 35–48; and Brian J. L. Berry, *America's Utopian Experiments: Communal Havens from Log-Wave Crisis* (Hanover, N.H.: University Press of New England, 1992). On the impact of the international economy on utopian literature, see Edgar Kiser and Kriss A. Drass, "Changes in the Core of the World System and the Production of Utopian Literature in Great Britain and the United States, 1883–1975," *American Sociological Review* 52 (April 1987): 286–93.

9. Karl Mannheim, *Ideology and Utopia*, trans. Louis Wirth and Edward Shils (New York: Harvest, 1936), p. 192. For a critique of Mannheim's positivistic and undialectical approach to utopianism in particular and the sociology of knowledge in general, see Martin G. Plattel, *Utopian and Critical Thinking* (Pittsburgh: Duquesne University Press, 1972), esp. pp. 66 and 77; also see Barbara Goodwin and Keith Taylor, *The Politics of Utopia: A Study in Theory and Practice* (New York: St. Martin's Press, 1982), pp. 77–80; and Theodor W. Adorno, "The Sociology of Knowledge and Its Consciousness," in *The Essential Frankfurt School Reader*, ed. Andrew Arato and Elkie Gebhardt (New York: Urizen Books, 1978), pp. 452–65.

10. Raymond Williams, *Marxism and Literature* (Oxford: Oxford University Press, 1977), pp. 108–14. For a brilliant use of Williams's distinction between oppositional and alternative formations, see Roy Rosenzweig, *Eight Hours for What We Will: Workers and Leisure in an Industrial City, 1870–1920* (Cambridge: Cambridge University Press, 1983), pp. 64, 189, 223–24, and *passim*.

11. Robert H. Wiebe, *The Search for Order, 1877–1920* (New York: Hill and Wang, 1967); also see Gabriel Kolko, *The Triumph of Conservatism* (Chicago: Quadrangle Books, 1963).

12. Studies of this period that take account of the contested and contradictory political and cultural terrain can be found, for example, in Peter Conn, *The Divided Mind: Ideology and Imagination in America, 1898–1917* (Cambridge: Cambridge University Press, 1983); Robert M. Crunden, *Ministers of Reform: The Progressives' Achievement in American Civilization, 1889–1920* (New York: Basic Books, 1982); Alan Dawley, *Struggles for Justice: Social Responsibility and the Liberal State* (Cambridge, Mass.: The Belknap Press of Harvard University Press, 1991), esp. pp. 17–294; Aileen Kraditor, *The Radical Persuasion, 1890–1917* (Baton Rouge: Louisiana State University Press, 1981); T. J. Jackson Lears, *No Place of Grace:*

Antimodernism and the Transformation of American Culture, 1880–1920
(New York: Pantheon, 1981); and Alan Trachtenberg, *The Incorporation of America: Culture and Politics in the Gilded Age* (New York: Hill and Wang, 1982).

Part I

Utopianism and Radicalism in Literary Expressions

The Ideological Matrix of Reform in Late Nineteenth-Century America: Reading Bellamy's Looking Backward

The late nineteenth century witnessed the beginnings of a profound transformation of political culture in the industrialized world. With the rise of reform movements concerned with labor, religion, women's rights, and a host of other matters, the winds of change blew around the globe.[1] In the United States the idea of and movement for reform emerged from a political culture that periodically resonated to calls for democratic change. Such calls were made even more urgent in late nineteenth-century America by crises in the legitimacy of the political, economic, and social systems buffeted by rapid demographic shifts.

In order to reconstitute the political culture of reform in late nineteenth-century America, I want to offer a model of cultural diffusion that can account for the production and predominance of ideological and discursive elements in a particular sociohistorical context. Part I will develop such a model and apply it to the currents of reform in America. Part II will look at how these ideological and discursive elements were embedded in the reader response to Edward Bellamy's utopian novel, Looking Backward. Because it was so widely read and discussed, Looking Backward provides an excellent vehicle through which to deconstruct and reconstruct the semiotic and political environment surrounding the novel and the ideologies of reform existent in the period.[2]

CULTURE AND IDEOLOGY IN THE
MATRIX OF REFORM

In order to explore the cultural and ideological dimensions of reform in late nineteenth-century America, it will be necessary first to consider theoretical models that account for the transmission and diffusion of culture and ideology. Such models, derived from quantum physics and the political philosophy of Antonio Gramsci, can account for the dynamic complexity and contradictions involved in such a transmission and diffusion. After outlining the interconnections of these theoretical models, I will move to a specific delineation and discussion of the cultural and ideological currents of reform at the end of the nineteenth century.

The model from quantum physics that seems particularly appropriate to the dynamic operation of ideas is known as the S-Matrix theory. The S-Matrix theory was first propounded by Werner Heisenberg to describe in terms of mathematical probabilities the interactions of subatomic particles which could, in turn, account for the indeterminancy and uncertainty of their position and momentum. It has since been formalized into a mathematical approach to strong interactions that aspires to combine quantum and relativity field physics. For purposes of this chapter, I want to concentrate on a few specific (and simplified) characteristics of the S-Matrix theory of particle interactions. First of all, the field of the S-Matrix is one of constant interaction that highlights the diffusion and alteration of particles. Thus, what emerges from the S-Matrix field is not precisely what entered; rather, it is a charged variant of the interacting particles. In the process of diffusion and alteration particles pass through networks and reactions channels where their resonance with these channels results in this recharged variant. While there are many more complicated components of the S-Matrix theory, the previous emphasis affords a basis for constructing a parallel model of a cultural and ideological matrix.[3]

Just as particles are exposed to particular changes in the S-Matrix field, so particles of culture (or cultural currents) are diffused through an ideological matrix. In this sense, particles of culture can be defined as flows of consciousness generated and mediated by historical and social forces that give direction to life. The ideological matrix is the domain through which particles of culture are charged by power relations. Within this matrix contingent and polyvalent meanings are articulated in systems of representation (ideas, beliefs—in short, ideology) and crystallized in discursive codes and chains. The production of systems of representations takes place in an interconnected field of social formations, constituting what can be designated as ideological networks. Within these networks chains of discursive codes regularize such systems of representations by influencing their trajectory in overt and covert ways. In turn, individuals within this network act as reaction channels or conductors of rearticulation or disarticulation, thus serving to valorize contingent meanings in a positive and/or negative sense. The positive sense embodies the activation of these individuals and others to realize those ideas and beliefs, while the negative sense implies a discounting or excluding of alternative ideas and beliefs. (Thus, the role of human agency in the ideological matrix raises issues about the indeterminancy of meaning just as Heisenberg's Uncertainty Principle does about the influence of the observer on the trajectory of particles.) In effect, the ideological matrix becomes the critical passageway for those flows of consciousness that inform and normalize political culture.[4]

The normalization of any political culture within the ideological matrix underscores the role that the hegemonic process plays as the unifying principle within that ideological matrix.[5] In effect, the hegemonic process, as the force which determines the field of contesting meanings of ideology and the diffusion of discursive codes and chains, is equivalent to the unified field theory in quantum physics. However, just as with this unified field theory, so the hegemonic process remains both elusive and unstable.[6] It is forever undergoing a means of reconstitution as it attempts to unify and direct the constitutive components of culture and ideology. However, in seeking to unify and direct the constitutive components or particles of culture and ideology, hegemony becomes a strategic force, reflecting contending social formations. Such political contestation represents the effort to realize what Gramsci has called a "historic bloc." The primary component behind this effort is a "moral and intellectual bloc" that facilitates the fusion of cultural particles and ideological elements. In such a fusion, the role of intellectuals as conductors of rearticulation and disarticulation becomes critical. Ultimately, the hegemonic process is contingent upon the historical conjunction or cathexis of social forces, cultural particles, and ideological elements within a determinate matrix.[7]

Having examined the theoretical parameters of what constitutes a matrix, I want to turn now to the ways in which cultural particles or currents are, as it were, ideologized in this matrix. In particular, I want to focus on the convergence and transformation of specific cultural particles that flowed out of those sociohistorical forces in late nineteenth-century America and generated the discursive practices of reform. Through an elaboration of the cultural currents of modernism, Anglo-Saxon revitalization, and technological utopianism, specific discursive codes and ideological networks will be linked to the hegemonic process as it emanated from the ideological matrix of reform in late nineteenth-century America. Elucidating those cultural currents will also render a requisite backdrop to the reading of Bellamy's *Looking Backward*.

The sociohistorical processes of urbanization, industrialization, bureaucratization, and secularization not only unleashed a crisis of moral authority in the late nineteenth century, but also engendered the cultural particle of modernism. Modernism can be defined as the self-consciousness and self-absorption of the values and norms propagated by modernization and its teleological push toward material growth and self-fulfillment. As a late nineteenth-century cultural current, modernism built on the most recent developments in the long wave of modernization in the west, especially in the securing of national transportation and communication links and the centralizing tendencies of government. The ideological adaptation of modernism by the liberal bourgeoisie would, however, transform material growth into a nascent compulsive consumerism and self-fulfillment into an obsessive search for personal regeneration. That personal regeneration, nevertheless, was projected onto society through an articulation of an ideological discourse suffused with the language of progress and morality. Thus, the bourgeois modernist sensibility attempted to integrate the profound changes in the late nineteenth century into an ideological matrix of reform.[8]

In the United States the effort to incorporate such changes necessitated a reformulation of traditional ethics and politics. In *Outlines of Cosmic Philosophy*, John Fiske sought to reconcile traditional Christian values with positivist and evolutionary thought, thus paving the way for a triumph of bourgeois modernist optimism. "The fundamental characteristic of social progress," averred Fiske, "is the continuous weakening of selfishness and the continuous strengthening of sympathy. Or—to use a more convenient and somewhat more accurate expression suggested by Comte— it is a gradual supplanting of egoism by altruism."[9] For Edward Bellamy the inevitability of social progress also was contingent on the emergence of altruism, but that altruism had to be institutionalized in an ethical state. In turn, the development of the ethical state required an acknowledgment of the moral imperatives of reform and the reformulation of traditional ethics and politics.

Such a reformulation of traditional ethics and politics was a consequence of both the ethical imperatives of reform and the social need to extend the functions of the state to realize those imperatives. The increasing demands of labor and of women for recognition and the calls for redistributive justice by farmers and others necessitated a "state conscience." The state had to become not just the balancing act that middle-class reformers envisioned, but an "educator" and incorporator in the Gramscian sense. As Gramsci notes, the interpenetration of civil society and the state is the result of "a new type or level of civilisation."[10] Gramsci's analysis makes clear that such an ethical state corresponds to "the needs of the productive forces of development."[11] In effect, the intellectual elite who would demarcate the ideological terrain of reform in America sought to foster a "state conscience" that would not only satisfy the modernist desire for material growth but also cement the merging of civil society and the state.

Another element in the modernist dynamic and the ideological matrix of reform was feminism. The growing emancipation of women from the domestic ideology of the home, particularly among the urban intelligentsia, provided an important impetus to the transformation of modernist self-fulfillment into the ideological discourse of reform represented in feminism.[12] Yet, the domestication of the public arena was integral to the feminist and reform agenda in late nineteenth-century America. Frances Willard, leader of the Women's Christian Temperance Union, urged WCTU members to "bring the home into the world" in order to "make the whole world homelike."[13] However, in seeking "the domestication of the public arena," one historian of the nineteenth century argues, women's activities "foreshadow a collapse of the distinction between the two spheres of public and private."[14] Reinforcing the interpenetration of civil society and the state, such feminism facilitated the incorporative function of the state. While contesting the exclusion of women from the public arena, feminism, as a ideological form of bourgeois modernism, reinforced the hegemonic reordering of domestic ideology.

Aiding and abetting the "grand domestic revolution" was the technological transformation of the environment, both in the home and world-at-large.[15] For the modernist bourgeois temperament, such technological transformation promised unlimited material growth and liberation from the drudgery of work. Thus, another cultural particle or current, this one being technological utopianism, became part of the ideological matrix of reform sweeping the developed world.[16] In effect, feminists and the heralders of technological utopianism welcomed the liberating and reform possibilities of a "grand domestic revolution."

Before writing *Looking Backward*, Edward Bellamy had boosted the efforts of feminists to break away from the "demon of housework." Writing in 1874 he seconded the reasoning of Mrs. Abby Morton Diaz (who would later return the favor by promoting Bellamy's novel) that women should be released from housework in order to seek their fulfillment and development in the public world.[17]

Integrating such sentiments into *Looking Backward*, Bellamy would reinforce precisely those modernist and technological utopian tendencies that buoyed the hopes of reformers and feminists in a new world order. With such missionary zeal, Ellen Swallow Richards, the first woman faculty member at MIT (Instructor in Sanitary Chemistry), attempted to convert the simple family kitchen into a technological and collective wonderland. Incorporating such experimental equipment as the Aladdin oven and cooker into her brave new world of the collective kitchen, Richards averred that "the mission of the Oven and Cooker is in the ideal life of the twentieth century as shown by Bellamy."[18]

This missionary zeal in advocating and implementing technological utopianism also had its parallels in the merging of another cultural particle with the ideological matrix of reform. From John Fiske to Josiah Strong, American social philosophers called for an Anglo-Saxon revitalization as a way to meet the crises at home and to foment reform abroad. While there were clearly racist overtones evident in the ideological adaptation of Anglo-Saxon revitalization, it shared with bourgeois modernism a sense of moral urgency, reform-mindedness, and a desire for regeneration in personal and social terms.[19] Josiah Strong in *Our Country* (1886) reveals those racist overtones while trumpeting the progress wrought by technology and democracy: "Only those races which have produced machinery seem capable of using it with the best results. It is the most advanced races which are its masters. Those races which, like the African and the Malay, are many centuries behind the Anglo-Saxon in development seem as incapable of operating complicated machinery as they are of adopting and successfully administering representative government."[20] Earlier John Fiske had argued that "only in the Aryan and some of the Semitic races . . . can we find evidences of a persistent tendency to progress." For Fiske, as for Strong and other reformers intoxicated by the progress and promise of the west, the rest of the world was in arrested development. "Half the human race," Fiske observes, "having surmounted savagery, have been arrested in an immobile type of civilization, as in China, in ancient Egypt, and in the East generally."[21]

Another tendency of Anglo-Saxon revitalization that endeavored to link its civilizing mission with a call to purify the social world was found in the ideology of feminism. While public crusades for purity in the world, such as women's involvement in the temperance movement, created a certain space for the empowerment of women, that very empowerment was circumscribed and limited by adopting an ascribed purity, especially in relationship to race regeneration.[22] "The commitment to race regeneration," asserts a historian of late

nineteenth-century feminism, "placed a premium on women's traditional duties and virtues."[23] Thus, Anglo-Saxon revitalization
unleashed reformist forces while reinforcing reactionary tendencies
within the ideological matrix of reform.

Nowhere were those contradictions more evident than in the
emphasis on the degenerating influences caused by urban life and
the obsession with racial regeneration through physical development. Bellamy, among many middle-class reformers, was troubled
by the degenerating influences of the urban industrial world. Moreover, he shared with many of these reformers an obsession with
physical development and race regeneration. Before *Looking Backward*, Bellamy had written about genetic utopias where proper
selection and breeding of the human stock would lead to renewed
hope in the future.[24] However, for Bellamy the mere tinkering with
various reforms could not facilitate the profound changes necessary
for a well-ordered future. Only a fusion of the currents of modernism, technological utopianism, and Anglo-Saxon revitalization could
transcend the limitations of previous reforms and command the
attention of those waiting for and wanting a brave new world.
Looking Backward would fuse those currents and galvanize the
ideological matrix of reform.

BELLAMY'S *LOOKING BACKWARD*: READING
FORMATIONS, IDEOLOGICAL NETWORKS, AND THE
DISCOURSE OF REFORM

When the author of *Looking Backward* died in 1898, the *American
Fabian* noted: "It is doubtful if any man, in his own lifetime, ever
exerted so great an influence upon the social beliefs of his fellow-
beings as did Edward Bellamy."[25] By the time of his death, *Looking
Backward* had sold over a half million copies in the United States
and hundreds of thousands worldwide. While *Looking Backward*
garnered an audience because of the propitious historical moment
for utopianism, the book was also read or half-read (or read about)
as a reflection of the "horizon of expectations" of its various readers.[26]

The success and influence of *Looking Backward* offer a way to
approach the novel as a historical artifact which demands decoding.
Moreover, the reception of the novel requires both a deconstruction
of the discourse generated by the novel and its readers and a
reconstruction of the historical moment of reception. In effect, the
reading of *Looking Backward* and its rearticulation and disarticulation as a "culturally activated" text affords an opportunity to analyze
the "material, social, ideological, and institutional relations in which

both text and readers are inescapably inscribed."[27] Thus, one focus of this section will be on the "inscribed audience" of *Looking Backward* and the reader response of that audience.[28]

The major focus, however, of this section will be on the interconnections of the reading formations, ideological networks, and discourse of reform surrounding the reading of *Looking Backward.* For literary theorist Tony Bennett "reading formations" are "a set of discursive and intertextual determinations which organize and animate the practice of reading, connecting texts and readers in specific relations to one another in constituting readers as reading subjects of particular types and texts as objects-to-be-read in particular ways."[29] For purposes of this chapter, particular reading formations will be identified through reviews and references to *Looking Backward.* In situating the reviews and references in the ideological matrix of reform, the role of the reviewer and respondent as a reaction channel, that is, a rearticulator or disarticulator, will be highlighted and connected to the ideological networks resonant with the reviewer/respondent.

While it may be the case, as one recent study of *Looking Backward* suggests, that "Bellamy's exploration of socialism was a moral inquiry proceeding from certain assumptions that he knew his listeners shared,"[30] not all of the listeners (readers/respondents) shared those assumptions in the same way. The meanings of particular words, as expressive of ideological discursive codes, not only meant different things to different people, but also underwent reformulation in the specific sociohistorical processes of the time. In decoding the language employed in various reviews and references to *Looking Backward,* this chapter will follow the contention of French sociolinguist Michel Pecheux: "The meaning of a word, an expression, a proposition, etc. doesn't exist 'in itself,' but is determined by the ideological positions brought into play in the sociohistorical process in which words, expressions, and propositions are produced."[31]

In locating the reading formations, ideological networks, and discursive codes associated with Bellamy's *Looking Backward,* it will be necessary to explore the ways in which these formations, networks, and codes are representative of the hegemonic process in the ideological matrix of reform. The success of cementing a historic bloc and achieving the ideological hegemony of reform will be more precisely sketched in the conclusion. What will be concentrated on now is the ways in which the reading formations, ideological networks, and discursive codes reflected a self-conscious effort on the part of an intellectual elite to enact a strategy of reform.

Nowhere is the response to Bellamy's *Looking Backward* by a self-conscious intellectual elite more reflective of an bid to enact a strategy of reform than in the creation of the Nationalist movement in the United States. The founding of that movement came in Boston with the leadership provided by two journalists and prominent members of the professional class. Those two journalists, Sylvester Baxter and Cyrus Field Willard, found in *Looking Backward* an answer to the waste and inefficiency that so bothered middle-class intellectuals in late nineteenth-century America.[32] *Looking Backward* had targeted that waste in Chapter XXII with the all-wise twentieth-century commentator, Doctor Leete, excoriating the industrial practices of nineteenth-century America. Telescoping the cultural currents of modernism, technological utopianism, and Anglo-Saxon revitalization into his criticism of such waste and inefficiency, Doctor Leete concludes his peroration with an attack that would resonate throughout the Nationalist movement: "Competition, which is the instinct of selfishness, is another word for dissipation of energy, while combination is the secret of efficient production; and not till the idea of increasing the individual hoard gives place to the idea of increasing the common stock can industrial combination be realized, and the acquisition of wealth really begin."[33] In the first issue of *The Nationalist*, the journal created for the promotion of Bellamy's ideas and the Nationalist movement, Sylvester Baxter echoed Doctor Leete's condemnation of nineteenth-century industrial society and rearticulated the collectivist solutions proposed in the novel: "The intricate complexity of multitudinous industrial antagonisms, keeping the national body in a chronic state of disease through the incomplete working of its various functions, will be reduced to simplicity by bringing all the diversified interests into harmonious and mutually helpful action under one central authority."[34] In the immediate aftermath of the publication of *Looking Backward* and in the context of an elite's fear of the dissipation of its energy and the concomitant dissolution of the social order, Nationalists like Sylvester Baxter looked toward the evolution of the state into a collectivist cure for all the ills that plagued late nineteenth-century America.

Such an obsession with the restoration of the physical and mental health of society was reflective of the discourse and ideology of the social formation represented by Baxter and most of the Nationalists. Constituting an ideological network of liberal collectivists, their discursive codes stressed the evolutionary development from an outmoded and discredited laissez-faire ideology to one of an interventionist and activist state.[35] As either declassed members of an older elite or "new social entrepreneurs," this particular network and reading formation was caught between its own contradictory longings for a restored republican past and a new social order where responsible collectivism would reign.[36] Their aspirations, nicely packaged by Bellamy in *Looking Backward*, would protect their own belief in upward mobility and progress while "[sanitizing] the process of social change."[37] In addition, through the promotion of specific practical reforms, such as changes in the civil service, such a social formation could insure its own elite position while trying to secure its ideological hegemony through its role in a moral/intellectual bloc of reform.[38]

Middle-class reformers drawn to Bellamy emphasized the positive role that the state could play as a moral arbiter of the conflicts raging in civil society. As members of an educated elite, these reformers in such professions as law and journalism underscored *Looking Backward*'s obsession with a system of merit and applauded Bellamy's transmutation of socialism into Nationalism.[39] As transitional figures to the middle-class socialists of the early twentieth century, these reformers embraced a political project that "would guarantee an equitable and uncapricious reward for hard work and individual initiative, preserve the family and best of traditional sex-roles, and tame an anarchic economy which threatened personal security and stability."[40] With their overall belief in progress and commitment to peaceful change, middle-class socialists came to regard *Looking Backward* as both a blueprint and a Bible.

That socialism of the late nineteenth century was dominated by a discourse of hope and faith underlines the contradictions inherent in such socialism and the splintering of the inchoate socialist networks in the American 1890s. In constituting particular reading formations surrounding *Looking Backward*, such socialist networks embodied ideological varieties that ranged from bureaucratic to technocratic to populist and evangelical. After retiring from the Nationalist movement, Cyrus Field Willard resurfaced in the short-lived 1890s Social Democracy movement. In a letter to Bellamy, Willard recalled the military and bureaucratic metaphors that abounded among the Nationalists: "The organization of Social Democracy is going on at lightning speed, and huge masses of men are being enrolled by competent and skillful officers, and it appears to be in fact the mustering of the industrial [army] which you portray."[41] As an editor of the *Coming Nation*, a socialist newspaper of the 1890s inspired by Bellamy's *Looking Backward*, Herbert Casson foreshadowed his own evolution from bureaucratic socialist to technocratic collectivist. Indicating his preference for a professional and managerial approach to industrial organization (which would later become his avocation as a writer on scientific management),

Casson endorsed "The Professionals . . . who believe in the organization of industry, so that the extra labor and wastefulness of competition shall be avoided."[42] The founder of the *Coming Nation*, Julius A. Wayland, had come to socialism via his entrepreneurial business successes and populist politics. Combining Bellamy's utopian visions and his own brand of evangelical populism, a brand that informed much of the socialism in the midwest and southwest, Wayland enscribed above the masthead of the *Coming Nation* a dedication to Bellamy's *Looking Backward*.[43] Not only did Wayland articulate a version of evangelical socialism resonant with Bellamy's socialist appeals, but he also set up a utopian socialist colony that tried to establish a microcosm of the "village utopianism" of Bellamy.[44] (For an extended discussion of this latter point, see Chapter 5.)

The envangelical message found in Bellamy's writings was what attracted religious reformers in America to Bellamy's *Looking Backward*. One such social gospel advocate was the Episcopalian Rev. W.D.P. Bliss. Bliss enlisted in the Nationalist cause as a Christian Socialist and soldier who wished to conquer the corrupt world through a socially engaged Christianity. Writing in an early issue of the *Nationalist*, Bliss preached that "Nationalism means essentially the application of ethics and equity through government to business. Its development means the development of righteousness in social order. And righteousness is Christianity."[45] Looking for secular salvation in the state, Christian Socialists like Bliss read *Looking Backward* as a "religious fable" which would sanctify both the coming industrial army and the Christianizing of America.[46] Attempting to overcome the paradox of Christian Socialism with its "simultaneous [commitment] to the patriarchal vertical of the 'fatherhood of God' and to the libertarian horizontal of the 'brotherhood of man,' " Bliss and the network he represented substituted "the application of ethics and equity through government" as a secular equivalent to the fatherhood of God.[47] Moreover, following the fusion of moral and material progress in *Looking Backward*, any misgivings held by radical religious reformers about a "conflict between spiritual growth and technological growth" could be resolved by holding to Bellamy's vision of the evolution of a religiously inspired future.[48]

The fusion of moral and material progress in *Looking Backward* also proved attractive to nineteenth-century American feminists. Frances Willard, temperance leader, women's rights advocate, and social reformer, believed that *Looking Backward* "might result in a 'practical working plan' for Christianity—in people's talking less about their religion and living it instead."[49] In particular, Willard considered *Looking Backward* as an opening to the salvation of women. Proclaiming the novel a "revelation," Willard wrote a friend at Bellamy's publisher: "Some of us think that Edward Bellamy must be Edwardina—i.e., we believe a big-hearted, big-brained woman wrote the book."[50] Willard's enthusiasm for the novel and the generally positive response of nineteenth-century American feminists can be attributed to several factors, not the least of which were the arguments Bellamy advanced in *Looking Backward* for women's emancipation from housework and their enfranchisement as full citizens and members of the industrial army, arguments expanded upon in journals such as *Good Housekeeping* and the *Ladies Home Journal*.[51] Beyond those positions, however, the approach that Bellamy took toward moral and material progress also inspired women readers. If Christian Socialists correctly saw that Bellamy's new nation was, in the words of *Looking Backward*, "a father who kept the people alive and was not merely an idol for which they were expected to die" (183), feminists could point to the maternal symbolism underlying a nation ordained to "[guarantee] the nurture, education, and comfortable maintenance of every citizen from the cradle to the grave" (85). Even more suggestive of this maternal nurturing was the encoding by Bellamy of female symbolism in the emblems and architecture of material prosperity in the novel. The main distribution store in Boston of the year 2000 has "above the portal standing out from the front of the building, a majestic life-size group of statuary, the central figure of which was a female ideal of Plenty, with her cornucopia" (92). The inside of the building "was a vast hall full of light, received not alone from the windows on all sides, but from the dome, the point of which was a hundred feet above" (92). This maternal and material suckling of consumers in Bellamy's *Looking Backward* not only valorized women's role as a significant symbol for and recipient of material progress in the year 2000, but also as, in the words of the novel, "wardens of the world to come" (192).

This feminist vision, albeit still embodying a commitment to a distinct women's sphere, encouraged women to continue in their efforts to domesticate the public world at the end of the nineteenth century. "We all became acquainted with the ideal picture in . . . *Looking Backward*," noted Mary Hinman Abel, a leading home economist of the period, "instead of fifty incompetent buyers at retail, one efficient buyer at wholesale; . . . the peripatetic housemaid and all other workers responsible to a bureau; the house heated from a central station, where a competent engineer shall extract from each pound of coal all the heat it should yield."[52] Abel took seriously Bellamy's vision of a collectivized and domesticated world through her involvement with the New England Kitchen. This large public kitchen opened in 1890 with the purpose of making nutritious food available to the masses. Beyond that, it proved to be a showcase for technological wonders such as the Aladdin Oven. Abel went on to help Ellen Richards, another Bellamy enthusiast, with the spectacular Rumford Kitchen at the Chicago World's Fair in 1893. "Material feminists" like Abel and Richards were part of a wave of women who rode a crest of modernism and technological utopianism into the public arena.[53] Emancipated from the private sphere of the home, feminist followers of *Looking Backward* in the United States extended domestic ideology into the public arena.

American feminists obviously saw in *Looking Backward* a vision of a future that might work for them as reformers in the present. They articulated their desires to be treated as first-class citizens not only through a discourse inspired by reformist visionaries like Bellamy but also through their own activities. Even if the struggle for first class citizenship was constrained by the vagaries of reform and limited to their role as voters and enlightened consumers, nineteenth-century feminists were at the cutting edge of the future. Feminists like Frances Willard were the vanguard of a modernism that demanded self-fulfillment and moral regeneration. Even when that fulfillment was circumscribed, the incorporation of woman as voter and manager and junior partner of domestic ideology was a major defining characteristic of the matrix of reform that swept throughout America and the western world at the end of the nineteenth century.[54]

CONCLUSION

The various reading formations and ideological networks previously identified constituted a moral/intellectual bloc which sought to articulate a discourse of reform and to effectuate the institutionalization of that reform. I want to conclude by elaborating a Gramscian perspective on the historic bloc and ideological hegemony of reform. In the context of the previous discussion, the reading formations and ideological networks reflect a range of social formations, albeit limited to the middle class. In seeking to promote an agenda of reform such a historic bloc must attempt to diffuse its vision of reform, its ideological agenda, throughout society. A historic bloc, thus, achieves ideological hegemony by incorporating disparate ideological elements and social formations into that vision and agenda.[55] In effect, what I want to suggest in this conclusion is that in America one sees the defusion of that vision and agenda through the splintering of the reform movement and the displace-

ment of reform through the strong emergence of imperialism, racism, and nativism in the 1890s.[56]

One way of tracking the successful diffusion of ideological hegemony is to review the dynamic by which various reading formations
and ideological networks articulated their understanding of Bellamy
vis-à-vis the state. It is particularly important to pay attention to
the way in which the state either expresses or reflects an active
historical agent—that is, the extension of a historic bloc of working
class and middle class interests, mounting a strategy of empowerment—or represents a reified conception of inevitable incorporation.
While there were certainly working-class readers and advocates of
Bellamy's vision and agenda in *Looking Backward*, those readers (as
indicated below) often expressed an ambivalent attitude toward
actual state power. On the other hand, most middle class supporters
tended to see the incorporating function of that state as an evolutionary march toward collective solutions. As William Dean Howells
wrote in his commentary on *Looking Backward*: "Mr. Bellamy's
allegorical state of A.D. 2000 is constructed exactly upon the lines
of Mr. Gronlund's *Cooperative Commonwealth*; and it is supposed
to come into being through the government acquisition of the vast
trusts and monopolies, just as the collectivist author teaches."[57]
One leader of the Bellamy movement in New York wrote in an 1889
Nationalist article: "Upon the ruins of the competitive state will arise
the Cooperative Commonwealth, with its system of equilibrated
production and consumption. Then private interest will no more be
hostile to public interest, but they will become identified."[58] Thus,
the reform-minded readers of *Looking Backward* looked to a tran-
scendental state to arbitrate the antagonisms that fueled the social
conflicts of the late nineteenth century.

While there were numerous instances of working class support
for such an idealized state, working-class readers of *Looking Backward* were less sanguine about the automatic evolution of this
idealized state as forecast by Bellamy's novel. A number of labor
leaders became active in the Nationalist movement, including an
official of the Cigar Makers Union who was instrumental in the
founding and organization of the Philadelphia Nationalist Club.[59]
Eugene Debs, leader of the Railway Workers Union and of the
Pullman strike of 1894, read *Looking Backward* and its sequel
Equality as "valuable and timely contributions to the literature of
Socialism . . . [which] not only aroused the people but started many
on the road to the revolutionary movement."[60] Thus, for Debs,
Looking Backward was an inspiration, but it was not an ideological
agenda. Given the bloody and repressive history of state intervention
against workers in the United States from the railroad strikes of

1877 to the Pullman strike of 1894, it is not surprising that working class leaders like Debs were suspicious and even antagonistic to the kind of state sponsorship embraced by middle class followers of Bellamy.[61]

Given the lack of ideological cohesion among the readers of *Looking Backward*, it is not surprising that finding a common political agenda, and thus cementing the Gramscian "historical bloc," proved impossible in the 1890s. As if to emphasize the disparate constituency in the Nationalist movement, one interpreter of Bellamy and his followers has identified Nationalism as a "haven for malcontents and 'declasse' intellectuals of every stripe—prohibitionists, disgruntled small businessmen, frustrated entrepreneurs, die-hard communitarians, feminists, anti-monopoly veterans, all with their own complaints against the new corporate capitalism."[62] While it is also true that "the new forms, ideas, and methods assumed by radical and revolutionary currents in the late 1890's and early 1900's emerged under the sign of *Looking Backward*," those currents often swirled into endless eddies and were at times swept aside by numerous counter currents such as racism and national chauvinism.[63] Finally, Bellamy and the readers of *Looking Backward*, whether reformist or radical, middle class or working class, were unprepared to articulate a cohesive ideological agenda that could unite the various reading networks and constituencies in a sustained political movement. Although offering a utopian vision and inspiration for change, *Looking Backward* could not provide its readers with the political will to create a transformative "historical bloc."[64]

NOTES

1. See, for example, E. J. Hobsbawm, *The Age of Empire, 1875–1914* (New York: Vintage, 1989), esp. pp. 84–141, 192–218.

2. On the historical use of the deconstructive and semiological approach to texts, see E. M. Henning, "Archaeology, Deconstruction and Intellectual History," in *Modern European Intellectual History: Reappraisals and New Perspectives*, ed. Dominick LaCapra and Steven L. Caplan (Ithaca, N.Y.: Cornell University Press, 1982), pp. 153–96; and Hayden White, *The Content of the Form: Narrative Discourse and Historical Representation* (Baltimore: The Johns Hopkins University Press, 1987), esp. pp. 196–208. On the intersection of ideology and discourse analysis, see John Frow, *Marxism and Literary History* (Oxford: Basil Blackwell, 1986), esp. pp. 51–82. For a review of discourse analysis in French, Anglo-American, and German historiography, see Peter Schottler, "Historians and Discourse Analysis," *History Workshop* 27 (Spring 1989): 37–65. For examples of the reconstructive approach to ideology and the reading of texts, see

Keith Michael Baker, "On the Problems of the Ideological Origins of the French Revolution," pp. 197–219, and Dominick LaCapra, "Rethinking Intellectual History and Reading Texts," pp. 47–85, in *Modern European Intellectual History*. Also, see Dominick LaCapra, *Rethinking Intellectual History: Texts, Contexts, Language* (Ithaca, N.Y.: Cornell University Press, 1983). Good general surveys of reader-response and reception theory can be found in *The Reader in the Text: Essays on Audience and Interpretation*, ed. Susan R. Suleiman and Inge Crosman (Princeton: Princeton University Press, 1980); and Robert C. Holub, *Reception Theory: A Critical Introduction* (London: Methuen, 1984).

3. For the most accessible and enlivening discussion of S-Matrix theory, see Fritjof Capra, *The Tao of Physics* (Berkeley: Shambhala, 1975), pp. 262–76, and Fritjof Capra, *The Turning Point: Science, Society, and the Rising Culture* (London: Fontana, 1983), pp. 83–88. For the more complicated and mathematical model developed by its leading contemporary proponent, see Geoffrey F. Chew, *S-Matrix Theory of Strong Interactions* (New York: W. A. Benjamin, 1962).

4. The following works have been particularly useful for my synthetic definition of the ideological matrix: Kenneth Thompson, *Beliefs and Ideology* (Chichester: Ellis Horwood, 1986); Anthony Giddens, *Central Problems in Social Theory: Action, Structure, and Contradiction* (London: The Macmillan Press, 1979), esp. pp. 165–97; *Politics and Ideology: A Reader*, ed. James Donald and Stuart Hall (Philadelphia: Open University Press, 1986), esp. pp. ix–xx; Terry Eagleton, "Ideology and Scholarship," in *Historical Studies and Literary Criticism*, ed. Jerome J. McGann (Madison: The University of Wisconsin Press, 1985), pp. 114–25; and Chantal Mouffe, "Hegemony and Ideology in Gramsci," in *Gramsci and Marxist Theory*, ed. Mouffe (London: Routledge and Kegan Paul, 1979), pp. 168–204.

5. Mouffe, *Gramsci and Marxist Theory*, pp. 194–95.

6. Raymond Williams, *Marxism and Literature* (London: Oxford University Press, 1977), pp. 112–13. Also see Mouffe, *Gramsci and Marxist Theory*, p. 195.

7. Gramsci's discussion of hegemony, the "historic bloc," and the "moral and intellectual bloc" can be found scattered throughout his prison notebooks. On his analysis of intellectuals, see *Selections from the Prison Notebooks*, trans. and ed. Quintin Hoare and Geoffrey Nowell Smith (New York: International Publishers, 1971), pp. 5–23. For relevant interpretations, see Walter L. Adamson, *Hegemony and Revolution: A Study of Antonio Gramsci's Political and Social Theory* (Berkeley: University of California Press, 1980), esp. pp. 140–201; Christine Buci-Glucksmann, *Gramsci and the State*, trans. David Fernback (London: Lawrence and Wishart, 1980); Joseph Femia, *Gramsci's Political Thought: Hegemony, Consciousness, and the Revolutionary Process* (Oxford: Clarendon Press, 1981), esp. pp. 23–60; Leonardo Salamini, *The Sociology of Political Praxis: An Introduction to Gramsci's Theory* (London: Routledge and Kegan Paul, 1981); the essays in Mouffe, *Gramsci and Marxist Theory*; T. J. Jackson Lears, "The Concept of Cultural Hegemony: Problems and Possibilities," *American*

Historical Review 90 (June 1985), 567–93: and Gwyn A. Williams, "The Concept of 'Egemonia' in the Thought of Antonio Gramsci: Some Notes and Interpretation," *Journal of the History of Ideas* 21 (October–December 1960): 586–99. On the interaction of hegemony and culture in the American historical context at the turn of the century, see T. J. Jackson Lears, *No Place of Grace: Antimodernism and the Transformation of American Culture, 1880–1920* (New York: Pantheon, 1981); and Roy Rosenzweig, *Eight Hours for What We Will: Workers and Leisure in an Industrial City, 1870–1920* (Cambridge: Cambridge University Press, 1983).

8. For a grounding of the definition of modernism, see Marshall Berman, *All That Is Solid Melts into Air: The Experience of Modernity* (New York: Simon and Schuster, 1982), esp. pp. 15–36. On the emergence of modernism in America, see George Cotkin, *Reluctant Modernism: American Thought and Culture, 1880–1900* (New York: Twayne, 1992); and Alan Tractenberg, *The Incorporation of America: Culture and Society in the Gilded Age* (New York: Hill and Wang, 1982). On the connections between modernism and anti-modernism in America, see Lears, *No Place of Grace*.

9. John Fiske, *Outlines of Cosmic Philosophy* (Boston: Houghton Mifflin, 1892), II, p. 201. *Outlines* was first published in 1874. On how Fiske's reconciliation opened the door to the positivist and modernist adaptation of traditional Protestant ethics, see Lears, *No Place of Grace*, pp. 22–23.

10. Gramsci, *Prison Notebooks*, p. 247. Commentaries on this interpenetration can be found in Adamson, *Hegemony and Revolution*, pp. 162–68; and Buci-Glucksmann, *Gramsci and the State*, pp. 70–71, 127, 384–86.

11. Gramsci, *Prison Notebooks*, p. 259.

12. On women's emancipation in the west and its political implications, see Hobsbawm, *The Age of Empire*, pp. 192–218. On the connections between bourgeois discourse and women's emancipation in the Progressive Era in the United States, see Carroll Smith-Rosenberg, *Disorderly Conduct: Visions of Gender in Victorian America* (New York: Oxford University Press, 1986), pp. 167–78. On feminism in nineteenth-century America, see Dolores Hayden, *The Grand Domestic Revolution* (Cambridge: MIT Press, 1981); William Leach, *True Love and Perfect Union: The Feminist Reform of Sex and Society* (London: Routledge and Kegan Paul, 1981); Ellen Carol DuBois, *Feminism and Suffrage: The Emergence of an Independent Women's Movement in America, 1848–1869* (Ithaca, N.Y:, Cornell University Press, 1978); and Mari Jo Buhle, *Women and American Socialism, 1870–1920* (Urbana: University of Illinois Press, 1981). On the rise of feminism in the west during this period, see Richard J. Evans, *The Feminists: Women's Emancipation Movements in Europe, America, and Australasia, 1840–1920* (London: Croom Helm, 1977). On feminism in England, see Phillippa Levine, *Victorian Feminism, 1850–1900* (London: Hutchinson, 1987). On the development of feminism and social reform which includes an insightful analysis of the social base and political implications of feminism and reform in Canada, see Carol Lee Bacchi, *Liberation Deferred? The Ideas of the English-Canadian Suffragists, 1877–1918* (Toronto: University of Toronto Press, 1983).

13. Quoted in Hayden, *The Grand Domestic Revolution*, p. 5. For a good biography of Frances Willard, see Ruth Bordin, *Frances Willard: A Biography* (Chapel Hill: University of North Carolina Press, 1986).

14. Levine, *Victorian Feminism*, p. 14. Also see Bacchi, *Liberation Deferred?*, pp. 116, 147.

15. See Hayden, *The Grand Domestic Revolution*, pp. 16–17 and *passim*. Also, see Hobsbawm, *The Age of Empire*, p. 215.

16. For a definition of technological utopianism and its impact in America, see Howard P. Segal, *Technological Utopianism in American Culture* (Chicago: University of Chicago Press, 1985).

17. Syliva E. Bowman, *The Year 2000: A Critical Biography of Edward Bellamy* (New York: Bookman Associates, 1958), p. 291.

18. Quoted in Hayden, *The Grand Domestic Revolution*, p. 148.

19. On Anglo-Saxon revitalization in America, see Lears, *No Place of Grace*, pp. 108–16. On the connections between Anglo-Saxon revitalization and nativism in the United States, see John Higham, *Strangers in the Land: Patterns of American Nativism 1860–1925* (New York: Atheneum, 1963), esp. pp. 234–63. On the white supremacist overtones in Anglo-Saxon revitalization, see Gail Bederman, *Manliness & Civilization: A Cultural History of Gender and Race in the United States, 1880–1917* (Chicago: University of Chicago Press, 1995), pp. 25–26, 41–42, and *passim*.

20. Quoted in Ronald T. Takaki, *Iron Cages: Race and Culture in Nineteenth-Century America* (Seattle: University of Washington Press, 1982), pp. 261–62. For Strong's missionary message and the foundations of American imperialism at the end of the nineteenth century, see Walter LaFeber, *The New Empire: An Interpretation of American Expansion 1860–1898* (Ithaca, N.Y.: Cornell University Press, 1963), pp. 72–80. Bellamy's sentiments in this seem to suggest a more uplifting approach to the "white man's burden." Doctor Leete, the voice of twentieth-century reason, responds to a question from Julian West whether "the societies of the Old World [have] also been remodeled?" "Yes," replied Doctor Leete, "the great nations of Europe as well as Australia, Mexico, and parts of South America, are now organized industrially like the United States, which was the pioneer of the evolution. The peaceful relations of these nations are assured by a loose form of federal union of worldwide extent. An international council regulates the mutual intercourse and commerce of the members of the union and their joint policy toward the more backward races, which are gradually being educated up to the civilized institutions." Edward Bellamy, *Looking Backward 2000–1887*, ed. and intro. Cecelia Tichi (New York: Penguin, 1984), p. 115.

21. Fiske, *Outlines of Cosmic Philosophy*, p. 255.

22. On the contradictory ideological and political dynamics in purity crusades among English feminists, see Levine, *Victorian Feminism*, pp. 150–51, and Frank Mort, "Purity, Feminism, and the State: Sexuality and Moral Politics, 1880–1914," in *Crises in the British State, 1880–1930*, ed. Mary Langan and Bill Schwarz (London: Hutchinson, 1985), pp. 209–25; among works on Canadian feminism, see Bacchi, *Liberation Deferred?* pp. 104–16. For studies of those dynamics in an American context, see Ruth

Bordin, *Women and Temperance: The Quest for Power and Liberty, 1873–1900* (Philadelphia: Temple University Press, 1981); and Barbara Leslie Epstein, *The Politics of Domesticity: Women, Evangelism, and Temperance in Nineteenth Century America* (Middletown, Conn.: Wesleyan University Press, 1981). On race regeneration in the writings of Charlotte Perkins Gilman, see Bederman, *Manliness & Civilization*, pp. 121–69.

23. Bacchi, *Liberation Deferred?*, p. 116.

24. On Bellamy's view of urban degeneration, see Bowman, *The Year 2000*, p. 249. On Bellamy's genetic utopias, see Arthur Lipow, *Authoritarian Socialism in America: Edward Bellamy and the Nationalist Movement* (Berkeley: University of California Press, 1982), pp. 51–53.

25. Quoted in Krishan Kumar, *Utopia and Anti-Utopia in Modern Times* (New York: Basil Blackwell, 1987), p. 133.

26. On the "horizon of expectations" and the reception of a text, see Holub, *Reception Theory*, p. 59. On utopianism and the historical moment, see Edgar Kiser and Kriss A. Drass, "Changes in the Core of the World System and the Production of Utopian Literature in Great Britain and the United States, 1883–1975," *American Sociological Review* 52 (April 1987): 286–93. On the proliferation of utopian literature and its relationship to the historical conditions of late nineteenth-century America, see Jean Pfaelzer, *The Utopian Novel in America, 1886–1900: The Politics of Form* (Pittsburgh: University of Pittsburgh Press, 1984); Kenneth M. Roemer, *The Obsolete Necessity: America in Utopian Writings, 1888–1900* (Kent, Ohio: Kent State University Press, 1976); and Charles J. Rooney, Jr., *Dreams and Visions: A Study of American Utopias, 1865–1917* (Westport, Conn.: Greenwood Press, 1985).

27. Tony Bennett, "Text, Readings, Reading Formations," in *Modern Literary Theory: A Reader*, ed. Philip Rice and Patricia Waugh (London: Edward Arnold, 1989), p. 216. On the text as historical artifact and its semiological decoding, see Hayden White, "The Context in the Text: Method and Ideology in Intellectual History," in *The Content of the Form*, p. 210. For an analysis of *Looking Backward* as a "culturally activated text," see Kenneth M. Roemer, "Getting 'Nowhere' Beyond Stasis: A Critique, a Method, and a Case," in *Looking Backward, 1988–1888: Essays on Edward Bellamy*, ed. Daphne Patai (Amherst: University of Massachusetts Press, 1988), pp. 126–46.

28. On the concept of the inscribed audience, see Susan R. Suleiman, "Introduction," in Suleiman and Crossman, *The Reader in the Text*, pp. 12 and 15.

29. Tony Bennett, "Texts in History: The Determinations of Readings and Their Texts," in *Post-Structuralism and the Question of History*, ed. Derek Attridge, Geoff Bennington, and Robert Young (Cambridge: Cambridge University Press, 1987), p. 70. Also see Bennett in *Modern Literary Theory*, p. 208.

30. John L. Thomas, *Alternative America: Henry George, Edward Bellamy, Henry Demarest Lloyd and the Adversary Tradition* (Cambridge, Mass.: The Belknap Press of Harvard University Press, 1983), p. 56.

31. Quoted in Frow, *Marxism and Literary History*, p. 72.

32. On the Nationalist movement as a formation of the educated middle class and professional intellectual elite, see Lipow, *Authoritarian Socialism in America*. Unfortunately, many of Lipow's insights are undermined by a tendentious and *post hoc* reading of *Looking Backward*. For other discussions of the Nationalist movement, see Everett W. Macnair, *Edward Bellamy and the Nationalist Movement, 1889–1894* (Milwaukee: Fitzgerald, 1957); Bowman, *The Year 2000*, pp. 123–30; and Thomas, *Alternative America*, pp. 266–76.

33. Bellamy, *Looking Backward*, p. 178. All further references to page numbers in *Looking Backward* will be cited in the text.

34. Quoted in Lipow, *Authoritarian Socialism in America*, p. 108. On the role of administrative efficiency for curing the industrial illnesses of late nineteenth-century America, see John F. Kasson, *Civilizing the Machine: Technology and Republican Values in America, 1776–1900* (New York: Penguin, 1976), p. 198.

35. On liberal collectivism, evolutionary thought, and the new organicism, see Michael Freeden, *The New Liberalism: An Ideology of Social Reform* (Oxford: Clarendon, 1978), esp. pp. 94–116. On the obsession with the physical and mental health of American society in the late nineteenth century, see Lears, *No Place of Grace*, esp. pp. 47–58; and Smith-Rosenberg, *Disorderly Conduct*, pp. 259–65.

36. On the "new social entrepreneurs" and the collectivist ideal, see James Gilbert, *Designing the Industrial State: The Intellectual Pursuit of Collectivism in America, 1880–1940* (Chicago: Quadrangle Books, 1972), p. 16. On the collectivist appeal of *Looking Backward* and Nationalism to a declassed elite, see Lipow, *Authoritarian Socialism in America*, *passim.*

37. Pfaelzer, *The Utopian Novel in America*, pp. 24–25.

38. On civil service reform, see Baxter's comments quoted in Lipow, *Authoritarian Socialism in America*, p. 207. On the role of an intellectual elite in cementing the moral/intellectual bloc and ideological hegemony, see Gramsci, *Prison Notebooks*, esp. pp. 5 and 60. Also, see Adamson, *Hegemony and Revolution*, esp. pp. 143–45; Buci-Glucksmann, *Gramsci and the State*, pp. 19–46; and Femia, *Gramsci's Political Thought*, esp. pp. 130–32.

39. Lipow, *Authoritarian Socialism*, pp. 104–47, and 136–59.

40. Robert Hyfler, *Prophets of the Left: American Socialist Thought in the Twentieth Century* (Westport, Conn.: Greenwood Press, 1984), p. 6.

41. Quoted in Lipow, *Authoritarian Socialism in America*, p. 91. On Bellamy's influence on the Social Democracy movement, see Albert Fried, *Socialism in America: From the Shakers to the Third International* (Garden City, N.J.: Doubleday, 1970), pp. 260–67; and Howard H. Quint, *The Forging of American Socialism: Origins of the Modern Movement* (Columbia: University of South Carolina Press, 1953), 72–102.

42. Quoted in Lipow, *Authoritarian Socialism in America*, p. 91; on the technocratic connections in socialism, see pp. 89–93. Also see Samuel Haber, *Efficiency and Uplift: Scientific Management in the Progressive Era* (Chicago: University of Chicago Press, 1964).

43. Cited in Quint, *The Forging of American Socialism*, p. 183; for biographical portraits of Wayland, see pp. 175–209. Also See Elliot Shore, *Talkin' Socialism: J. A. Wayland and the Role of the Press in American Radicalism 1890–1912* (Lawrence: University Press of Kansas, 1988). On the continuity of populist and socialist ideology and its relationship to the millennial and evangelical politics of the southwest, see James R. Green, *Grass-Roots Socialism: Radical Movements in the Southwest, 1895-1943* (Baton Rouge: Louisiana State University Press, 1978), esp. pp. 12-52.

44. On Wayland's evangelical socialism, see Paul Buhle, *Marxism in the United States: Remapping the History of the American Left* (London: Verso, 1987), p. 82; also see Shore, *Talkin' Socialism*. On Bellamy's "village utopianism," see Daniel Aaron, *Men of Good Hope: A Story of American Progressivism* (New York: Oxford University Press, 1961), pp. 92–132. On Wayland and the utopian socialist colony of Ruskin, see W. Fitzhugh Brundage, *A Socialist Utopia in the New South: The Ruskin Colonies in Tennessee and Georgia, 1894–1901* (Urbana: University of Illinois Press, 1996), pp. 20–40; John Egerton, *Visions of Utopia: Nashoba, Rugby, and the "New Communities" in Tennessee's Past* (Knoxville: The University of Tennessee Press, 1977), pp. 64–86; and Francis Shor, "Contradictions in the Emergence of American Socialism and the Utopian Ruskin Colony of Tennessee," *Journal of American Culture* 12 (Winter 1989); pp. 21–27.

45. Quoted in Sidney Fine, *Laissez Faire and the General Welfare State* (Ann Arbor: University of Michigan Press, 1964), p. 299. On Bliss and Christian Socialism, see Arthur Mann, *Yankee Reformers in the Urban Age* (New York: Harper Torchbooks, 1966), pp. 90–99. On the social gospel and Christian Socialism in America, see Fine, *Laissez Fair and the General Welfare State*, pp. 169–97; Robert M. Crunden, *Ministers of Reform: The Progressives' Achievement in American Civilization, 1889–1920* (New York: Basic Books, 1982), pp. 41–51; and R. C. White and C. H. Hopkins, *The Social Gospel: Religion and Reform in Changing America* (Philadelphia: Temple University Press, 1976).

46. On *Looking Backward* as a "religious fable," see Thomas, *Alternative America*, pp. 237–41. On the significance of the industrial army for the Christian social gospel, see Lipow, *Authoritarian Socialism in America*, p. 205.

47. On this paradox of Christian Socialism, see Darko Suvin, *Metamorphoses of Science Fiction: On the Poetics and History of a Literary Genre* (New Haven: Yale University Press, 1979), p. 191.

48. Pfaelzer, *The Utopian Novel in America*, p. 33. Bellamy's religious subtext for *Looking Backward* followed from such comments in his unpublished manuscripts: the "idea that men being brothers should live together as brothers is as old as the first aspirations of humanity. It is the heart of all religion and the express meaning of Christ. . . All I have done in *Looking Backward*, all I aim . . . to do is to show certain ways whereby men can realize this ideal." Quoted in Bowman, *The Year 2000*, p. 189.

49. Quoted in Sylvia E. Bowman, *Edward Bellamy Abroad: An American Prophet's Influence* (New York: Twayne: 1962) p. 416. On Willard's

commitment to social gospel Christianity, see Bordin, *Frances Willard*, pp. 155–74.

50. Quoted in Bowman, *The Year 2000*, p. 120. For *Looking Backward*'s influence on Willard, see Bordin, *Frances Willard*, pp. 145–48.

51. For the positive and critical responses of nineteenth-century American feminists to *Looking Backward*, see Bowman, *The Year 2000*, esp. pp. 274–76; Mari Jo Buhle, *Women and American Socialism*, pp. 74–82; Hayden, *The Grand Domestic Revolution*, esp. pp. 135–37; and William Leach, "Looking Forward Together: Feminists and Edward Bellamy," *democracy* 2 (January 1982): 120–34.

52. Quoted in Hayden, *The Grand Domestic Revolution*, p. 152.

53. "Material feminism" is Hayden's term. On Able and Richards in the New England Kitchen and Chicago World's Fair, see ibid., pp. 158–59. For an overview of the Chicago World's Fair and the role of women in the fair, see Reid Badger, *The Great American Fair: The World's Columbian Exposition and American Culture* (Chicago: University of Chicago Press, 1979).

54. For a discussion of the circumscribed radicalism and liberal contradictions of feminism, see Bacchi, *Liberation Deferred*; Mari Jo Buhle, *Women and American Socialism*; and Leach, *True Love and Perfect Union*, esp. pp. 347–51. On the global significance of feminism and women's emancipation, see Evans, *The Feminists*; and Hobsbawm, *The Age of Empire*, pp. 192–218. On feminism and suffrage in the United States in the nineteenth century, see DuBois, *Feminism and Suffrage*. On women as managers and the junior partners of domestic ideology in America, see Hayden, *The Grand Domestic Revolution*; and Barbara Ehrenreich and Deidre English, *For Her Own Good* (New York: Anchor Doubleday, 1979), pp. 141–81.

55. For an elaboration of the Gramscian perspective on historic bloc and ideological hegemony, see Adamson, *Hegemony and Revolution*, pp. 170–79; Buci-Glucksmann, *Gramsci and the State*, esp. pp. 275–90; Femia, *Gramsci's Political Thought*, pp. 23–60; Salamini, *The Sociology of Political Praxis, passim*; and Lears, "The Concept of Cultural Hegemony," p. 571.

56. For a concise overview of the defusion and displacement of reform in the United States in the 1890s, see Nell Irvin Painter, *Standing at Armageddon: The United States, 1877–1919* (New York: W. W. Norton, 1987), esp. pp. 72–169. The splintering of the American socialist movement in the 1890s can also be attributed to the "impossible expectations" loaded onto a "small movement" which tried "to cut through the webs of non-class reform and radicalism." See Paul Buhle, *Marxism in the United States*, p. 24. On imperialism in this period, see LaFeber, *The New Empire*; on nativism, see Higham, *Strangers in the Land*; on racism, primarily in the south, see Joel Williamson, *A Rage for Order: Black-White Relations in the American South Since Emancipation* (New York: Oxford University Press, 1986).

57. Quoted in Robert L. Shurter, *The Utopian Novel in America, 1865–1900* (New York: AMS Press, 1973), p. 177.

58. Quoted in Franklin Rosemont, "Bellamy's Radicalism Reclaimed," in *Looking Backward, 1988–1888*, p. 170. Rosemont tends to interpret *Looking Backward* through Bellamy's more activist orientation in the 1890s, a period when he expressed a decidedly more pro-labor, populist, and feminist agenda than revealed in *Looking Backward*.

59. Ibid, p. 160.

60. Quoted in Lipow, *Authoritarian Socialism in America*, p. 23. For Debs's own path to the revolutionary movement, see Nick Salvatore, *Eugene V. Debs: Citizen and Socialist* (Urbana: University of Illinois Press, 1982).

61. Hyfler, *Prophets of the Left*, p. 6.

62. Quoted in Thomas, *Alternative America*, p. 270.

63. Rosemont in *Looking Backward, 1988–1888*, p. 168.

64. For a criticism of Bellamy and *Looking Backward* along these lines, see Jonathan Auerbach, " 'The Nation Organized': Utopian Impotence in Edward Bellamy's *Looking Backward*," *American Literary History* 6 (Spring 1994): 24–47. Howard Quint's evaluation of Nationalism also parallels my final assessment: "Nationalism was a movement which exploded in all directions at the same time. That was its principal weakness. Its energies were never channelized. It had little organization, less leadership, and almost nothing in the way of a co-ordinated working program." Quint, *The Forging of American Socialism*, p. 101.

2

The "New Woman" in Turn-of-the-Century Utopian Fiction: Bellamy's Equality and Gilman's "A Woman's Utopia"

Given the exalted rhetoric that "elevated" the Victorian woman in the industrialized world of the late nineteenth century to a reputed moral superiority, the actual social position of women still lagged behind that of men. Nevertheless, as the nineteenth century drew to a close, the accumulation of a "grand domestic revolution" and the transformation in birth rates opened up the social space for middle class women to seek a more emancipated position in society. Through clubs and other women-centered organizations, middle class women experienced a growing sense of confidence in their public roles. With an increasing number of women participating in enlarged service and public sectors of the economy, women moved out of the home and into the waged world. By 1900 over 21 percent of the female population over sixteen in the United States worked for wages. Although those wages were far below the average male wage in a masculinized economy, women's expectations for advancement reflected a new perception of what women could achieve. In effect, "an enhanced sense of self, gender, and mission" propelled a "new woman" onto the world stage.[1]

In America the break from earlier stereotypes that obstructed the progress of women was not clean and immediate. Writing in the *Atlantic Monthly* in 1901, Caroline Ticknor conveyed the conflicted condition of the new woman in light of the fall from grace from "true womanhood": "Hail the new woman—behold she comes apace! Woman, once man's superior, now his equal!"[2] While there were residual elements of the cult of "true womanhood" which persisted, impeding the full emergence of the new woman, certain continuities were revised to give birth to modern feminism. Stressing redefined concepts of self-reliance, physical fitness, and maternal service, the developing ideal of the new woman, especially for the middle class in the United States, opened up additional possibilities on the eve of the twentieth century. Expectations concerning changing social status were, in turn, translated into a woman-centered culture and social psychology.[3]

As the horizons of expectations for women were raised, representations of the "new woman" found their way into the literature of turn-of-the-century America. As readers and writers of utopian fiction, women were engaged in a process of interrogating what social conditions impeded their ultimate emancipation and envisioning alternative social formations. As Carol Kolmerten has noted: "From 1890 through 1919, more than thirty American women wrote utopian novels depicting their versions of a better world."[4] This reconceptualization of women in turn-of-the-century utopian fiction was not, however, the sole province of women writers. A number of men also envisioned women as equal partners in the construction of a better world. Nevertheless, both male and female utopian writers could not escape gender and other sociocultural contradictions inherent in an age where women were still predominantly typecast as both the weaker sex and an eternal source of goodness.[5]

Among the most prominent utopian writers in turn-of-the-century America were Edward Bellamy and Charlotte Perkins Gilman. The publication of Bellamy's *Looking Backward* in 1888 became a magnet for advocates of the "new woman," including Gilman. In fact, Gilman became active as a spokesperson in the Nationalist movement that sprang up in California and around the country in the aftermath of the publication of *Looking Backward*.[6] Bellamy, himself, was transformed from a rather reclusive writer to an activist in the burgeoning adversarial politics of the 1890s.[7] As political activists, both Bellamy and Gilman necessarily translated their utopian expectations, especially for women, into their cultural work as utopian writers. For Bellamy that meant taking into account the critique of the role of women in *Looking Backward* by his feminist allies in the Nationalist movement and incorporating such criticisms into the changes for women in his sequel, *Equality* (1897).[8] For Gilman that meant telescoping her activism and writing as a Nationalist, Fabian socialist, and material feminist in the 1890s and early 1900s into her utopian writings of the period 1907–1916.[9]

Because Bellamy's *Equality* and Gilman's "A Woman's Utopia" (1907) come at the end of a period of intense political activism and are so rarely deemed significant texts in their oeuvres and in representations of the utopian and radical thinking of the time, they will be the focus of this chapter. In particular, I want to determine how the conceptions and contradictions of the "new woman" were elaborated in these two less considered works of turn-of-the-century utopian fiction. It will be my contention that Bellamy and Gilman inscribed a feminist audience in the above texts as a consequence of their involvement with particular tendencies within the women's movement and radical politics at the turn of the century.[10] In turn, by analyzing the representations of the "new woman" in these two texts, one can better decode the political and cultural context of Bellamy's and Gilman's feminism and that of their audiences.

Even though women embraced Bellamy's *Looking Backward* with such effusive praise as Frances Willard's contention that it was "the route to female salvation," there were expressions of disappointment with the limitations Bellamy had imposed on women, from his creation of a separate industrial army for women to their exclusion from certain occupations.[11] A number of Bellamy's feminist supporters, such as Mary Ford, Abby Morton Diaz, and Mary Livermore, reproached Bellamy for keeping women in what they construed as subservient roles. Bellamy's response to these criticisms was evident in a developing articulation in the 1890s of the need for women's full economic equality. In his talks and writings on Nationalism, Bellamy contended that "the equality of women with men can never be anything but a farce as long as the mass of the feminine sex remains dependent upon the personal favor of men for their means of support."[12] According to Bellamy's revamped Nationalist program, a woman's "means of support will be an income equal to that of all citizens, and whether she be married or unmarried, will be her personal right, and received through no other person. She will, that is to say, through life, be not only economically equal with every man, but absolutely independent of any man."[13]

As a consequence of Bellamy's heightened sensitivity to the demands of the "new woman," *Equality* no longer consigns women to a separate and restricted sphere of work as did *Looking Backward* with its gender division of the industrial army. As emphasized in *Equality*: "There is not a trade or occupation . . . in which women do not take part."[14] Even Edith Leete, that hapless and demure contradiction of Victorian sentimentality and "new woman" consumerism, is transformed into a vigorous manager of farm work, albeit reliant on the miracles of advanced technology. She conveys this change in women's social condition in the following dialogue with Julian West: "It is partly because we are physically much more vigorous than the poor creatures of your time that we do the sorts of work that were too heavy for them, but it is still more on account of the perfection of machinery" (44). It is precisely those miracles of advanced technology that eliminate any vestiges of domestic drudgery still evident in *Looking Backward*. Moving beyond the socialization of domestic work cherished by material feminists such as Gilman, Bellamy creates recycled and disposable clothes and household items in *Equality* which require no tending by women, except perhaps for the replacement labor for such items.[15] Women thus achieve economic equality through a realization of a feminized and socialized Declaration of Independence which Dr. Leete cites as containing "the entire statement of the doctrine of universal economic equality guaranteed by the nation collectively to its members individually" (16).

While Bellamy's revision of economic equality in *Equality* retains its allegiance to the idealized universalism in both the original (1776) and Seneca Falls (1848) version of the Declaration of Independence, his commitment to the social and spiritual evolution of women leads him to foreground the critical role that women played in the revolutionary changes evident in the year 2000. In one of the longest chapters in *Equality*, entitled "What the Revolution Did for Women," Bellamy acknowledges that women were the key in converting society to an inclusive material and moral welfare. "If to the men the voice of the revolution was a call to a higher and nobler plane of living, to woman it was as the voice of God calling her to a new creation" (131). Thus, women's critical role becomes the assumption of the birthing of a transfigured citizenry, a citizenry which would be morally uplifted by women. In turn, Bellamy also asserts in this chapter that the revolution "gave free mothers to the race—free not merely from physical but from moral and intellectual fetters" (138). In effect, Bellamy inscribes the crusades for social purity spearheaded by women in the late nineteenth century into *Equality* with those religious, reform Darwinist, and Victorian sensibilities he shared with many of the middle class feminists of the times.[16]

"What the Revolution Did for Women" also delineates the "triple yoke" that oppressed women: (1) the "class rule of the rich"; (2) personal subjugation to the husband; and (3) a slavish conformity "to a set of traditions and conventional standards calculated to repress all that was spontaneous and individual, and impose an artificial uniformity upon both the inner and outer life" of women (135–36). For each component of this triple yoke, Bellamy provides the example of the emancipated women. From a "system which permitted human beings to come into relations of superiority and inferiority," Bellamy poses equality as "the only moral relation between human beings" (133). Of course, it is significant that Bellamy transposes this class conflict into a matter of morality, thus making moral suasion the key to a transformed America. Nevertheless, Bellamy's responsiveness to feminist criticism of the persistence of traditional marital and sexual relations in *Looking Backward* leads to a liberated sense of partnership where women no longer change their name in marriage. Children also follow this liberated path where "girls take the mother's last name with the father's as a middle name, while with boys it is just the reverse" (139). Finally, Bellamy heeds the call of women's dress reform, a call that was also crucial for Gilman's personal and political life, by ending the ridiculous dress requirements that were still evident in *Looking Backward*.[17]

It is no surprise, therefore, that the chapter following "What the Revolution Did for Women" should focus on the physical and moral health of the "new woman" of the future. As noted in conversation with Julian West: "Women's invalidism was one of the great tragedies of your civilization, and her physical rehabilitation is one of the greatest single elements in the total increment of happiness which economic equality has brought to the human race" (149). While women's physical vigor is in keeping with late nineteenth-century feminists' desire for women's independence, the stress on physical exercise in turn-of-the-century America does indicate that Bellamy is not at all out of sync with the dominant culture.[18] Moreover, the implicit and explicit message inscribed in *Equality*, as well as in Bellamy's earlier utopian fiction and that of feminist writers from Mary H. Lane in *Mizora* (1889) to Gilman's *Herland* (1915), is on the role of women as mothers of a revitalized Anglo-Saxon race.[19] Thus, although Bellamy and many of his middle class feminist allies locate an emancipated role for women in the present and future, they retain a racialized Victorian sense of motherhood.

On the other hand, *Equality* demonstrates that Bellamy saw the need to develop a bolder agenda for women in keeping with the demands of his feminist audience and his own political evolution. Before the publication of *Equality*, Bellamy had editorialized in an October 1893 edition of his paper, the *New Nation*, that the "present worldwide agitation for the equality of the sexes is one of the main forces that is making necessary and inevitable the radical economic reorganization of society for which we work and wait. It is fitting that in this greatest of all revolutions, men and women should move abreast."[20] In conjunction with this sentiment and in recognition of his inscribed feminist audience for *Equality*, toward the end of the novel Bellamy notes: "In this matter of the place of woman in the new order, you must understand that it was the women, themselves, rather than the men, who insisted that they must share in full the duties as well as the privileges of citizenship" (369). Thus, the "new woman" of Bellamy's *Equality* assumes that role of full citizenship for which Bellamy and middle class feminists agitated in turn-of-the-century America.

As one of the most ubiquitous agitators and prolific writers among turn-of-the-century feminists, Charlotte Perkins Gilman began her public career in the 1890s as a spokesperson for Nationalism and Fabian socialism. Bellamy's *Looking Backward* inspired her not because of his originality but because of "the daring imagination, the careful practical planning of detail, and the immense human love."[21] Moreover, Gilman, like other middle class supporters of Nationalism, welcomed a vision of the future free of class conflict. According to Gilman, under Nationalism "class distinctions would disappear, and social instincts would unite instead of separating us."[22] In her autobiography Gilman made clear her commitment to a non-Marxist socialism: "My Socialism was of the early humanitarian kind, based on the first exponents, French and English, with the American enthusiasm of Bellamy. The narrow and rigid 'economic determinism' of Marx with its 'class consciousness' and 'class struggle' I never accepted."[23]

Although Nationalism as an Americanized form of socialism was, in Gilman's estimation, the "most practical form of human development," gender equality was "the most essential condition of that development."[24] Beyond her campaigning for Nationalism and Fabian socialism, Gilman made the realization of gender equality the core of her practical and theoretical work. The most seminal expression of the need for gender equality came with the publication in 1898 of *Women and Economics*. The preface to that work completely telescopes the theoretical influences that would remain critical to all of her writings, both nonfictional and fictional.[25] Adopting the voice of the moralist and reform Darwinist, the preface claims the book will "show how some of the worst evils under which we suffer, evils long supposed to be inherent and ineradicable in our natures are but the result of certain arbitrary conditions of our own adoption, and how, by removing those conditions, we may remove the evils resultant" (xxxix). Evident in this passage is a "Lamarckian idealism" that assumes "ideas could modify both human heredity and social environment" and that "goes considerably beyond Bellamy's belief that freedom from economic constraints would liberate the natural goodness inherent in the human soul."[26]

While Gilman's Lamarckian idealism informs her adaptation of evolutionary thought in the service of gender equality, Gilman's

Victorian feminist emphasis on women's role in the moral uplift of society fashions her appeal to her female audience. Gilman makes that appeal in the preface—"To reach in especial the thinking women of to-day, and urge upon them a new sense, not only of their social responsibility as individuals, but of their measureless racial importance as makers of men" (xxxix). Embedded in this passage, as well as conspicuous throughout *Women and Economics*, is Gilman's debt to the American sociologist Lester Frank Ward and his popular 1888 article "Our Better Halves." In that article Ward asserted: "Woman is the race and the race can be raised up only as she is raised up. . . . True science teaches that the elevation of woman is the only sure road to the evolution of man."[27] In *Women and Economics* Gilman reinforces this Victorian moral reading of motherhood by calling motherhood "the common duty and the common glory of womanhood" (246). On the other hand, *Women and Economics* also attempts to demonstrate that socializing maternal care and love by freeing women from the individual home and developing a specialized and professional approach to domestic tasks, such as cooking, cleaning, and child-care, will benefit not only women but the species as well.[28]

Gilman followed up her success with *Women and Economics* with a number of other books and articles continuing her call for the feminist transformation of work, home, and child-care. In her attempts to reach a wide audience with this agenda for the "new woman," Gilman began to write utopian fiction. Focusing, as one critic suggests, "not upon the macrostructure of a capitalist economy (as did Bellamy in *Looking Backward* and *Equality*) but the microstructure of everyday living," Gilman's utopian fiction "seeks to dislodge traditional gender ideology by presenting alternative, realizable possibilities for more egalitarian gender roles."[29] Although only a five-chapter fragment (four of which were published in a short-lived monthly magazine), her 1907 "A Woman's Utopia" brings together the sociological nonfiction writings and her activist feminist sensibilities.[30] By inscribing both her evolutionary feminism and her female audience into the story, "A Woman's Utopia" provides an excellent opportunity to track the representation of Gilman's version of the "new woman."

Gilman introduces "A Woman's Utopia" by linking her Lamarckian idealism with a feminized utopian vision of universal "betterment" (216). In claiming an "instinctive demand for happiness . . . [and] for heaven, not after death, but here" (215), Gilman grounds her utopian appeal in evolution. "What a species is born desiring, is good for it," Gilman contends. Further arguing that previous utopias, generated by men like Plato, More, and Wells, "have been of a large and glittering generality . . . [assuming] extreme differences" (216), Gilman sees the progress inherent in the present offering a "glorious future" that "begins here and now" (216). Overlooking women's utopian writing, Gilman nonetheless notes how "vocal" contemporary women are by citing their increasing public voice, albeit a "complaining" one (216). Insisting that "[n]ow is the time for practical Utopias," Gilman identifies the agent of that practical utopia as "the Mother" (216), that great nurturer who would be the icon for her and many of her Victorian feminist supporters.

If the introduction to "A Woman's Utopia" underscores an elevating maternalism, it also reveals a consistent condescending paternalism derivative of Bellamy and Gilman's Nationalist origins.[31] Citing the importance of science and education in advancing the common mind, Gilman avows that "we can see in the years behind us how our progress was needlessly impeded by the density, the inertia, the prejudice and cowardice and sodden ignorance of the multitude. A century of science has helped the common mind. Our socialized schools and libraries, our freedom of thought and speech, and our undeniable achievements, all make us better able to take further steps" (216). Those further steps described in "A Woman's Utopia" will thus necessarily rely on the class pretensions and cultural biases shared by Gilman and her middle class audience, irrespective of their level of feminist consciousness.

It should come as no surprise that the instrument for the practical betterment of society, elaborated in Chapter I, entitled "The Proposition," is the intervention of a wealthy intellectual named Morgan G. Street, the appropriate skeptical male narrator. Gilman and other utopian writers of the time relied on the agency of "benevolent capitalism" as a consequence of their middle class fear of class conflict and inability to envision a transformation that would not be based on evolutionary right thinking.[32] Street falls in love with his cousin Hope Cartwright (shades of Gilman's own marriage to her cousin Houghton Gilman?), whom he accompanies to the vaguely socialist R.G.U. Club ("argue" club, Street calls it—217). He dismisses the denizens of this club as "all with the humanitarian bee in their bonnets, mad with the notion of helping the world" (217). As a taunt to these hopeless optimists, Street decides to give the club members twenty million dollars "to play with" (218) for twenty years while he travels the world.

Discounting Hope's faith in an entrepreneurial and scientific utopian figure she calls the "Social Inventor" (219), Street also derisively dismisses Hope's women colleagues at the club as faddists who were concerned with "baby-culture," "cooking," and "dressmaking" (217). While Street exhibits his sexist biases, this allows Gilman to acknowledge those reform movements that were important to Gilman and her feminist audience. Street assumes that "pretty soon they'd all be married and could practice their fine theories where they belonged—at home" (217), little realizing that Hope Cartwright and her R.G.U. comrades will instead use the twenty million dollars offered by Street to accomplish what Victorian feminists from Frances Willard to Gilman articulated—"to make the whole world home-like."[33] In fact, it is very likely that the "Social Inventor" that Gilman had in mind who could accomplish the task "to make the whole world home-like" was Gilman's close friend from her California days and Hope Cartwright namesake, Helen Campbell. Campbell, like Gilman, was a tireless reformer and women's rights advocate whose writings on socializing household economics and involvement with the National Consumers League suggested the kind of practical utopian possibilities central to "A Woman's Utopia."[34]

When Street returns after his twenty-year absence, he immediately notices several "mechanical improvements" and "certain indefinable alterations in the women" (219). He is also visibly struck by the "absence of smoke" in the clean and aesthetically pleasing city environment. Demonstrating a trope that is to inform much of her utopian fiction, especially in *Herland*, Gilman conflates the emancipation of women with an environmentally sound society built to human scale. While it is tempting to laud Gilman's advanced ecological sensitivity, it is evident in her descriptions of the smokeless and uncluttered urban environment that she shares with Bellamy and other middle class utopian writers a revulsion of the disorder caused not only by industrial capitalism but also by immigrant hordes residing in the city. This xenophobia and racism, evident in the nativist movements of the turn of the century, is also an unfortunate prime component of adversaries of the dominant order like Gilman whose Victorian feminism's emphasis on social purity conveyed obvious ethnocentric biases.[35]

Those ethnocentric biases are particularly unmistakable in Gilman's description of the Lower East Side of New York City as "that ghastly blot on our civilization, that hotbed of consumption and worse evils still" (502). The Lower East Side has been transformed in the year 1927 into "broad, tree-shaded avenues, parks and parklets everywhere" (502). Partly as a consequence of feminized city planning, the old slums have been demolished to make way for "flowery, sunlit, open courts" (502). Slum dwellers and surplus labor, all of a darker hue than the middle class saviors of society, were inducted into a Bellamy-like industrial army where they did road-building and other hard labor. While being compensated for their work, it is clear in these references, especially to how such disciplined work "settled the negro [sic] problem" (504), that Gilman and her readers could be assured that practical utopias would carry out a much needed Anglo-Saxon revitalization of society and the underclass. As noted in Gail Bederman's recent study of the intersection of gender and race in the turn-of-the-century discourse on civilization, Gilman's "feminism was inextricably rooted in the white supremacism of 'civilization.' "36

In the unpublished Chapter V we are taken into an apartment in the former Lower East Side slum where an obviously immigrant and working class husband and wife now live productive lives with their children well cared for by professional child-caretakers in a rooftop day-care center. What is so striking about this little interlude is that Gilman feels compelled to Anglicize the Jewish names from Weisberg to Whiteberg as a further expression of the moral and social uplift that this practical utopia achieved. Moreover, the dialogue with the Whitebergs, the mother from Russia and the father from Germany, provides an occasion for a disquisition on the new scientific and judicious immigration restriction and Americanization policies (503–504). In addition, while eschewing a racialized forced eugenics plan (at least at this point in time), Gilman has Mrs. Whiteberg speak up for a more socially conscious birth control policy by practicing intelligent selection of mates. Thus, says Mrs. Whiteberg: "We will not marry the inferior men" (596), dooming them to extinction. Through such changed social conditions and education, Gilman illustrates for her native middle class audience the ethnocentric benefits of "A Woman's Utopia."

This exercise in social missionary work among poor immigrants is also reflective of the key mechanism that led to the conversion of society—the "new religion." Chapter III is devoted to explaining the interconnections between the new religion and the feminist cultural revitalization in the practical utopia of the future. Echoing a theme that had been basic to the Social Gospel movement and the work of Bellamy-inspired Christian Socialists like W.D.P. Bliss and Walter Rauschenbush, Gilman put her faith in secular religion that emphasized conversion to the Cooperative Commonwealth.37 Adding her own feminist and Lamarckian twist, Gilman describes how a movement started by a vaguely Christian Socialist called Henry St. John put "ethics on a practical basis" (371). Spread throughout society by "thousands of missionaries" (372), children and others are taught such lessons as "the social danger of lying" by studying "lying as we were studying cancer and consumption when you left" (372). Moreover, "the great fountain head of lying was the position of women" (373). With Street responding incredulously, his guide at this point, "Dale Edwards, the manager-in-chief of the Upgrade Publication Co" (371), avers: "The idea is that women were maintained in a primitive relation to man, a subordinate, dependent position; taking no part in our social growth. This kept them like a lower race among us, and preserved in them vices and weaknesses of the lower races" (373). Gilman's configuring of women's subordination and dependence with primitive and lower races reveals how the civilizing mission she envisioned in her fiction and nonfiction writing was bound up with white supremacist ideology. In her 1903 publication, *The Home: Its Work and Influence*, the drudgery forced upon women in the privatized home reduced them to the level of the savage "squaw." Reinforcing sexual differences of this type would, according to Gilman, impede both racial advancement and civilization. In turn, sexual equality would lead to racial advancement and the uplifting of civilization to a new and higher stage of evolution.[38]

In linking the moral uplift of society with the role of women, Gilman not only reiterates her Ward-inspired analysis in *Women and Economics*, but she also reveals how that message of the social uplifting of women contains a racialized Lamarckian core. As "A Women's Utopia" makes clear once "women really became people— independent, self-supporting citizens"—lying was "educated out of the stock" (373). Moreover, women could then assume a socialized maternal role that helped transform everything from child-care to cooking. Again echoing *Women and Economics*, "A Woman's Utopia" underscores the movement from "egoism to socioism" (373), rendering in the process a vital sense of "social service" as "Christian duty." In effect, Gilman establishes in this work of utopian fiction what she will argue for in her last work, *His Religion and Hers: A Study of the Faith of Our Fathers and the Work of Our Mothers*: "tak[ing] the nineteenth-century notion of maternal service and ma[king] it the foundation of an ethical system and a guide for the conduct of everyone."[39] Thus, in the new world of the future "it is vulgar and ignorant to be selfish, like bad table manners. Now women and men alike recognize that the one all-embracing duty is to love and serve humanity, and to learn how" (375).

Ultimately, the instruction to learn how to love and serve humanity in "A Woman's Utopia" is the task that Hope Cartwright takes on in her education of Morgan Street. In Chapter IV, Street is not only confronted with his own sexist biases, but the reader is engaged in either discovering or reconfirming the key components of Gilman's feminist perspective for the "new woman" and of a utopian hope for a new and better world. Street's challenge to Hope Cartwright, reflective of his unwillingness to imagine human betterment, contains the springboard to his (and the reader's) education in utopian possibilities. "If you can show me human nature to be in any degree wiser, kinder, truer, stronger, nobler, purer, braver, sweeter; if you can show me better health, better morals, better manners; more virtue and happiness, less dishonesty and greed, less vice, crime, disease, misery, and general cussedness—clear proof of change in any or all of these points—in twenty years—why you win the argument, and I lose" (499). The argument, of course, is one that Gilman had lampooned in her first publication, the satirical poem "Similar Cases." Published in the April 1890 *Nationalist*, the Bellamy-inspired monthly journal, the poem ridiculed the social conservatism of those whose claim "You'd have to change human nature!" was patently contradicted by the record of evolutionary transformations.[40]

The key for Hope Cartwright's victory over Morgan Street's social conservatism resides in the central tenet of Gilman's work dating from *Women and Economics*, namely that in freeing women from the oppressiveness of domestic slavery and economic dependence you liberate humanity and open up the future to massive positive change. Thus, she poses the "average woman" of the past who "had few interests beyond her home and children, cared little for business, politics, or general progress, cared much for personal decoration, was a slavish observer of fashion and convention, had little physical strength and a rapidly waning beauty, and was a profound individualist and conservative" (499) to that of "the average woman of to-day [who] is interested in the improvement of the whole world, her own country, and especially her own city; [who] . . . takes a large part in business and politics, art and science, all industry and trade; [who] . . . has become stronger, more beautiful, and dresses with wise good taste and personal distinction; [who] . . . is now organized and united in splendid co-ordination in every city, throughout the country and internationally as well; and [who] is hand in hand with men in the highest progress" (499). By such contrast, Gilman not only recapitulates the perspectives found in Bellamy's *Equality* but also in her own theoretical treatises from *Women and Economics* through *The Home: Its Work and Influence* (1903) and *Human Work* (1904).

To explain the change Hope points to the "tremendous progress" women had made by 1907 through their activities in "clubs and federations" and the increasing scientific study of "Domestic Economy" and "Child Culture" (500), topics that Gilman and her material feminist sisters had been writing about and putting into practice for years.[41] What provided the real catalyst was the "new religion" which "illuminated all the confused problems of the time" (500). Combining this "religious fervor" with "mother-love and the new pride of free womanhood," women organized into the "New World Party" and won "municipal suffrage for women, everywhere, within five years." As a consequence, "[b]etter civic management was so clear and practical an issue that majorities agreed on that almost at once" (500). Thus, with little or no strife, and certainly no class conflict, a radical transformation in the political order was effectuated with women at the helm. Enacting the programs that had been the hallmark of material feminists like Gilman and her predecessors—collective kitchens, professional chid-care, and other reforms that gave women and children a more liberated role in society—the "New World Party" put into practice a socialized motherhood reflective of Gilman's own brand of Victorian feminism.[42]

Because of Gilman's focus on "civilized motherhood" (596) as the cornerstone of the dramatic changes in "A Woman's Utopia," she perpetuates the Victorian ideology of maternal service for the betterment of humanity.[43] Although thoroughly liberating women from the domestic service inherent in conservative Victorian ideology through the techniques and technology advanced by material feminism, Gilman's socialization of maternal service roots her feminism in a bygone era, one that would become increasingly out of date with the birth of a more modern feminism that eschewed religious precepts and Victorian sexuality.[44] Thus, Gilman's "new woman" embodies ideals all too consonant with certain features of her "Nationalist-Fabian origins" that "were characteristic elements of Gilded Age socialist evolutionism."[45]

If both Gilman's and Bellamy's utopianism was constrained by the ideological contradictions of their age, they nonetheless managed to project visions of change and social betterment in keeping with their desire for gender equality in the future. While projections of the "new woman" in *Equality* and "A Woman's Utopia" were in keeping with the advances in the sociocultural conditions for women and feminist activism and expectations, those projections all too easily reflected the Victorian feminist sensibilities of both their authors and their inscribed audience. Not able to escape the class and ethnic/racial biases of middle class progressives, the utopian fiction of Bellamy and Gilman engendered a future no-place that was not, unfortunately, far removed from the prejudices of the present places inhabited by Bellamy, Gilman, and their readers.[46]

NOTES

1. Nancy Woloch, *Women and the American Experience*, 2d ed. (New York: McGraw-Hill, 1994), p. 269. On the "new woman" in the modern

industrial world, see E. J. Hobsbawm, *The Age of Empire, 1875–1914* (New York: Vintage, 1989), pp. 192–218. On the "new woman" in turn-of-the-century America, see Woloch, *Women and the American Experience*, pp. 269–307. On the contradictions confronting the new woman in Victorian America, see Carroll Smith-Rosenberg, *Disorderly Conduct: Visions of Gender in Victorian America* (New York: Oxford University Press, 1985). On the impact of the "grand domestic revolution" for women in America, see Dolores Hayden, *The Grand Domestic Revolution* (Cambridge: MIT Press, 1981).

2. Quoted in Jean Pfaelzer, *The Utopian Novel in America, 1886–1896: The Politics of Form* (Pittsburgh: University of Pittsburgh Press, 1984), p. 150. For a discussion of Ticknor's article, "The Steel Engraving Lady and the Gibson Girl," see ibid., pp. 143–44. On the "Gibson Girl" as a figure compatible with the "new woman," even Gilman's version, see Martha Patterson, " 'Survival of the Best Fitted': Selling the American New Woman as Gibson Girl, 1895–1910," *ATQ* 9 (June 1995): 73–85.

3. On the transformation from true or ideal womanhood to the new woman, see Frances B. Cogan, *All-American Girl: The Ideal of Real Womanhood in Mid-Nineteenth-Century America* (Athens: University of Georgia Press, 1989), pp. 257–63. On the birth of modern feminism, see Nancy Cott, *The Grounding of Modern Feminism* (New Haven: Yale University Press, 1987), esp. pp. 13–50. On the emergence of a woman-centered culture and social psychology, see Rosalind Rosenberg, *Beyond Separate Spheres: Intellectual Roots of Modern Feminism* (New Haven: Yale University Press, 1982), esp. pp. 36–83.

4. Carol A. Kolmerten, "Texts and Contexts: American Women Envision Utopia, 1890–1920" in *Utopian and Science Fiction by Women: Worlds of Difference*, ed. Jane L. Donawerth and Carol A. Kolmerten (Syracuse: Syracuse University Press, 1994), p. 107. On the "horizon of expectations" in literary texts, see Robert C. Holub, *Reception Theory: A Critical Introduction* (London: Methuen, 1984), p. 59; and Susan R. Suleiman, "Introduction," in *The Reader in the Text: Essays on Audiences and Interpretation*, ed. Susan R. Suleiman and Inge Crossman (Princeton: Princeton University Press, 1980), pp. 35–37. On those horizons of expectations in utopian literature, see Peter Ruppert, *Reader in a Strange Land: The Activity of Reading Literary Utopias* (Athens: University of Georgia Press, 1986).

5. For a discussion of those gender constructions in turn-of-the-century utopian fiction in America, see Kolmerten, "Texts and Contexts," pp. 107–25; and Pfaelzer, *The Utopian Novel*, pp. 141–58.

6. On Bellamy and the development of the Nationalist movement, see Arthur Lipow, *Authoritarian Socialism in America: Edward Bellamy and the Nationalist Movement* (Berkeley: University of California Press, 1982); and Everett W. Macnair, *Edward Bellamy and the Nationalist Movement, 1889–1894* (Milwaukee: Fitzgerald, 1957). For a discussion of *Looking Backward*'s impact on the women's movement, see Mari Jo Buhle, *Women and American Socialism, 1870–1920* (Urbana: University of Illinois Press, 1981), pp. 75–81; Hayden, *Grand Domestic Revolution*, esp. pp. 135–37; and William Leach, "Looking Forward Together: Feminists and Edward Bel-

lamy," *Democracy* 2 (January 1982): 120–34. For two slightly different perspectives on Gilman's role in the Nationalist movement, see Mary A. Hill, *Charlotte Perkins Gilman: The Making of a Radical Feminist, 1860–1896* (Philadelphia: Temple University Press, 1980), pp. 170–85; and Gary Scharnhorst, *Charlotte Perkins Gilman* (Boston: Twayne, 1985), pp. 20–33.

7. John L. Thomas, *Alternative America: Henry George, Edward Bellamy, Henry Demarest Lloyd and the Adversary Tradition* (Cambridge: The Belknap Press of Harvard University Press, 1983), *passim.*

8. On the changes in women's roles from *Looking Backward* to *Equality*, see Sylvia Bowman, *Edward Bellamy* (Boston: Twayne 1986), esp. pp. 98–109; Sylvia Strauss, "Gender, Class, and Race in Utopia," in *Looking Backward, 1988–1888: Essays on Edward Bellamy,* ed. Daphne Patai (Amherst: University of Massachusetts Press, 1988), pp. 88–89; Kenneth M. Roemer, "Getting 'Nowhere' Beyond Stasis: A Critique, a Method, and a Case," in Patai, *Looking Backward 1988–1888,* pp. 138–42; and Ruth Levitas, " 'Who Holds the Hose?' Domestic Labour in the Work of Bellamy, Gilman and Morris," *Utopian Studies* 6 (1995): 66–70.

9. For the most complete presentation of Gilman's background to and development of her utopian writings, see Carol Farley Kessler, *Charlotte Perkins Gilman: Her Progress Toward Utopia with Selected Writings* (Syracuse: Syracuse University Press, 1995), pp. 1–114. For other concise considerations of Gilman's translations from her activism and nonfiction writings to her utopian fiction, see Hayden, *The Grand Domestic Revolution,* pp. 183–205; and Polly Wynn Allen, *Building Domestic Liberty: Charlotte Perkins Gilman's Architectural Feminism* (Amherst: University of Massachusetts Press, 1988), pp. 83–102.

10. On the "inscribed audience" in the literary text, see Suleiman in *The Reader in the Text,* pp. 12 and 15. On the similar role of the implied reader in the utopian text, see Ruppert, *Reader in a Strange Land,* pp. 48–49 and *passim;* and Roemer in "Getting 'Nowhere' Beyond Stasis: A Critique, a Method, and a Case," in *Looking Backward,* pp. 134–35.

11. Quoted in Sylvia E. Bowman, *The Year 2000: A Critical Biography of Edward Bellamy* (New York: Bookman Associates, 1958), p. 275. On feminist criticism of *Looking Backward,* see Bowman, *Edward Bellamy,* p. 57, and Strauss, "Gender, Class, and Race in Utopia," pp. 77–78.

12. Quoted in Daphne Patai, "Introduction: The Double Vision of Edward Bellamy," in Patai, *Looking Backward, 1988–1888,* p. 14.

13. Ibid., p. 15.

14. Edward Bellamy, *Equality* (New York: D. Appleton, 1897), p. 43. All further references will be noted in the text.

15. Levitas, "'Who Holds the Hose?' " p. 69.

16. As an example of the social purity crusades of the times, see Ruth Bordin, *Women and Temperance: The Quest for Power and Liberty, 1873–1900* (Philadelphia: Temple University Press, 1981). On Bellamy's religious, reform Darwinist, and Victorian feminist sensibilities, see Bowman, *Edward Bellamy,* pp. 80–109; Mark Pittenger, *American Socialists and Evolutionary Thought, 1870–1920* (Madison: University of Wisconsin

Press, 1993), pp. 65–71; and Strauss, "Gender, Class, and Race in Utopia," pp. 68–90.

17. On Bellamy's change toward dress reform, see Strauss, "Gender, Class, and Race in Utopia," p. 79.

18. For a discussion of the emphasis on physical exercise in the 1890's, albeit on a masculinized sensibility, see John Higham, "The Reorientation of American Culture in the 1890's," *The Origins of Modern Consciousness*, ed. John Weiss (Detroit: Wayne State University Press, 1965), pp. 25–48. On Gilman's own involvement with physical culture of late nineteenth-century America, see Jane Lancaster, " 'I could easily have been an acrobat': Charlotte Perkins Gilman and the Providence Ladies' Sanitary Gymnasium 1881–1884," *ATQ* 8 (March 1994): 33–52.

19. See Lipow, *Authoritarian Socialism in America*, pp. 51–53. On the role of motherhood and its interface with Anglo-Saxon revitalization in women's utopian fiction, see Pfaelzer, *The Utopian Novel in America*, pp. 146–58.

20. Quoted in Franklin Rosemont, "Bellamy's Radicalism Reclaimed," in Patai, *Looking Backward*, 1988–1888, p. 175; Rosemont's positive assessment of Bellamy's connection to the women's movement and to the radicalism of the period can be seen in pp. 147–209.

21. Quoted in Hill, *Charlotte Perkins Gilman*, p. 171.

22. Quoted in ibid.

23. Charlotte Perkins Gilman, *The Living of Charlotte Perkins Gilman: An Autobiography* (New York: D. Appleton-Century, 1935), p. 131.

24. Quoted in Hill, *Charlotte Perkins Gilman*, p. 182.

25. Charlotte Perkins Gilman, *Women and Economics*, ed. Carl Degler (New York: Harper Torchbooks, 1966). All references in the text will be made to this edition.

26. Pittenger, *American Socialists and Evolutionary Thought*, pp. 72 and 75. Other commentary on Gilman's reform Darwinism and Lamarckian reading of evolutionary theory can be found in Lois N. Magner, "Darwinism and the Woman Questions: The Evolving Views of Charlotte Perkins Gilman," *Critical Essays on Charlotte Perkins Gilman*, ed. Joanne B. Karpinski (New York: G. K. Hall, 1992), pp. 115–28; and Scharnhorst, *Charlotte Perkins Gilman*, pp. 64–65.

27. Carl Degler, "Introduction," in Gilman, *Women and Economics*, xxxiv.

28. For a fuller discussion of *Women and Economics*, see Ann J. Lane, *To Herland and Beyond: The Life and Work of Charlotte Perkins Gilman* (New York: Pantheon, 1990), pp. 233–54.

29. Carol Farley Kessler, "Consider Her Ways: The Cultural Work of Charlotte Perkins Gilman's Pragmatopian Stories, 1908–1913," in *Utopian and Science Fiction by Women*, p. 131; and Kessler, *Charlotte Perkins Gilman*, p. 8.

30. The first four chapters appeared in the 1907 January, February, and March editions of *The Times Magazine*. The last chapter and fourth installment is available only in page proofs in the Gilman Papers at Radcliffe. There is no evidence that the novel was ever completed. All

references in the text will be to the extant page numbers. I am indebted to Gary Scharnhorst for supplying me with a full copy of what remains of "A Woman's Utopia."

31. Hill, *Charlotte Perkins Gilman*, p. 173.

32. Hayden, *The Grand Domestic Revolution*, p. 197. Carol Farley Kessler notes the number of utopian stories and novels by Gilman that rely on inheritances or gifts from wealthy individuals to construct the better society. See Kessler, *Charlotte Perkins Gilman*, pp. 42–81.

33. On Willard's statement to "make the whole world more home-like," see Hayden, *Grand Domestic Revolution*, p. 5. On Gilman's commitment to that principle, see Lane, *To Herland and Beyond*, p. 303. In an article entitled "The Passing of the Home in Great American Cities," published in the December 1904 edition of *Cosmopolitan*, Gilman gives credence to the "expansion of the home life into 'society life.' " Cited in Kessler, *Charlotte Perkins Gilman*, p. 45. On how "home" can be read during this era as a code word for Anglo-Saxon superiority, social purity, and reform, see Woloch, *Women and the American Experience*, p. 270.

34. On Campbell's connection to and influence on Gilman, see Hill, *Charlotte Perkins Gilman*, pp. 238–41; and Hayden, *The Grand Domestic Revolution*, pp. 185–86.

35. On nativism and Anglo-Saxon prejudices in American culture, see John Higham, *Strangers in the Land: Patterns of American Nativism 1860–1925* (New York: Atheneum, 1963), esp. pp. 234–63. On Gilman's xenophobia and racism, see Kessler, *Charlotte Perkins Gilman*, pp. 45–48, 50–52, 73–77.

36. Gail Bederman, *Manliness & Civilization: A Cultural History of Gender and Race in the United States, 1880–1917* (Chicago: University of Chicago Press, 1995), p. 122.

37. Hill, *Charlotte Perkins Gilman*, p. 174. On Bliss and Christian Socialism, see Arthur Mann, *Yankee Reformers in the Urban Age* (New York: Harper Torchbooks, 1966), pp. 90–99. On the Social Gospel movement, see R. C. White and C. H. Hopkins, *The Social Gospel: Religion and Reform in Changing America* (Philadelphia: Temple University Press, 1976). On Gilman's religious views and their connection to the Social Gospel movement, see Frank G. Kirkpatrick, " 'Begin Again!': The Cutting Social Edge of Charlotte Perkins Gilman's Gentle Religious Optimism," in Karpinski, *Critical Essays on Charlotte Perkins Gilman*, pp. 129–43.

38. Bederman, *Manliness & Civilization*, pp. 132, 136–40, 145.

39. Lane, *To Herland and Beyond*, p. 289.

40. For a brief discussion of and excerpt from the poem, see Scharnhorst, *Charlotte Perkins Gilman*, pp. 22–24.

41. On Gilman's intersection with the material feminists, see Hayden, *The Grand Domestic Revolution*, pp. 183–205.

42. On Gilman's sense of "social motherhood," see Scharnhorst, *Charlotte Perkins Gilman*, pp. 64–69. On Gilman's approach to feminist reform of the social and built environment, see Allen, *Building Domestic Liberty*, pp. 55–141.

43. On the influence of Victorian ideology in Gilman's work, see Barbara Scott Winkler, "Victorian Daughters: The Lives and Feminism of Charlotte Perkins Gilman and Olive Schreiner," in Karpinski, *Critical Essays on Charlotte Perkins Gilman*, pp. 173–83. On the emphasis of motherhood in Gilman's nonfiction and utopian fiction, see Kessler, *Charlotte Perkins Gilman*, p. 29 and *passim*.

44. On the birth and nature of modern feminism, see Cott, *The Grounding of Modern Feminism*, pp. 13–50.

45. Pittenger, *American Socialist and Evolutionary Thought*, p. 87.

46. For an even harsher criticism of the lack of radical utopianizing primarily by Gilman, but also Bellamy, see Thomas Galt Peyser, "Reproducing Utopia: Charlotte Perkins Gilman and *Herland*," *Studies in American Fiction* 20 (Spring 1992): 1–16.

3

Racial Boundaries and "Hidden" African-American Utopias: Griggs's Imperium in Imperio *and* Hopkins's *"Of One Blood"*

For African-Americans, the turn of the century witnessed an up-surge in white supremacist thought and practice, leading one historian of this period to designate it as the "nadir" of modern black life.[1] During the 1890s, in the aftermath of the failed interracial solidarity of the Populist movement and in the face of a depressed economy, African-Americans, especially in the South where 90 percent of them resided, were under siege. On both an institutional and ideological level racial boundaries were redrawn to exclude blacks from the center stage of public life. Disfranchisement and segregation became the vehicles by which white supremacy pushed black citizens to the margins of political and social existence. When such institutional and legal oppression did not satisfy white su-premacists, extra-legal means such as lynching were utilized, es-tablishing a reign of terror in the South. As George Fredrickson has noted: "Lynching was . . . symptomatic of a conviction that the legal mechanisms of repression that accompanied segregation and dis-franchisement did not go far enough."[2]

Nevertheless, the legal mechanisms of repression and oppression continued apace in the South during the 1880s and 1890s. While the redrawing of racial boundaries saw an increase in the passage of state laws mandating segregation, it was the U.S. Supreme Court that sanctioned the institutionalization of white supremacy in public life. Striking down the Civil Rights Act of 1875, the Supreme Court in 1883 gave the green light to states seeking to exclude blacks from equal protection of the law through "Jim Crow" legislation. When the Supreme Court voted to uphold an 1890 Louisiana statute segregating rail passengers in *Plessy v. Ferguson*, it did more than validate "separate but equal" as the law of the land. As one interpreter of the ruling contends: "*Plessy* was a landmark case not because it drastically altered the direction of legislation and judicial thought, but because it concluded the process of transfiguring dual *constitutional* citizenship into dual *racial* citizenship which had unfolded since the end of Reconstruction"[3] (author's emphasis).

In redefining racial boundaries, the ideology of white supremacy played as significant a role as the institutional realignment authorized by legal and political provisions. If one understands race as "a highly contested representation of relations of power between social categories by which individuals are identified and identify themselves," then the ideological deployment of race becomes a "discursive tool for both oppression and liberation."[4] During this turn-of-the-century period, white supremacists articulated an ideological discourse that at best projected a paternalistic representation of African-Americans and, at worst, created an image of black degeneracy and bestiality. While genteel moderate whites of the "New South" argued for a "benevolent guardianship" that would protect their infantile image of African-Americans from further depredations of modern life and help "elevate" blacks, radical white racists enunciated a belief in black barbarism as an ideological cover for repressive legislation and violent acts towards African-Americans.[5] Ideological ranting about black bestiality was not only a discursive tool of southern demagogues like South Carolina Senator Benjamin Tillman, but it also found its way into the social Darwinist-tinged pseudo-science of the turn of the century. A professor of medicine at the University of Virginia opined at a 1900 conference that "all things point to the fact that the Negro as a race is reverting to barbarism with the inordinate criminality and degradation of that state."[6]

Against such ideological diatribes that inscribed black inferiority into the discourse of turn-of-the-century life, African-American writers and intellectuals attempted to develop a discursive response to white supremacy.[7] In renegotiating the ideology of racial boundaries, black writers such as Charles Chestnutt endorsed a "literature of necessity" which required discursive strategies to contest white supremacist representations.[8] In effect, the black intellectuals' response to the ideological debasement by white supremacy was the creation of a "New Negro" as "a counterforce of self-definition and achievement."[9] The black minister and writer Sutton E. Griggs underscored this redefinition by noting in his 1899 novel *Imperium in Imperio*: "The cringing, fawning, sniffling, cowardly Negro which slavery left, had disappeared, and a new Negro, self-respecting, fearless, and determined in the assertion of his rights was at hand."[10]

On the other hand, the assertion of rights and the redefinition of racial boundaries and identity by African-Americans were not without their ambiguities and contradictions, reflecting at times the resonance of a mainstream ideological discourse and at other moments the emergence of a nationalist sensibility. Given the necessity of underscoring genteel and middle class values as a counterforce to images of black degeneracy and barbarism, African-American discursive strategies, even in nationalist form, often embodied bourgeois and Victorian reformist ideologies. As Wilson Jeremiah Moses has argued: "Black bourgeois nationalism was not a fantasy, nor was it an escape from reality; it was a rational attempt to manipulate the hostile environment in which it was conceived."[11] Moreover, the emphasis on racial uplift in African-American literature at the turn of the century reinscribed "civilizationist" and "elitist" ideals into black discursive strategies, sometimes merging with a rhetoric that reinforced imperialist ideology emergent in U.S. policy.[12] Finally, the ideology of Christian humanism, while consistent with a reformist Social Gospel of the time, often led to a "messianic self-conception" that overlapped with an "Ethiopian mysticism" evident in black intellectuals and writers at the turn of the century.[13]

Two African-American writers who stood out in this period and whose novels attempted to redefine the ideology of racial boundaries in concert with the aforementioned discursive strategies were Sutton E. Griggs and Pauline Hopkins.[14] Both writers developed major characters who, in keeping with Arlene Elder's survey of African-American fiction at the time, "are meant to be counterstereotypes, drawn with the intent of demonstrating the race's beauty, nobility, intelligence, determination, and ambition, and, thereby appeasing the Black middle-class reading public."[15] Furthermore, by keeping in sync with the "literature of necessity," both Griggs and Hopkins articulated a didactic ideal in their fiction. For Hopkins, such didacticism led her to assert in the preface to her 1900 novel *Contending Forces* a desire "to raise the stigma of degradation from my race."[16] Even more attuned to the propagandistic value of such literature, Griggs noted: "To succeed as a race we must move up out of the age of the voice, the age of direct personal appeal, and live in an age where an idea can influence to action. . . . When the time arrives that the Negroes are capable of being moved to action on a

large scale by what they read, a marked change in the condition of
the race will begin instantly and will be marvelous in its propor-
tions."[17]

While it is clear that both Griggs and Hopkins aimed their
discursive strategies at the small black middle class at the turn of
the century, they also replicated the moral message found in
abolitionist and temperance literature of an earlier era in order to
reach out to whites of good conscience. As indicated in a biographical sketch of Hopkins in a 1901 issue of the *Colored American
Magazine* (for which Hopkins was the literary editor from the
journal's inception in 1900 to its takeover by the allies of Booker T.
Washington in 1904): "Her ambition is to become a writer of fiction,
in which the wrongs of her race shall be handled as to enlist the
sympathy of all classes of citizens."[18] In order to enlist the sympathy
of all classes of citizens, their fiction on one level conformed to the
conventions of the fiction of their era. On the other hand, where it
differed from white popular fiction was in making an "appeal to
action in the speaker's or writer's own experience of injustice and
in personal, eyewitness instances of suffering."[19] Thus, the novels
of Griggs and Hopkins have constant references to the tragic
implications of lynching, rape, and segregation and the white supremacist ideology of the times.

With such references to the institutional and ideological horrors
confronting African-Americans at the turn of the century, it may
seem surprising that both Griggs and Hopkins produced a literary
text that could be classified as utopian. Certainly, unlike the other
utopian novels of this period, neither Griggs's utopian 1899 novel
Imperium in Imperio, or Hopkins's serialized magazine novel "Of One
Blood" (serialized from November 1902 to November 1903 in the
Colored American Magazine) spend much time exploring the ideal
characteristics of the utopian societies portrayed in their texts.[20]
(Griggs devotes less than a third and Hopkins less than a quarter.)
On the other hand, both texts do satisfy the definition of utopian
literature "as works of the imagination, as symbolic constructs,
which function not to represent islands of social perfection but to
serve as thought-provoking catalysts whose value is in their shock
effect on readers."[21] Given the intense need to provide a counterforce
argument to the ideology of white supremacy and to move their
readers to action, the literary utopias of Griggs and Hopkins seek
to challenge and subvert the claims of white supremacist thought
about the backwardness of African-Americans and to reconfigure
racial boundaries at the turn of the century.[22]

What is particularly striking about the utopian societies in both
novels, however, is that they are hidden. In *Imperium in Imperio* the

utopian society is an underground black government outside (of all places) Waco, Texas. In "Of One Blood" the utopian society is the intact hidden city of Telassar, buried beneath the ruins of the ancient Ethiopian city of Meroe. Instead of classifying such hidden sites as typical of utopian escapes or enclaves of refuge, I want to suggest that part of the reason for their hidden quality has to do with the symbolic construction of what anthropologist James Scott calls the "hidden transcript." For Scott the hidden transcript is an "offstage discourse" by oppressed people away from the hegemony of the dominant group where "resistance can be nurtured and given meaning."[23] Moreover, in connecting the role of utopia to such hidden transcripts, Scott notes: "Most traditional utopian beliefs can, in fact, be understood as a more or less systematic negation of an existing pattern of exploitation and status degradation as it is experienced by subordinate groups."[24] Thus, Griggs constructs a symbolic hidden site whose utopian function negates, among other things, the political practice and ideology of disfranchisement while Hopkins's construction of Telassar negates the dominant view of Africa as backward and African-Americans as barbaric.

Another key component of the utopian function of the hidden sites in the texts of Griggs and Hopkins is the wish fulfillment embedded in the hidden transcript. In effect, such wish fulfillment, as noted by Ernst Bloch, becomes essential to the creation of an anticipatory consciousness whose social imaginary provides hope for a better world.[25] Understandably, such hope was constrained by the deplorable situation facing African-Americans at the turn of the century. Moreover, the inconsistencies and contradictions embedded in every utopian text were further compounded by the fact that, as African-American middle class intellectuals, Griggs and Hopkins had to contend with validating their existence as enlightened members of a despised race.[26] Thus, their literary texts become symbolic constructs not only of constrained utopianism and radicalism, but also of the terrible urgency of overcoming the ideological oppressiveness of white supremacy. It is to the specifics of each literary text that we must now turn.

Imperium in Imperio is the story of the intertwining lives of two charismatic African-American males—dark-skinned Belton Piedmont and light-skinned Bernard Belgrave. Although they attend the same Reconstruction public school, their paths separate, to be joined later in the novel when they become the leaders of a secret underground government. While Bernard's career is highly successful as a consequence of his mulatto background and a prominent, but mostly absent, white father, Belton's career suffers all of the harsh setbacks that confronted many educated members of the black middle class. In particular, Griggs uses the experiences of Belton to replicate the marginalization, repression, and terror that faced African-Americans in the 1880s and 1890s, especially in the aftermath of *Plessy*. By constructing situations where Belton is denied both his rights and any respect as a citizen and a black man, Griggs is able to comment on the ideological climate at the turn of the century and to calculate the dialectical equation of hope and despair that demarcates literary utopias.[27] Finally, in making both assimilationist and nationalist appeals for citizenship rights, social equality, and human dignity through the travails of Belton, Griggs demonstrates his own ideological commitment to political reformism, middle class respectability and elitism, and Christian humanism prevalent among African-American writers and intellectuals at the turn of the century.[28]

In appealing for rights and respect as African-Americans, Griggs also incorporates the racialist conceptions prominent in an era when evolutionary thought posited certain traits endemic to particular ethnic groups. As one critic of Griggs's writings asserts: "Griggs, like most of his contemporaries, contrasted Afro-Americans with Anglo-Saxons, seeing in each group certain inherent racial vices and virtues."[29] Thus, the configuration of political rights is cast in the black struggle to achieve Anglo-Saxon liberty and the failure of white America to honor the universal message inscribed in Anglo-Saxon liberty. It is not surprising then that Belton Piedmont's graduation oration is entitled: "The Contribution of the Anglo-Saxon to the Cause of Human Liberty" (32). Moreover, Belton's white sponsor, V. M. King, the "ultraliberal" (41) editor of the *Richmond Daily Temps*, and "an outspoken advocate of giving the negro every right accorded him by the Constitution of the United States" (41), underscores the connection between the struggle for liberty and the political contributions of Anglo-Saxonism. King ruminates on the fact that "it was only a matter of a few years before the negro would deify liberty as the Anglo-Saxon race had done, and count it a joy to perish on her altar" (42).

King's tutelage of Belton becomes a further occasion for a racialist polemical appeal to the reader combining Anglo-Saxon liberty with the social gospel of Christian humanism. "[King] knew that it was more humane, more in accordance with right, more acceptable with God, to admit to the negro that Anglo-Saxon doctrine of the equality of man was true, rather than to murder the negro for accepting him at his word, though spoken to others" (43–44). (This absence of the beneficence of granting Anglo-Saxon liberty to African-Americans recalls the earlier comments of black intellectual and teacher Anna Julia Cooper in her 1892 collection of essays, *A Voice from the South*, regarding the "problematical position at present occupied by descendants of Africans in the American social polity—growing . . . out of the continued indecision in the mind of the more powerful descendants of the Saxons as to whether it is expedient to apply the maxims of their religion to their civil and political relationships."[30]) King's ultimate message for Belton is one rooted in seeking liberty through political reform mitigated by Christian charity toward whites of good conscience, a message sure to assuage the concerns of whatever white readers there were for *Imperium in Imperio*. Belton's thankfulness for King's largess and instruction leads him to conclude that "from that moment to never class all white men together, whatever might be the provocation, and to never regard any class as totally depraved" (47).

Such instruction in political reform tempered with Christian humanism is further reinforced when Belton graduates from Stowe University (modelled undoubtedly on Fisk University). Although Belton had led a successful revolt of black students against the segregated dining facilities for white and black faculty at Stowe under the banner of "Equality or Death" (58), that rebellious spirit is mitigated by the graduating sermon delivered by the white president of Stowe, Dr. Lovejoy. Using the Christian humanist ideal of "The Kingdom of God is within us" (64) as his text, Dr. Lovejoy exhorted the graduates to consider the following:

> You shall be called upon to play a part in the adjusting of positions between the negro and Anglo-Saxon races of the South. The present state of affairs cannot possibly remain. The Anglo-Saxon race must surrender some of its outposts, and the negro will occupy these. To bring about this evacuation on the part of the Anglo-Saxon, and the forward march of the negro, will be your task. This is a grave and delicate task, fraught with much good or evil, weal or woe. Let us urge you to undertake it in the spirit to benefit the world, and not merely to advance your own glory. (66)

Besides evoking racialist ideology as part of the tactical nonviolent war (as much a Gramscian war of ideological position as one of logistical politics), Lovejoy's sermon refers to the leading role that will be played by men like Belton. Further, alluding to their role as "commanders" who would either become "true patriots" or "time-serving demagogues" (67), Lovejoy's sermon foreshadows the rest of Belton's career and the ultimate conflict he will wage with Bernard in the hidden utopian site over strategy for the future.

Before that conflict with Bernard, Belton returns to Richmond and, with the messages of King and Lovejoy still ringing in his ears, founds a journal which he manages in addition to his regular teaching job. After denouncing election fraud and alleging "that practicing fraud was debauching the young men, the flower of the Anglo-Saxon race" (126), Belton is dismissed from his teaching position. Although he is able to attain a postal clerk position by a political appointment, Belton loses the job when the political winds change. Buffeted by those winds and the racial discrimination of the times, Belton begins to despair about finding any job that will accord with his education and middle class status. Betraying a certain amount of elitism, Belton reflected on the fact that "If a man of education among the colored people did such manual labor, he was looked upon as an eternal disgrace to the race" (129). Here echoing Alexander Crummell's elitist philosophy that was the motivation for the founding in 1897 of the American Negro Academy, Griggs displays his alarm at the failure of the nation to live up to its Reconstruction promises about the uplift of African-Americans, especially by an educated black elite dedicated to a program of "character building and moral regeneration."[31]

The obvious hindrance to character building and moral regeneration, as experienced by Belton and other educated members of the black middle class, was racial discrimination. The frustration over the persistence of such discrimination through color prejudice and legal restriction causes Griggs to spell out how educated black men might begin to "execrate a national government that would not protect them against color prejudice, but on the contrary actually practiced it itself" (131). Belton's "alarm" at this "state of affairs" (131) leads him to disguise himself as a woman and secure the position of a nurse in white households with the intention of surreptitiously surveying white attitudes toward blacks. Although there may be grounds for seeing this cross-dressing sequence as a symbolic expression of emasculation by the racism of the time, another reading would emphasize how oppressed groups often resort to disguises or posing to practice what Scott calls "infrapolitics" as a form of hidden or unobtrusive resistance.[32] One of the prime discoveries Belton makes using this disguise is the abysmal white ignorance of African-American life and the blindness about the offstage political activity of black folks. Thus, as Griggs notes, "whites never dreamed of this powerful inner circle that was gradually but persistently working its way in every direction, solidifying the race for the momentous conflict of securing all the rights due them according to the will of their heavenly Father" (133–34).

Another lesson that Belton learns by posing as a female nurse concerns the gender dimension of respect and dignity. When the young white men of the families act out their stereotypical belief in the lasciviousness of black women, trying to importune Belton for lustful reasons, Griggs's comments reveal not only a Victorian sensibility about sex and the virtue of true womanhood but also a defensive validation of the integrity of black women in a charged atmosphere of disrespect toward African-American men and women.[33] Griggs's Victorian sensibility is especially evident in an earlier incident where Belton employs a white cab driver to drive a woman friend to the train station. Discovering that he lacks the money to fully compensate the driver, Belton physically prevents the driver from accosting the woman for the money. This allows Griggs to comment in a way that brings together a racial message of black pride with a gender salute to supposed Anglo-Saxon virtues:

> At Stowe University, Belton had learned to respect woman. It was in these schools that the work of slavery in robbing the colored women of respect, was undone. Woman now occupied the same position in Belton's eye as she did in the eye of the Anglo-Saxon. There is hope for that race or nation that respects its women. . . . The Negro race had left the last relic of barbarism behind, and this young negro, fighting to keep that cab driver from approaching the girl for a fee, was but a fore-runner of the negro, who, at the voice of a woman, will fight for freedom until he dies. (81–82)

The mix of race pride and gender has profound implications for Bernard also. When the woman he loves commits suicide in the belief that she would be contributing to the demise of the race by marrying a mulatto, Bernard starts on the path that will take him to the hidden secret black government. In her suicide note she exclaims: "If miscegenation is in reality destroying us, dedicate your soul to the work of separating the white and colored races. Do not let them intermingle. Erect moral barriers to separate them. If you fail in this, make the separation physical; lead our people forth from this accursed land" (175). While such black separatism might imply a radical nationalist agenda (one that Bernard will, in fact, articulate), the meaning for Griggs is ultimately tied into a challenge of white hegemonic power and black resistance mitigated by a struggle not for racial citizenship as *Plessy* valorized but for actual political citizenship.

The denial of that political citizenship, based on a belief in the universalist message of "liberty and justice for all," and the outrages of southern legal and extra-legal repression become the final catalyst propelling Belton into the hidden black utopia of the underground government. After Belton accepts a position as a president of a small black college in Louisiana, he is forced to submit to a series of humiliations and terrors that replicate the social and political repression facing African-Americans in the South at the turn of the century. Evicted from a first class coach seat on a train in Louisiana (reflecting the actual case in the *Plessy* decision), he is tossed by angry whites into a muddy ditch. After lecturing on the rights and responsibilities of voting, he learns about the recent violent history of disfranchisement from a sympathetic black father of a student and retreats from political involvement (here echoing the political posture of Booker T. Washington). Finally, when Belton mistakenly decides to seat himself next to a white woman in a white church, he incurs the wrath of the locals who organize a lynching party. Trusting in God, Belton miraculously escapes from the mob after being shot and having to kill a white doctor, for which he is eventually tried and found guilty by an outraged all-white jury. Through the timely intervention of Bernard, his conviction is over-turned, leading eventually to Belton's journey to the hidden utopia and his reuniting with Bernard.

That reuniting in the utopian site is both a climax of the critique of the dominant white supremacist ideology and the collision of alternative discursive strategies for African-American betterment. The detailing in the final portion of *Imperium in Imperio* of a manifesto for black self-determination is both a form of the utopian narrative and the elaboration of a contradictory and ambiguous black nationalism.[34] While the utopian narrative is embodied in Belton's role as Bernard's guide to the underground black govern-ment, the Imperium, the struggle between Belton and Bernard over what direction to take vis-à-vis the United States government, the Imperio, leads to an eventual split and to an open-ended conclusion of racial betrayal but national patriotism. Tracing those steps to the conclusion should help to clarify the ideological negotiation of the racial and utopian boundaries of *Imperium in Imperio*.

Belton's invitation to Bernard to join him outside of Waco, Texas, finds them at a "stone wall enclosure" surrounding a "building four stories high" (178). Carved into the steps leading to the building were the words "Thomas Jefferson College" (179). This is as much a key to the political aspirations of the secret black government as it is a ruse to cover the hidden utopia of the underground resistance housed on the site. After Bernard passes a death-defying test of his racial loyalty, Belton inducts him into the Imperium. The Imperium was founded in the "early days of the American Republic" when "a negro scientist who won an international reputation by his skill and erudition" contributed politically and financially to gathering free blacks "to endeavor to secure for the free negroes all the rights and privileges of men, according to the teachings of Thomas Jefferson" (191). Belton goes on to explain that "Jefferson's writings" were used to educate the "negro to feel that he was not in the full enjoyment of his rights until he was on terms of equality with any other human being that was alive or had ever lived" (192).

With the failure to realize Jefferson's ideals and the institutionalization of white supremacy in the aftermath of the Reconstruction, Belton reveals to Bernard how black secret societies were united under a hidden political structure that literally produced a complete shadow government. Needing only a president to crown the achievements of a united black government, Bernard is drafted to that office. After a short time in office, two events precipitate a denouement for the Imperium—the war in Cuba and the murder of a black postmaster in South Carolina. Calling together the Congress of the Imperium, Bernard announces this as "an appropriate time for us to consider what shall be our attitude, immediate and future, to this Anglo-Saxon race, which calls upon us to defend the fatherland and at the same moment treats us in a manner to make us execrate it" (207). Further reviewing the denial of civil and social rights, Bernard alludes to the Supreme Court's "shameful" decision in *Plessy* which "has lent its official sanction to all such acts of discrimination" (213) and concludes with a request for action beyond either the ballot— "snatched from our hands"—or the bullet whose "modern implement of revolutions has been denied us" (220).

Bernard thus sets the stage for the debates and arguments over strategy which give meaning to the hidden transcript at the core of the Imperium's utopianism and to the inconclusive resolution of Grigg's black nationalist and reformist agenda. If, as Scott contends, "the social location par excellence for the hidden transcript lies in the unauthorized and unmonitored secret assemblies of subordinates,"[35] the impassioned analysis and heated arguments in the Imperium encapsulate the discursive core of the hidden utopia. When the resolutions are articulated in the aftermath of Bernard's call to action, they run the gamut from extreme assimilationism to emigration to Africa to civil insurrection, recalling the extensive history of African-American discursive strategies. It is up to Belton to try to navigate between the extremes, in turn requiring Griggs to outline his own position beyond accommodationist, assimilationist, or separatist ideologies.

In elucidating his alternative to a declaration of war, Belton proposes a number of points in the form of a resolution that probably represents Griggs's perspective on the need for political and educational reforms. In noting the need to "secure possession" of the "stolen ballot box" (241), Belton thus criticizes Washington's apolitical accommodationism. Furthermore, Belton underscores the need for assertiveness—but still with a sense of Christian humanism and humility. Thus he declaims: "Before we make a forward move, let us pull the veil from before the eyes of the Anglo-Saxon that he may see the New Negro standing before him humbly, but firmly demanding every right granted him by his maker and wrested from him by man" (244). This is to be done over a period of time by unveiling the Imperium and then educating the "Anglo-Saxon" to the point that African-Americans "have arrived at the stage of development as a people, where we prefer to die in honor rather than live in disgrace" (245). If all else fails, blacks should emigrate to Texas and form a separate nation. Although Belton's resolution passes unanimously, Bernard counters with a modified and secret plan of war which Belton claims is treasonous. This, in turn, leads to Belton's execution and a final note from a follower of Belton to blow the cover of the Imperium out of his duty to "mankind . . . humanity . . . civilization" (204).

The final note of the novel, in fact, refers back to the introduction—a declaration by one Berl Trout in which he acknowledges while he may be a race "traitor" he is a true "patriot" with "the interest of the whole human family of which my race is but a part" (2). This dilemma, cited by Griggs as the framing mechanism of the novel, is apparent not only in his other writings but also in the writings of other African-American middle class intellectuals at the turn of the century. In her review of Griggs's writings, Arlene Elder asserts: "Griggs posits as valid two kinds of patriotism: national and racial. When a choice must be made between the two, it is the racial that frequently comes first, ironically, because the nation has failed to provide African-Americans with an acceptable alternative."[36] While this claim has a certain validity, I believe there is another dimension to the two kinds of patriotism embodied in Trout's declaration and discussed by Elder. That dimension is a profound recognition that the political is personal, or, in this case, psychological. In other words, this schizoid-type split is what W.E.B. Du Bois meant by his analysis of "double-consciousness" or "two-ness." As Du Bois wrote about this condition in the 1903 publication, The Souls of Black Folk: "One ever feels his two-ness—an American, a Negro; two souls, two thoughts, two unreconciled strivings; two warring ideals in one dark body, whose dogged strength alone keeps it from being torn asunder. . . . He simply wishes to make it possible for a man to be both a Negro and an American, without being cursed and spit upon by his fellows, without having the doors of Opportunity closed roughly in his face."[37] Clearly, this constrained utopian aspiration of being respected as a Negro and an American is at the heart and soul of the hidden utopia of Griggs's Imperium in Imperio.

Also obsessed with this two-ness, but at an even more profound psychological level with clear Pan-African overtones, is Pauline

Hopkins's "Of One Blood," subtitled "The Hidden Self." Hopkins and Du Bois deploy the psychological studies of William James to explore double-consciousness at an individual and collective level. According to Eric Sundquist: "For both Hopkins and Du Bois, James provided the key to a theory of diasporic consciousness that was capable of yoking together the conception of a split-off, perhaps hidden but in any case culturally oppositional 'personality' and the conceptions of race nationalism comprised by the ideological watchword 'African Personality.' "[38] Thus, the announcement at the beginning of the novel by Reuel Briggs, a Harvard medical student passing for white, "the wonders of the material world cannot approach the undiscovered country within ourselves—the hidden self lying quiescent in every human soul" (448). Not only will Reuel ascertain his individual hidden self as an African-American, but also he will discover in an expedition to Africa that takes him to the hidden city of Telassar both the individual and collective authentic "African personality." It is this process of dual discovery that provides the novel with its fantastic plot and its critical exploration of ideological racial boundaries.

While some critics see the fantastic component in "Of One Blood" as overshadowing the serious social message found in other novels by Hopkins, Thomas Otten maintains that the use of the fantastic is not "merely entertaining" but part of a discursive strategy for the relocation of the self in the charged atmosphere of racial relations at the turn of the century.[39] Acknowledging "however fantastic the story," Dickson Bruce does admit that "Hopkins wove the cruel ironies of interracial romance into her work."[40] Although certainly containing elements of romance, "Of One Blood" is also a utopian fable about the implications of the racial past for the present. Such fabulist components facilitate the utopian function of "defamiliarizing and restructuring" perceptions in order to highlight historical circumstances on a social and personal level.[41] Moreover, the struggle of Reuel Briggs to realize his own racial past through contact with his submerged self and the hidden utopian city of Telassar reveals what Ernst Bloch sees as the "not-yet-conscious or forward dawning" of the utopian social imaginary.[42]

While Reuel's journey to realize his hidden self through the discovery of his authentic individual and collective racial identity drives the dynamic of the narrative, that journey is awash in the fabulist exploration of conventional and popular genres of the period. In shifting between genres, Hopkins is able to probe the different selves that Reuel engages in the story as an element of the political unconsciousness that the fabulist components of the story come to represent. Thus, instead of using the direct and didactic narrative of the manifesto found in *Imperium in Imperio*, Hopkins relies on the hidden qualities of the fable to comment on the racial boundaries at the turn of the century and to construct a discursive strategy of transfiguration necessary not only for the symbolic function of her story but also for the ultimate social liberation of African-Americans from the ideological impediments imposed by white supremacy.[43]

We first meet Reuel Briggs in his room at Harvard contemplating the meaning of "The Unclassified Residuum" (442), a book whose theories on multiple consciousness and the power of "mind-cures" provides a link to the psychological theories of the day, as popularized by William James in an essay on "The Hidden Self" originally published in *Scribner's Magazine* in 1890 and later revised for inclusion in James's 1897 book, *The Will to Believe*.[44] Beyond the fabulist overtones of the mystical qualities of these psychological theories, Hopkins twice emphasizes a reference to the "effects of the imagination" (442 and 443) and Reuel's belief in his ability through his powers of mind to do what one subject in his readings is capable of doing—"transcend her *possible* normal consciousness" (443, author's emphasis). Thus, Reuel's desire to transcend normal consciousness by his will and mind becomes a vehicle for the romantic and fabulist elements of the plot, the utopian imagination underlying the plot, and the symbolic political unconscious represented in ideological boundaries of race uncovered in the story and linked to the social relations confronting African-Americans at the turn of the century.[45]

Reuel's first opportunity to use his will and powers of mind comes when the beautiful mulatto, Fisk Jubilee singer Dianthe Lusk, has been injured in a train accident. Reuel had first seen Dianthe in a mystical vision (446) and then at a concert where the transcendent power of her singing of African-American spirituals awakens his own sense of the past sufferings of his race (454). Only later, after Dianthe has been injured in a train accident and appears dead, does Reuel attempt to apply a "solution of one of life's problems: *the reanimation of the body after seeming death*" (464, author's emphasis). While Reuel's use of a form of "animal magnetism" (468) to revive Dianthe is consonant with the fabulist and romantic elements of the plot, it also is strikingly resonant with the charismatic role Reuel will play later in the novel when he discovers his Ethiopian princely status and assumes leadership of the hidden utopian site.[46] Moreover, the symbolic transformation that Reuel has engendered in Dianthe could be a commentary by Hopkins on the need for black intellectuals to revivify the deadened masses to challenge such legally sanctioned segregation practices as separate passenger cars on trains.

Reuel's resuscitation of Dianthe leads to a melodramatic and conventional love story between them which is compounded by the evil intrigue of Aubrey Livingston, an erstwhile friend of Reuel who turns out to be related to both Dianthe and Reuel as a consequence of their common slave-holding father. Beneath this bizarre plot, Hopkins locates the legacy of miscegenation and the artificiality of racial boundaries. As one critic suggests in following the symmetry and logic of the story: "[W]hen the artificial boundaries between seeming opposites break down, the result is the violent end in which Aubrey forces suicide upon Dianthe before receiving the same sentence from Reuel."[47] The revelation of this blood tie between Reuel, Dianthe, and Aubrey by a living legacy from slavery's past, Dianthe's grandmother Hannah, allows Hopkins to comment on the present ideology of white supremacy and tie the title, "Of One Blood," to the subtitle, "The Hidden Self," through a reference to another transcendent and hidden power:

> The slogan of the hour is "Keep the Negro down!" but who is clear enough in vision to decide who hath black blood and who hath it not? Can any one tell? No, not one; for in His own mysterious way He has united the white race and the black race in this new continent. By the transgression of the law He proves His own infallibility: "Of one blood have I made all nations of men to dwell upon the whole face of the earth," is as true today as when given to the inspired writers to be recorded. No man can draw the dividing line between the two races, for they are both of one blood! (607)[48]

Beyond the references to divine inspiration for racial equality found in "Of One Blood," Hopkins's exposing of the ideological absurdity of racial separation necessitated both a monogenetic theory of origin and a development of a Pan-African ideal that would invert white supremacist beliefs about the backwardness of Africa.[49] The plot device utilized by Hopkins to redefine the significance of Africa is an archaeological expedition to locate "the ancient Ethiopian capital Meroe" (520). The head of the expedition, Professor Stone, believes "in placing the Ethiopian as the primal race" (521), thus confounding "the theories of prejudice" (520) that prevent whites from acknowledging the role of Africa in the development of civilization. In retelling the glories of ancient Ethiopia (531–32) and its capital city of Meroe, Professor Stone is met by the following incredulous response of a white American on the expedition: "Great Scott! . . . you don't mean to tell me that all this was done by niggers?" (532). To which Stone replies: "Undoubtedly your Afro-Americans are a branch of the wonderful and mysterious Ethiopians who had a prehistoric existence of magnificence, the full record of which is lost in obscurity" (532).

It is up to Reuel, as the doctor of the expedition and as a descendent of Ethiopian royalty, to unlock the past hidden story of Meroe and "return and restore the former glory of the race" (535). Reuel accomplishes this first by accident and then by the magnetism of his will. In examining the pyramids of Meroe by himself and late at night, Reuel loses consciousness before a Sphinx (542–44). Waking up in a place of "bewildering beauty" (545)—"the hidden city of Telassar" (546)—Reuel is introduced to this utopian site by a conventional utopian guide who, in the fabulist plot in "Of One Blood," is Ai, the "faithful prime minister" (547) of the returning king. Crowned King Ergamenes and hailed by the inhabitants of the outer city (554), Reuel must make his way to the inner city to join with the Virgin Queen Candace. When the narrow path to the inner city is blocked by a lion, Reuel uses "the full force of his personal magnetism" (566) to chase the lion away, eliciting praise for his "admirable intrepidity" (566). Thus, Reuel fulfills his destiny in the fable as an Ethiopian king while restoring a sense of nationalist pride in African-American ancestry.[50]

Part of that pride was intimately bound up with Hopkins's efforts to recast gender relations in a way that would deliver black men and, especially, black women from negative stereotypes and the ideology of white supremacy. In her earlier novel, Contending Forces, Hopkins had written: "[W]e must ourselves develop the men and women who will faithfully portray the inmost thoughts and feelings of the Negro with all the fire and romance which lie dormant in our history."[51] While obviously concerned about expressing pride in the racial past, Hopkins, like other African-American women writers of the time, "had to define a discourse of black womanhood which would not only address their exclusion from the ideology of true womanhood but, as a consequence of this exclusion, would also rescue their bodies from a persistent association with illicit sexuality."[52] Thus, Queen Candace is described by Hopkins as "the embodiment of all chastity" (569). In linking the personal features of Candace to Dianthe, Hopkins attempts to redeem both the body and spirit of Dianthe from the sins of white rape and lust.[53] In the union of Candace and Ergamenes/Reuel, while reinscribing a form of patriarchalism, Hopkins, nonetheless, establishes a repositioned black masculinity and femininity that disputes the racialized fantasies of white supremacist ideology.

On the other hand, Hopkins does succumb to a racialized reading of Africa and African-Americans that casts both as the embodiment of certain "soft" feminine ideals. The fact that the inner city of Telassar is a place ruled by a Virgin Queen seems to indicate that at the heart of Africa is a form of the Eternal Feminine. Moreover, in describing the sights and sounds of Telassar as luxuriant and "sonorous" (546–48), Hopkins not only renders a fabulist utopian narrative of the hidden city as a paradisaical refuge, but also enacts an ideological posture that can be found in the writings of other African-American intellectuals of the time. For Anna Julia Cooper, African-Americans were "ballast" because of their "tropical warmth and spontaneous emotionalism," countering the "cold and calculating Anglo-Saxon."[54] For Du Bois, part of the genius and distinctiveness of African-Americans was their feminine qualities.[55] Thus, Hopkins and other black intellectuals of the time framed the contributions of Africa and African-Americans to the regenerative powers of a feminine ideal.

Central to that feminine ideal and to the underlying message in "Of One Blood" is an evangelical sense of spiritual uplift. The civilizing mission which late nineteenth-century feminists and Victorian reformers were spreading with the gospel of purity and moral regeneration found parallels in the social activities and writings of black women.[56] In the conclusion to her 1892 novel *Iola Leroy*, Frances Harper wrote: "I have woven a story whose mission will not be in vain if it awakens in the hearts of our countrymen a stronger sense of justice and a more Christlike humanity."[57] In "Of One Blood," Hopkins has Ai comment that the downfall of ancient Ethiopia was "because of her idolatries" (547) and that the restoration of her greatness will require the spiritual uplift of Christianity. "But there was a hope," Ai avers, "held out to the faithful worshippers of the true God that Ethiopia should stretch forth her hand unto Eternal Goodness, and that then her glory should again dazzle the world" (547–48). Echoing a Christianized Pan-African millennial ideal taken from Psalms 68:31, "Princes shall come out of Egypt, [and] Ethiopia shall soon stretch forth her hands to God," Hopkins makes clear through Ai's obeisance to Reuel ("O Ergamenes, your belief shall be ours, we have no will but yours"—563) that the acceptance of Christianity will be the key to reviving the fortunes of the people of Telassar, and, indeed, the continent of Africa. By merging spiritual uplift and a refurbished notion of the civilizing mission, Hopkins brings to her Pan-African ideal a sensibility that ultimately reflects a westernized and nostalgic vision of Africa and her hidden legacy.[58]

As with Sutton Griggs, Pauline Hopkins struggled to convey through a hidden utopia a way out of the oppressive ideological racial boundaries imposed by white supremacy. Both writers in-

scribed in those hidden utopias a Christian humanism whose social
gospel they were convinced would be redemptive for all races, but
especially for African-Americans. Both writers placed their hope for
that redemption in a form of "authoritarian collectivism," defined by
Wilson Jeremiah Moses as "a belief that all black people could and
should act unanimously under the leadership of one powerful man
or group of men, who would guide the race by virtue of superior
knowledge or divine authority."[59] This elitism was an obvious
consequence of a black middle class who felt under siege by the
reconstituting of racial boundaries that further marginalized and
disrespected them. It should not be surprising, therefore, that the
discursive strategies by which Griggs and Hopkins hoped to rene-
gotiate ideological racial boundaries away from oppression and
toward liberation were tainted with constricting and contradictory
elitist and civilizationalist beliefs. On the other hand, in creating
this constrained utopianism and radicalism in their respective
novels, Griggs and Hopkins raised the hope that African-Americans
could find their way to a less troubled future, one inspired by the
thought-provoking catalysts of *Imperium in Imperio* and "Of One
Blood."

NOTES

1. Rayford W. Logan, *The Betrayal of the Negro: From Rutherford B.
Hayes to Woodrow Wilson* (New York: Collier-Macmillan, 1972).

2. George M. Fredrickson, *The Black Image in the White Mind: The
Debate on Afro-American Character and Destiny, 1817–1914* (Middletown,
Conn.: Wesleyan University Press, 1987), p. 275. On the redrawing of
institutional and ideological racial boundaries in the South, see Edward L.
Ayers, *The Promise of the New South: Life After Reconstruction* (New York:
Oxford University Press, 1992); and Joel Williamson, *The Crucible of Race:
Black-White Relations in the American South Since Emancipation* (New
York: Oxford University Press, 1984). On the institutional and ideological
impact of white supremacy on the nation, see Fredrickson, *The Black
Image in the White Mind*; and Logan, *The Betrayal of the Negro*. On
lynching, see Ayers, *The Promise of the New South*, p. 157; Fredrickson,
The Black Image in the White Mind, pp. 272–82; and Joel Williamson, *A
Rage for Order: Black-White Relations in the American South Since Emancipation* (New York: Oxford University Press, 1986), esp. pp. 84–85, 120–26;
189–90.

3. Eric J. Sundquist, *To Wake the Nations: Race in the Making of
American Literature* (Cambridge, Mass.: Belknap Press of Harvard University Press, 1993), p. 241. On the Supreme Court's rulings towards African-
Americans during this time, see Logan, *The Betrayal of the Negro*, pp.
105–24.

4. Evelyn Brooks Higginbotham, "African-American Women's History and the Metalanguage of Race," *Signs* 17 (Winter 1992): 252, 253.

5. On paternalistic white supremacy, see Fredrickson, *The Black Image in the White Mind*, pp. 198–227. On racial radicalism, see Williamson, *A Rage for Order*, pp. 78–205.

6. Quoted in Fredrickson, *The Black Image in the White Mind*, p. 252.

7. Dickson D. Bruce, Jr., *Black American Writing from the Nadir: The Evolution of a Literary Tradition, 1877–1915* (Baton Rouge: Louisiana State University, 1989), p. 2.

8. Quoted in Sundquist, *To Wake the Nations*, p. 276.

9. Ibid., p. 277.

10. Sutton E. Griggs, *Imperium in Imperio* (Miami: Mnemosyne, 1969), p. 62. All future references cited in the text will be to this edition.

11. Wilson Jeremiah Moses, *The Golden Age of Black Nationalism, 1850–1925* (New York: Oxford University Press, 1978), p. 29. On the influence of middle class values and the cultivation of gentility in African-American writing at this time, see Bruce, *Black American Writing from the Nadir*, pp. 6–10, 19–22.

12. Moses, *The Golden Age of Black Nationalism*, p. 7. On the connections between racial uplift and imperialism, see Kevin Gaines, "Black Americans' Racial Uplift Ideology as 'Civilizing Mission': Pauline E. Hopkins on Race and Imperialism," in *Cultures of United States Imperialism*, ed. Amy Kaplan and Donald E. Pease (Durham: Duke University Press, 1993), esp. p. 437.

13. Moses, *The Golden Age of Black Nationalism*, p. 11. On the connection between racial reformers, both white and black, and the Social Gospel movement, see Ronald C. White, Jr., *Liberty and Justice for All: Racial Reform and the Social Gospel* (New York: Harper and Row, 1990).

14. For a concise discussion of the writings of Hopkins and Griggs, see Bruce, *Black American Writing from the Nadir*, pp. 144–55, 155–63.

15. Arlene A. Elder, *The "Hindered Hand": Cultural Implications of Early African-American Fiction* (Westport, Conn.: Greenwood Press, 1978), p. 31.

16. Pauline E. Hopkins, *Contending Forces* (Carbondale: Southern Illinois Press, 1978), p. 13.

17. Quoted in Moses, *The Golden Age of Black Nationalism*, pp. 170–71.

18. Quoted in Elizabeth Ammons, *Conflicting Stories: American Women Writers at the Turn into the Twentieth Century* (New York: Oxford University Press, 1991), p. 78. On the abolitionist and temperance influence on the moral didacticism of the black literature of the late nineteenth century, see Elder, *The "Hindered Hand,"* p. 9.

19. Elder, *The "Hindered Hand,"* p. 37.

20. For surveys of the utopian literature of the period, see Carol A. Kolmerten, "Texts and Contexts: American Women Envision Utopia, 1890–1920," in *Utopian and Science Fiction by Women: Worlds of Difference*, ed. Jane L. Donawerth and Carol A. Kolmerten (Syracuse: Syracuse University Press, 1994), pp. 107–25; Jean Pfaelzer, *The Utopian Novel in America, 1886–1896: The Politics of Form* (Pittsburgh: University of Pittsburgh Press, 1984); Kenneth M. Roemer, *The Obsolete Necessity: America in Utopian Writings, 1888–1900* (Kent, Ohio: Kent State University Press,

1976); and Charles J. Rooney, Jr., *Dreams and Visions: A Study of American Utopias, 1865–1917* (Westport, Conn.: Greenwood Press, 1985). Of the two latter surveys of the period when Griggs's utopian novel *Imperium in Imperio* was published, only Roemer mentions it. See Roemer, *The Obsolete Necessity*, pp. 74–75. Neither Kolmerten nor Rooney cites Hopkins's "Of One Blood." "Of One Blood" can be found in *The Magazine Novels of Pauline Hopkins* (New York: Oxford University Press, 1988), pp. 441–621. All further references cited in the text will be to this edition.

21. Peter Ruppert, *Reader in a Strange Land: The Activity of Reading Literary Utopias* (Athens: University of Georgia Press, 1986), p. xiii.

22. On the role of utopian literature in challenging and subverting dominant consciousness and values and as a spur to action, see Pfaelzer, *The Utopian Novel in America*, p. 14; and Ruppert, *Reader in a Strange Land*, pp. 5, 19, and *passim.*

23. James C. Scott, *Domination and the Arts of Resistance* (New Haven: Yale University Press, 1990), pp. 5, 20. For a brilliant application of Scott to African-American resistance during the 1930s and 1940s, see Robin D. G. Kelley, " 'We Are Not What We Seem': Rethinking Black Working-Class Opposition in the Jim Crow South," *The Journal of American History* 80 (June 1993):77–78 and *passim.*

24. Ibid., p. 81.

25. Ernst Bloch, *The Principle of Hope*, Vol. I, trans. Neville Plaice, Stephen Plaice, and Paul Knight (Cambridge: MIT Press, 1986), pp. 77–113. On wish fulfillment and the hidden transcript, see Scott, *Domination and the Arts of Resistance*, p. 38.

26. On utopian literature as "contradictory and inconsistent," see Ruppert, *Reader in a Strange Land*, p. xii. On the middle-class contradictions evident in the writings of African-American intellectuals like Griggs and Hopkins, see Bruce, *Black American Writing from the Nadir*, pp. 6–10, 144–63.

27. On the dialectical connection between hope and despair in written utopias, see Melvin J. Lasky, *Utopia and Revolution* (Chicago: University of Chicago Press, 1976), p. 9.

28. On the middle-class nationalist roots of Griggs's writings, see Elder, *The "Hindered Hand,"* pp. 69–103; and Moses, *The Golden Age of Black Nationalism*, pp. 170–93.

29. Moses, *The Golden Age of Nationalism*, p. 186. For Griggs's incorporation of evolutionary theory in his writings, see ibid., p. 27 and *passim.* On the application of racialist theory to reactionary and anti-black ideology of the period, see Fredrickson, *The Black Image in the White Mind*, pp. 228–55. On the contradictions of racialist theory for progressive evolutionary thought related to blacks and other marginalized people, see Mark Pittenger, *American Socialists and Evolutionary Thought, 1870–1920* (Madison: University of Wisconsin Press, 1993), pp. 167–98.

30. Anna Julia Cooper, *A Voice from the South* (New York: Oxford University Press, 1988), p. 185.

31. On Crummell's Academy and the role of educated blacks, see Moses, *The Golden Age of Black Nationalism*, p. 73.

32. On the analysis of this scene as symbolic emasculation, see Moses, *The Golden Age of Black Nationalism*, pp. 185–86. On Scott's definition of infrapolitics and the disguises and poses of subordinate groups, see Scott, *Domination and the Arts of Resistance*, pp. 183–201.

33. On Griggs's Victorian ideal, see Moses, *The Golden Age of Black Nationalism*, p. 184. On the charged atmosphere of race and sex in the South of this time, see Williamson, *A Rage for Order*, pp. 186–91; and on the discourse of true womanhood for black women, see Hazel V. Carby, *Reconstructing Womanhood: The Emergence of the Afro-American Woman Novelist* (New York: Oxford University Press, 1987), p. 32.

34. On the manifesto form in utopian literature, see Pfaelzer, *The Utopian Novel in America*, p. 18. On the contradictions and ambiguities of Griggs's black nationalism in *Imperium in Imperio*, see Elder, *The "Hindered Hand,"* pp. 73–77; and Moses, *The Golden Age of Black Nationalism*, pp. 170–193.

35. Scott, *Domination and the Arts of Resistance*, p. 121.

36. Elder, *The "Hindered Hand,"* p. 103.

37. W.E.B. Du Bois, *The Souls of Black Folk* (Greenwich, Conn.: Fawcett Premier, 1961), p. 17. For discussion of Du Bois and the presentation of double-consciousness, see Bruce, *Black American Writing from the Nadir*, pp. 203–12; David Levering Lewis, *W.E.B. Du Bois: Biography of a Race, 1868–1919* (New York: Henry Holt, 1993), esp. pp. 281–83; Moses, *The Golden Age of Black Nationalism*, pp. 136–38 and *passim*; and Sundquist, *To Wake the Nations*, pp. 459–63 and *passim*.

38. Sundquist, *To Wake the Nations*, p. 571. For a discussion of the influence of James on Du Bois as a student at Harvard and in his writings, see Lewis, *W.E.B. Du Bois, passim*. For commentary on Jamesian references in "Of One Blood," see Thomas J. Otten, "Pauline Hopkins and the Hidden Self of Race," *ELH* 59 (Spring 1992): 227–56. On the Pan-African ideal in Hopkins, see Moses, *The Golden Age of Black Nationalism*, p. 200.

39. Otten, "Pauline Hopkins and the Hidden Self of Race," p. 236. For critics who observe that the use of the fantastic is entertaining or disconcerting in "Of One Blood," see Bruce, *Black American Writing from the Nadir*, p. 154; and Carole McAlpine Watson, *Prologue: The Novels of Black American Women, 1891–1965* (Westport, Conn.: Greenwood Press, 1985), p. 144.

40. Bruce, *Black Writing from the Nadir*, p. 154.

41. Ruppert, *Reader in a Strange Land*, p. 166. On the links between romance and the utopian fable, see Pfaelzer, *The Utopian Novel in America*, p. 18.

42. Bloch, *The Principle of Hope*, pp. 114–78.

43. On the discursive and its link to the symbolic and social, see John Frow, *Marxism and Literary History* (Oxford: Basil Blackwell, 1986), p. 58. For a discussion of the connection between the political unconscious and transfigured states, see Fredric Jameson, *The Political Unconscious: Narrative as Socially Symbolic Act* (Ithaca: Cornell University Press, 1981), p. 112. On genre-shifting and different selves in "Of One Blood," see Otten, "Pauline Hopkins and the Hidden Self of Race," p. 246. On the use of

popular conventions, Carby claims that Hopkins "was the first Afro-American author to produce a black popular fiction that drew on the archetypes of dime novels and story papers" in *Reconstructing Womanhood*, p. 144.

44. Sundquist, *To Wake the Nations*, p. 570.

45. On the utopian imagination, see Tom Moylan, *Demand the Impossible: Science Fiction and the Utopian Imagination* (New York: Methuen, 1986), pp. 20–26.

46. Sundquist, *To Wake the Nations*, p. 572. On the role of charisma, personal magnetism, and the hidden transcript, see Scott, *Domination and the Arts of Resistance*, pp. 221–24.

47. Otten, "Pauline Hopkins and the Hidden Self of Race," p. 251. On the role of miscegenation in Hopkins's fiction and its link to the racial facts of African-American life, see Carby, *Reconstructing Womanhood*, p. 128.

48. On the biblical roots for this passage and the link between Hopkins and Du Bois on this issue, see Sundquist, *To Wake the Nations*, pp. 571–72.

49. On the exposing of racial ideology in Hopkins's fiction, see Carby, *Reconstructing Womanhood*, p. 140. On the monogenetic argument in "Of One Blood," see Sundquist, *To Wake the Nations*, p. 571. On the Pan-African ideal in "Of One Blood" and its Ethiopianist implications, see Moses, *The Golden Age of Black Nationalism*, p. 200; and Otten, "Pauline Hopkins and the Hidden Self of Race," p. 244. On the "Western-dominated" nature of that Pan-African ideal, see Gaines, "Black Americans' Racial Uplift Ideology as 'Civilizing Mission,' " p. 435 and *passim*.

50. Otten, "Pauline Hopkins and the Hidden Self of Race," p. 237.

51. Hopkins, *Contending Forces*, p. 14.

52. Carby, *Reconstructing Womanhood*, p. 32.

53. Sundquist, *To Wake the Nations*, p. 572.

54. Cooper, *A Voice from the South*, p. 173.

55. Lewis, *W.E.B. Du Bois*, p. 173. On the mystical genius of race in Du Bois and Hopkins, see Ammons, *Conflicting Stories*, p. 82.

56. On social purity, Victorian reformism, and black women's clubs of the 1890s, see Moses, *The Golden Age of Black Nationalism*, pp. 123–24. On black feminist thought and writings, see Carby, *Reconstructing Womanhood*, pp. 95–120; and Watson, *Prologue*, pp. 9–31.

57. Quoted in Watson, *Prologue*, p. 14.

58. Gaines, "Black Americans' Racial Uplift Ideology as 'Civilizing Mission,' " p. 445. On Ethiopianism and the links to biblical prophecy, Christianity, and "Of One Blood," see Sundquist, *To Wake the Nations*, 553–55, and 573. On the black nationalist reading of Ethiopianism that "the divine providence of history was working to elevate the African peoples," see Moses, *The Golden Age of Black Nationalism*, p. 24.

59. Moses, *The Golden Age of Black Nationalism*, p. 11.

4

Socialism and Its Discontents: London's The Iron Heel and Reader Response

Seven years after the publication of *The Iron Heel* (1907), Jack London wrote to a friend that he would not consider "writing another book of that sort. It was a labor of love and a dead failure as a book. The book buying public would have nothing to do with it and I got nothing but knocks from the socialists."[1] Although *The Iron Heel* was scorned by some contemporary socialist critics and nonsocialist reviewers of fiction, London's visionary and cataclysmic tale of abortive revolution and counterrevolution captured the attention of later critics and generations schooled in the actualities of post–World War I revolutions and the fascist counterrevolutions that followed in the 1920s and 1930s. That *The Iron Heel* would be resurrected from its "dead failure as a book" precisely because of what a later generation would see as its prophetic power seems to contradict Jack London's own assessment that he "didn't write the thing as a prophecy at all."[2]

On the other hand, London was certainly committed to making *The Iron Heel* into a propaganda device for criticizing capitalism and advancing socialism. It is clear that in the immediate aftermath of an exhaustive year of lecturing as president of the Intercollegiate Socialist Society (1905–1906), he was preoccupied with spreading the gospel of revolutionary socialism. Yet London's effort to translate socialist propaganda into a form of utopian literature created problems not only for contemporary readers of the novel but also for future critics. In locating the immediate reader response to *The Iron Heel*, this chapter will explore how the ideological discourse of socialism was articulated in the novel and then rearticulated in its contemporary reception.

It has generally been acknowledged that *The Iron Heel* falls within the broad category of utopian literature even though the categorization of the novel has ranged from that of a "heuristic utopia" to a "dystopia utopia."[3] London himself was unclear about what kind of utopian literature it was other than announcing in a letter to a friend that "it's sort of a different proposition from the average Utopias. And it certainly deals with the live thing of to-day."[4] In determining how to situate *The Iron Heel* in the broad context of utopian literature, Jean Pfaelzer's definition of utopian fiction as a "category of prose fiction in which the author's political statement controls the narrative structure" helps to highlight the particular literary form of *The Iron Heel*. Moreover, her discussion of the "interacting forms" of "manifesto" and "fable" offers a way to locate the formal construction of the ideological discourse and narrative action of *The Iron Heel*.[5]

Nevertheless, accounting for the ideological discourse and literary style that inform the utopian components of *The Iron Heel* requires, in addition, connecting it to the specific sociohistorical context. As Peter Ruppert contends in his book on reading the literary utopia: "The real power of utopian literature is in the capacity to reveal the present as a moment in history, that is, as a temporal horizon of possibilities that is constantly changing."[6] Thus, criticism that sees the novel's utopian thrust as primarily a dystopic obsession with conflict and destruction without providing more of a context than London's mind-set undermines an understanding of how the novel is part of the discursive practices of the period and a "strategic site for the contestation of dominant ideological subject identities."[7] In particular, London's adherence to the discursive practices of naturalism, notwithstanding the sentimental and romantic components found in *The Iron Heel*, helps to configure the conflictual and dystopic elements of the novel as utopian fiction. Moreover, London's use of marginal notes to convey the social character of the utopian future also helps to locate the political context of London's perspective on utopian possibilities and socialism.

A key to understanding that political context is the way in which marginalization as a social and psychological process shaped the ideological discourse of radicals like London, his socialist comrades of the time, and the characters that inhabit his fiction. The connection between marginalization and utopianism can be seen in the following definition of utopianism as "the characteristic attitude of those groups in society which are so fundamentally dissatisfied with the existing order that they refuse to integrate themselves into it, and work instead to establish an alternative system in which they believe they (and possibly everyone else as well) can achieve complete happiness and fulfillment."[8] While a number of interpreters of reform and radical politics have noted the constancy of utopianism in American life, the particular period of London's adult years (from the 1890s through his death in 1916) proved to be a time when there was an especially prolific representation of utopian ideas and movements, precisely as a consequence of the crisis of legitimacy of the political-economic-cultural order and the resulting dissatisfaction of significant sectors of the population. The merging of such utopian aspirations with the emergent socialist politics of turn-of-the-century America not only gave such politics a millennial coloring, but also the fragmenting tendencies inherent in working class culture of the time doomed such socialist politics to an ultimate, albeit vibrant, marginalization. Both in London's life and in his characters the effects of such marginalization led to an eclectic radical critique of the present and an unrealized (perhaps even unrealizable) hope for the future.[9]

Of all the characters in *The Iron Heel*, Ernest Everhard probably comes closest to representing many, but not all, of those radical critiques and idealized hopes of Jack London. Ernest Everhard is not only a vehicle for the articulation of Jack London's political manifesto but also for a mediation of the ideological discourse of the age. According to Joan London, "Ernest Everhard was the revolutionist Jack would have liked to be if he had not, unfortunately, also desired to be several other kinds of men."[10] While Everhard's embodiment of masculine power and virile radicalism represents certain historically validated social and cultural characteristics, those characteristics also demarcate specific discursive practices. By tracing the discourse that London uses to describe Everhard, to identify his demeanor, and to qualify his message, we may be better able to evaluate the ideology embedded in the various masculinities London projects.[11]

In both physical and psychological make-up, London and Everhard seem to share certain attributes. Especially, in the articulation of an ideological discourse of socialism, much of what motivates London seems to run through Everhard's message. In describing the emotional roots of socialism for London as "a cry for justice, a fear of degradation, a loathing of the waste of human potential," Andrew Sinclair could also be outlining the passionate appeals of Ernest Everhard.[12] In noting that "[s]ocialism was Jack London's holy war . . . [giving] him the psychic release of a religion and the physical release of a fight," Joan Hedrick could also be describing the framing of Everhard's demeanor.[13]

We come to know Ernest Everhard through the so-called Everhard Manuscript, a journal kept by Avis Everhard of the critical events between 1912 and 1932 and edited by Anthony Meredith, the interlocutor from the utopian Brotherhood of Man society located some seven centuries into the future. In the "Foreward" to the Everhard Manuscript Meredith discounts the overblown estimation by Avis of her husband Ernest and decries his errors of interpretation. In a warning to readers that could well serve as a self-conscious comment by London on his own ideological fervor, Meredith chides Avis on her lack of "perspective." "She was too close to the events she writes about," Meredith continues. "Nay, she was merged in the events she has described."[14]

On the other hand, Meredith singles out the Everherd Manuscript as "especially valuable . . . in communicating to us the *feel* of those terrible times. Nowhere do we find more vividly portrayed the psychology of the persons that lived in that turbulent period—their mistakes and ignorance, their doubts and fears and misapprehensions, their ethical delusions, their violent passions, their inconceivable sordidness and selfishness. These are the things that are so hard for us to understand" (1, author's emphasis). By distancing Meredith in time and tone, London attempts to explain the strengths and weaknesses of the characters and their story in light of the future. Such a device both facilitates a utopian critique of the present and provides an alienating or estranged framework within which one can read the characters and conditions that produce them.[15] Much like Joan London's following comment on her father's work, we are forewarned about the need to link the characters' lives with their environment: "Any attempt to judge Jack London's work without appreciating the environmental forces which shaped his life and his work is certain to produce unsatisfactory results."[16]

In portraying the physical and psychological characteristics of Everhard, London does more than provide some insight into his own psyche; he presents the reader with an opening to deconstruct what Hayden White elsewhere calls the "context in the text."[17] When Avis refers to her "Eagle, beating with tireless wings the void, soaring towards what was ever his sun, the flaming ideal of human freedom" (5), she deploys an image that is to appear throughout the novel of this fierce, proud, and American bird of prey. Linking that bird to Ernest's devotion to the cause for which he gave his "manhood," London reveals what was part of the struggle of American socialists like Eugene Debs (also often referred to as an eagle)—to rescue their manhood through an American application of socialism.[18]

In describing the physical characteristics of Everhard, London not only fixes Everhard as a masculine hero of the working class, but also allows that portrait to be subverted by the seemingly androgynous editor, Meredith. In characterizing his ill-fitting suits, Avis notes that "the cloth bulged with his muscles, while the coat between the shoulders, what of the heavy shoulder-development, was a maze of wrinkles. His neck was the neck of a prize-fighter, thick and strong" (7). The allusion to the prize-fighter allows Meredith to remark in the footnotes that "it was the custom of men to compete for purses of money. They fought with their hands. When one was beaten into insensibility or killed, the survivor took the money" (7). London's distancing of this masculinist characteristic may have something to do with his own effort to transcend a "manhood" that is associated with "the lower class values of the Oakland street culture" out of which he emerged and from which, according to Joan Hedrick and others, he was trying to escape.[19] It also may have to do with what Clarice Stasz calls London's "visionary conception of masculinity and femininity," which, although "no feminist's dream, is a male chauvinist's nightmare."[20]

Elsewhere, in depicting Everhard's argumentative style, there is further evidence of the masculinist and class basis for the character and his message. Referring to the "war-note in his voice," Avis goes on to contend that in such arguments Ernest "took no quarter and gave none" (16). The reference to taking no quarter allows Meredith once more to comment that the expression "arises from the customs of the times. When, among men fighting to the death in their wild-animal way, a beaten man threw down his weapons, it was at the option of the victor to slay or spare him" (16). Beyond the obvious distancing from such barbaric times, Meredith utilizes a reference to animal-like behavior London was noted for and that was part of the discourse of naturalism, particularly related to issues of class struggle. In fact, as pointed out by one interpreter of naturalism, "the fear of class warfare that is part of the material worked by naturalism must be recognized as a powerful element of the ideology of the period."[21]

London's discourse on class warfare found throughout *The Iron Heel* is replete with references to irrational male behavior and atavistic social ethics, especially in the annotations by Meredith. In Everhard's debate with the bishop he demonstrates what was a bedrock of London's social Darwinist beliefs about the innate selfishness of all classes. Citing a tenet of revolutionary socialism in the "irreconcilable conflict" (23) between labor and capital, London nonetheless allows Meredith to denounce such conflicts as strikes in the following revealing manner:

> These quarrels were very common in those irrational and anarchic times. Sometimes the labourers refused to work. Sometimes the capitalists refused to let the labourers work. In the violence and turbulence of such disagreements much property was destroyed and many lives lost. All this is inconceivable to us—as inconceivable as another custom of that time, namely, the habit the men of the lower classes had of breaking the furniture when they quarrelled with their wives. (23)

In this instance the double point of view captures what in another instance Joan Hedrick refers to as "sympathy for the manhood that inspired [such revolts] and fear of consequences it provoked."[22]

Yet London was too immersed at the time he wrote *The Iron Heel* in the ideological discourse of revolutionary socialism to shy away from embracing the logic of class confrontation and conflict. In setting the confrontation between Ernest Everhard and the representatives of the California ruling class in the Philomath Club, London repeats the political arguments that he had been delivering in his speeches and writings during 1906. Moreover, the chapter follows an earlier moral indictment of capitalism as a system through Avis's investigation of the responsibility for the loss of one worker's arm. I want to turn now to the iconic significance of "Jackson's arm" for further elaboration of the ideological discourse in *The Iron Heel.*

Jackson's arm becomes the metaphorical, or, more precisely, metonymical vehicle for educating both Avis and the reader about the brutal dynamics of capitalism and the political system that supports it.[23] In effect, there exists a manifest and latent quality to that discourse that requires not only a reconstruction of those social and historical conditions that frame the ideological discourse of the novel but also a deconstruction or decoding of the images and language deployed by London.[24] Thus, by identifying how London's ideological discourse emerges out of the context and becomes embedded in the icons, images, and language of the text, one can better discern sociohistorical meanings in *The Iron Heel.*

Jackson's arm assumes the manifest role of exposing the inherent exploitative and unjust operation of corporations and the courts and the biases of the press precisely because of London's ideological commitment to presenting how such interlocking corruption has robbed working men of their capacity to be productive members of society. Building on a actual story that London had read in one of the muckraking journals of the day of a worker named Jackson who had been maimed in an industrial accident, London traces the unraveling of the conspiracy against this one worker through Avis's investigation.[25] By personalizing the tragedy afflicting one worker and the disillusionment of the innocent Avis with the lack of fairness toward this man, London may have hoped to arouse the conscience of his middle class readers against the scandals of industrial capitalism and those institutions that supported and legitimatized it. (In a short story set in a dystopian future and published soon after *The Iron Heel*, entitled "A Curious Fragment" [1908], London again uses the severing of an arm in an industrial accident to condemn the brutishness of capitalism and to appeal to the conscience of his readers.)

Through the ideological icon of Jackson's arm London was able to excoriate the brutal, arrogant, and uncaring power of the industrial machine while further testifying to the ways in which that industrial system emasculated and made slaves of working men. Thus, London could incorporate an anticapitalist critique found in progressive journals and socialist tracts of the times by representing through "Jackson's arm" what historian Nell Painter Irvin has noted of the period: "During the early years of the century working men, women, and children had no effective statutory protection to limit working hours, set minimum wages, provide compensation for accidents on the job, old-age pensions, unemployment compensation, or occupational safety. At the same time the incidence of industrial accidents in the United States was the highest in the world. About half a million workers were injured and 30,000 killed at work every year."[26] London's special emphasis on Jackson's reduction to a peddlar and his attendant loss of income suggests not merely a symbolic castration of this worker but an iconic representation of the loss of manhood in a era when making a decent living was the measure of true masculinity, especially for men in the working class.[27]

In the chapter entitled "Jackson's Arm" London takes the naive Avis through a series of meetings with those men associated with the fictitious Sierra Mills where Jackson lost his arm in an industrial accident and those involved in the court case where Jackson sought compensation. London allows Avis's outraged innocence to indict the men and the positions they represent in protecting the company and industrial capitalism against the charges of Jackson for just compensation. Moreover, Meredith's annotations help to reinforce the ideological critique of the exploitative and irrational economic practices of the day. In one telling passage on the utopian transcendence of such practices, Meredith notes:

In those days thievery was incredibly prevalent. Everybody stole property from everybody else. The lords of society stole legally or else legalized their stealing, while the poorer classes stole illegally. Nothing was safe unless guarded. Enormous numbers of men were employed as watchmen to protect property. The houses of the well-to-do were a combination of safe deposit, vault, and fortress. The appropriation of the personal belongings of others by our own children of today is looked upon as a rudimentary survival of the theft-characteristic that in those early times was universal. (31)

While this critique is a predictable indictment by London of the cozy ruling circles that include the characters of Colonel Ingram, corporate lawyer for Sierra Milis, and Judge Caldwell, lodge buddy of Ingram and the trial judge who dismissed Jackson's claims, Avis and the reader are confronted with the duplicity committed by a fellow worker, Peter Donnelly, against Jackson. Donnelly justifies his siding with the company on the grounds of the need to protect his livelihood in order to feed his family. When Avis reports her findings to Ernest, whom she calls, in an obvious nod to patriarchal authority, her "father confessor" (38), Ernest retorts that "not one of them was a free agent. . . . They were all tied to the merciless industrial machine. And the pathos of it and the tragedy is that they are tied by their heart-strings" (38). This sets up London's ideological denunciation of a class system that rewards those wealthy members of society with dividends made from the tragedies of working men like Jackson, while making wage slaves out of men like Donnelly who only wish to feed their families.

Another ideological icon that ties Jackson's arm to the larger indictment of industrial civilization is the image of blood. In fact, according to one interpreter of *The Iron Heel*, the "central unifying image throughout the novel is blood."[28] From Ernest's charge that "[o]ur boasted civilisation is based upon blood" (38) to Avis's acknowledgment that she "saw the blood of Jackson upon my gown as well" (41) the "scarlet stain" (38) seems to wash over everyone and every incident in the novel. (London's apocalyptic short story, "The Scarlet Plague" [1912], transforms this indictment of civilization's bloodshed into a decimating disease that destroys so-called advanced civilization and returns the remnants of humanity to "cave-man" existence.) In immersing the novel in the image of blood, London thus telescopes a manifested ideological critique of power through socialist (the bloodshed caused by capitalism and the red revolution embraced by Ernest), Christian (Ernest as the potential Christ-like blood sacrifice), and naturalist (the animal-like bloodletting of contending forces) lenses.

On another level, the image of blood exemplifies the gender contradictions that London and the culture embodied. Such contradictions are evident in the phallocentric violation that Ernest imposed on Avis by accusing her of having a "gown . . . stained with blood" (28), which, in turn, caused Avis to remark that she "had never been so brutally treated in my life" (28). Ernest's aggressive indictment of Avis's blood-stained complicity with destructive capitalism and her naivety about the roots of the tragedy of Jackson's arm not only reveal the masculinist inclinations of Everhard, but also underscore the patriarchal politics of an age when men welcomed public blood-letting through their embrace of conflict. Thus, Jackson's arm and the image of blood reflect and refract an ideological discourse that made London both a spokesman for socialism and symbol of the contradictions of gender prerogatives of the age.[29]

In turning to other discursive elements in *The Iron Heel*, one can begin to see more clearly the ideological terrain upon which London and other revolutionary socialists stood. London's own need to demonstrate his intellectual superiority and the superiority of the ideological discourse articulated through Everhard attempts to move the structure of the novel from a didactic to dramatic moment in the Philomath Club confrontation, foreshadowing in the process the ultimate violent confrontation described in "The Chicago Commune" chapter. Nonetheless, much of the what transpires in the Philomath Club and the immediate follow-up chapters aims at convincing Avis and other members of the middle class through ideological set-pieces that they will have to "awaken to the inescapable choice between a past and future, between capitalism and socialism."[30]

Everhard has a pugnacious stance toward the denizens of the upper-class Philomath Club: he revels in challenging their failed economic leadership, repeating in the process not only London's amalgamation of socialist and progressive tracts of the period but also previous utopian treatises on the inefficiencies and immorality of capitalism. What sets London's language off from that of Bellamy in *Looking Backward* or the speeches of Debs is the naturalist tone of the discursive chains. For example, Ernest says to Avis: "I shall menace their money bags. That will shake them to the roots of their primitive natures. If you can come, you will see the cave-man, in evening dress, snarling and snapping over a bone. I promise you a great caterwauling and an illuminating insight into the nature of the beast" (50). As June Howard points out in her study of naturalism, "in the rhetoric of the period, the powerful as well as the powerless can be brutes."[31]

Everhard's excoriation of the ruling class focuses not only on their brutishness but also their "intellectual stupidity" (53). In denouncing the selfishness and materialism of the master class, Everhard links their lack of Christian morality to their class hatred and hypocrisy. Talking about his involvement with members of the upper class, Everhard averred: "I met men . . . who invoked the name of the Prince of Peace in their diatribes against war and who put rifles in the hands of Pinkertons with which to shoot down strikers in their own factories. I met men incoherent with indignation at the brutality of prize-fighting, and who, at the same time were parties to the adulteration of food that killed each year more babes than even red-handed Herod had killed" (53–54).

In the above passage London manages to hold up to ridicule a ruling class that decries the vices of a lower class, such as prize-fighting (a vice from which he had previously distanced himself) while perpetrating even greater crimes of violence on the working and lower class. By alluding to the adulteration of food, London reiterates the muckraking charges made by Upton Sinclair in *The Jungle* while focusing, as did Sinclair, on the heinous disregard by men of wealth for the well-being of innocent children. Such criticism allows London to deplore the flawed manhood of upper class males who look down their noses at the vices of the poor without recognizing their own responsibility for the suffering of the less well-off. Furthermore, by connecting the crimes of a ruling class to Herod and the neglect of the message of the "Prince of Peace," London recalls the social gospel and Christian Socialist discourse of the time, as well as propagating his own brand of evangelical socialism.[32]

As one critic notes, *The Iron Heel* is "framed by the Marxist dialect, . . . the apocalyptic vision of Christianity, and the naturalistic imagery of social Darwinism."[33] There are, as demonstrated above, traces of all three ideologies in the discourse enunciated by Everhard. However, when the focus shifts exclusively to a discussion and debate over power, a form of crude, but poetic, Marxism takes precedence. For instance, as part of the challenge to expropriate the wealth and possessions of the ruling class, Everhard remonstrates: "Here are our hands. They are strong hands. We are going to take your government, your palaces, and all your purpled ease away from you, and in that day you shall work for your bread even as the peasant in the field or the starved and runty clerk in your metropolises. Here are our hands. They are strong hands!" (55). This Marxist vision of working class expropriation of society's wealth and power and the attendant ruling class loss of power and destitution is also at the core of London's 1909 futuristic short story, "The Dream of

Debs." The repetition of the reference to hands as the metaphorical equivalent of labor power here conveys the discursive code of class struggle, with the lines anticipating and perhaps even inspiring the last stanza and chorus of the song "The Preacher and the Slave" written by Wobbly balladeer and martyr Joe Hill:

> Workingmen of all countries unite,
> Side by side we for freedom will fight;
> When the world and its wealth we have gained
> To the grafters we'll sing this refrain:
>
> You will eat, bye and bye,
> When you've learned how to cook and to fry;
> Chop some wood, 'twill do you good,
> And you'll eat in the sweet bye and bye.[34]

In fact, there was much of an overlap in the ideological discourse between Jack London and the Wobblies, especially those itinerant members from the West whose own background mirrored some of the same experiences that London had as a young man. Wobblies like Joe Hill and "Big Bill" Haywood (a leader of the Industrial Workers of the World in the aftermath of their founding convention in Chicago in 1905) were marginalized members of a working class and self-taught alienated intellectuals whose uncompromising vision of class struggle and revolutionary millennialism challenged not only the ruling elites but also reformers in both labor and socialist circles. Indeed, London's short story "South of the Slot" features a Haywood-like character called "Big" Bill Totts who is the schizoid virile radical half of the effete academic Freddie Drummond. This story concludes with Drummond/Totts abandoning his comfortable bourgeois life and delicate fiancee Catherine Van Vorst for the robust life of a labor leader, resident of a working class ghetto, and husband of the firebrand President of the International Glove Workers Union No. 974, Mary Condon.

There were also among the Wobblies, as with London at this time, contradictory currents of Nietzschean, Darwinist, and syndicalist thought. Where, however, there was some clearly common thread was on the matter of power. When George Speed, an early friend and comrade of London's at the turn of the century in Oakland and an IWW organizer, asserted that "power is the thing that determines everything today," he not only expressed the sentiments of the Wobblies but also the discourse of Everhard in this particular section of *The Iron Heel* when he asserts: "Power will be the arbiter, as it always has been the arbiter" (64).[35]

Of course, the challenge that Everhard launches against those in the Philomath Club does not go unanswered. However, the answer is not a philosophical refutation of those arguments mounted by Everhard, but in the language of power, a language that expresses a curious symmetry between Everhard's revolutionary challenge and the ruling class response to this challenge.[36] "Our reply," says Wickson, an outraged member of the Philomath audience, "will be couched in terms of lead. We are in power. Nobody will deny it. By virtue of that power we shall remain in power" (63). To try to heighten the dramatic moment of this confrontation of an otherwise static screed, Avis comments: "He turned suddenly upon Ernest. The moment was dramatic" (63). Such an interjection attempts a rather heavy-handed reinforcement of the drama of the confrontation as a prelude to the overkill of the following aggressive language: "When you reach out your vaunted strong hands for our palaces and purpled ease, we will show you what strength is. In roar of shell and shrapnel and in whine of machine-guns will our answer be couched" (63). Meredith's annotation at the end of this sentence further fixes the political conflict embedded in the language of the speaker: "To show the tenor of thought, the following definition is quoted from 'The Cynic's Word Book' (A.D. 1906), written by one Ambrose Bierce, an avowed and confirmed misanthrope of the period: 'Grape shot, n. *An argument which the future is preparing to the demands of American socialism*' " (63, author's emphasis).

The future these passages presage and the seven centuries that Meredith looks back on certainly attest to London's orthodox Marxist sensibility that overcoming capitalism will take a long time and that capitalism must pass through several stages. In fact, both near the beginning of his involvement with socialism and after his resignation from the Socialist Party near the end of his life, London expressed a Darwin-tinged vision of class struggle that could only see socialism, at best, as a distant, albeit inevitable, goal. In a letter to Cloudsley Jones in 1901 London wrote:

> I should like to have socialism yet I know that socialism is not the very next step; I know that capitalism must live its life first. That the world must be exploited to the utmost first; that first must intervene a struggle for life among the nations, severer, intenser, more widespread, than ever before. I should much more prefer to wake tomorrow in a smoothly-running socialistic state; but I know I shall not; I know that a child must go through its child's sicknesses ere it becomes a man. So, always remember that I speak of the things that are: not of the things that should be.[37]

Not only does this letter reveal London's pessimism about an easy and bloodless transition to socialism, but it also indicates some insight into the morbidity that would plague London and his times. Reflecting on the struggle for socialism in Italy at a little later time, the more dialectical Italian marxist Antonio Gramsci commented: "The crisis consists in the fact that the old is dying and the new cannot be born; and in this interregnum a great variety of morbid symptoms appears."[38]

Beyond the morbid symptoms that Gramsci and London allude to, the aforementioned letter by London also helps to frame the dystopic utopian structure and ideological discourse found in *The Iron Heel*. Furthermore, it provides additional evidence of the seemingly anomalous connections between the socialist, naturalistic, and masculinist orientation of much of London's writings. While there is a sense that any anomalies in *The Iron Heel* can be explained by the "antinomies of (London's) own protean mind and character," such antinomies are part and parcel of the naturalist project and the social contradictions of the time.[39] There was a sense of crisis and cataclysm in the United States and the West in general that promised both reform and repression, elements that are evident in the discourse and narrative of *The Iron Heel*.[40] Furthermore, in the character and language of Ernest *Everhard* (my emphasis) there is a continuous masculinist posturing that reflects London's own concern with his manhood, the ethos of naturalism, and the strong emphasis on virile power, especially for important segments of the radical working class.[41]

The mano-a-mano confrontation between Everhard, the revolutionary spokesman of the working class, and Mr. Wickson, the leader of the pack of the Philomath elite, reflects the class and gender dynamics evident throughout *The Iron Heel* and refracts London's own emotional and ideological orientation. In London's 1903 article on "How I Became a Socialist" he highlights that orientation in the following revealing way: "And I looked ahead into long vistas of a hazy and interminable future into which playing what I conceived to be a MAN'S game, I should continue to travel with unfailing health without accidents, and with muscles ever vigorous. As I say, this future was interminable. I could see myself only raging through life without end like one of Nietzsche's blond beasts, lustfully roving and conquering by sheer superiority and strength."[42] Given London's attraction to *Ubermensch* socialism, it should be no surprise that Ernest Everhard is described in the following manner: "He was a natural aristocrat—and this in spite of the fact that he was in the camp of the non-aristocrats. He was a superman, a blond beast such as Nietzsche has described, and in addition he was aflame with democracy" (8).[43]

Of course, the irony is that both Everhard and London had little faith in democracy, or, for that matter, the avoidance of bloodshed. When London contended that he looked "to the strong man, the man on horseback to save the state from its own rotten futility,"[44] he was reflecting both his infatuation with Nietzsche and his part in the trajectory of authoritarian socialists who stretched from Bellamy to De Leon.[45] (In a utopian short story published soon after *The Iron Heel* called "Goliah," London's protagonist changed from a working-class superman to a scientist superman while retaining the authoritarian socialist cast.) Finally, London's own assessment near the end of his life about what lies ahead in the future reiterated the pessimistic tone in the discourse over power and the obsession with the endless violence that marked the fable-like latter half of *The Iron Heel*: "[E]verything appears almost hopeless; after long years of labor and development, the people are as bad off as ever. There is a mighty ruling class that intends to hold fast to its possessions. I see years and years of bloodshed. I see the master class hiring armies of murderers to keep the workers in subjection, to beat them back should they attempt to dispossess the capitalists. That's why I am a pessimist. I see things in light of history and the laws of nature."[46]

Such pessimism is deeply embedded in the lead-up to the cataclysmic events of "The Chicago Commune" denouement of *The Iron Heel*. Halfway through the novel, Everhard realizes that even with the socialist advances in the electoral arena, the counterrevolution has begun to seal the fate of those seeking immediate radical change. Everhard reflects: "I had hoped for a peaceable victory at the ballot-box. I was wrong. Wickson was right. We shall be robbed of our few remaining liberties; the Iron Heel will walk upon our faces; nothing remains but a bloody revolution of the working class. Of course we will win, but I shudder to think of it" (112). Even with the obligatory nod to a deterministic reading of history and revolution, London betrays a well-earned fear of the repressive apparatus of the state. From his own experiences as a teenager in Coxey's army, that ragtag assembly of unemployed workers heading towards Washington, D.C. to protest the economic conditions of the 1890s, to the continual intervention of police, military, and para military forces to repress working class struggles during this time, London was keenly aware that the entrenched power of the capitalists could call upon such repressive forces to retain its privileges and prevent social change.[47]

On the other hand, London's understanding of the workings of capitalism and the lure of its contradictory powers compels him in

The Iron Heel to focus on something other than repression, namely cooptation, as a contributing factor to undermining an easy and bloodless transition to socialism. Retaining his orthodox marxist and De Leonist-tinged distrust of mainstream unions, London highlights that distrust through Everhard's prophetic denunciations of coopted unions:

> In the favoured unions are the flower of American workingmen. They are strong, efficient men. They have become members of those unions through competition in place. Every fit workman in the United States will be possessed by the ambition to become a member of the favoured unions. The Oligarchy will encourage such ambition and the consequent competition. Thus will the strong men, who might else be revolutionists, be won away and their strength used to bolster the Oligarchy. (141)

It is also clear from this passage that such cooptation plays off of the lure of competition for workingmen whose manhood is defined by their ability to achieve recognition for their skills as efficient workers. In an era when efficiency and ambition are measurements of manhood, London is particularly attuned to the undermining of the message of revolutionary change for workingmen.[48]

From the criticism of the "aristocracy of labour" to the establishment of the clandestine cadre of revolutionists, London's *The Iron Heel* recalls Lenin's 1902 pamphlet "What Is to Be Done?" Especially in the emergence of the "Fighting Groups," the underground and secretive revolutionary organization that was to extract revenge and wreak mayhem on the Iron Heel, the counterrevolutionary organization of the Oligarchy, London demonstrates a characteristic emphasis on the efficacy of violence.[49] Although admittedly brutal in their treatment of their enemies and traitors within their own ranks, Avis's memoir notes that the "comrades of the Fighting Groups were heroes all, and the peculiar thing about it was that they were opposed to the taking of life. They violated their own natures, yet they loved liberty and knew of no sacrifice too great to make for the Cause" (155–56). Meredith's long commentary on the Fighting Groups acknowledges the inspiring influence of Russian revolutionists and the history of martyrdom by the men and women of the Fighting Groups leading up to the utopian Brotherhood of Man. He concludes his commentary with the following: "We, who by personal experience know nothing of bloodshed, must not judge harshly the heroes of the Fighting Groups. They gave up their lives for humanity, no sacrifice was too great for them to accomplish, while inexorable necessity compelled them to bloody expression in an age of blood" (157).

If the "inexorable necessity" of revolution led London to cast the struggle over power into bloody class warfare, then those who embraced revolutionary conflict would have to be transformed into class warriors. In the chapter entitled "Transformations" London's revolutionaries become estranged from their previous lives, taking on in the process those gender codes that defined London's own ideological discourse. Avis is required to alter her looks and demeanor in order to develop an effective disguise so that she may infiltrate the Oligarchy. In transforming herself she will not only inure herself to the coming violence, but also take on the role of an independent "new woman." In effect, at Ernest's request, Avis must become less of the naive and helpless middle class maiden and more of a strong comrade-mate, not surprisingly unlike London's real-life "mate-woman" Charmian Kittredge.[50]

Like Avis, the other men and women who were inexorably pulled into the orbit of the revolution had to throw off any bourgeois sentimentality in order to harden themselves for battle. In describing their transformations London also demonstrated his gendered readings of what constituted weaknesses and failures of nerve. Freed from their responsibilities to feed their families, the characters Jackson and Peter Donnelly seek class and gender revenge through the revolution. As Peter Donnelly says when joining the 'Frisco Reds: " 'tis revenge for my blasted manhood I'm after' " (178). In the character of Anna Roylston, dubbed the "Red Virgin" in the novel (179), London reveals once more, in the words of Joan Hedrick, how "the bourgeois virtues [are associated] with a narrow, effeminate way of seeing,"[51] and in transcending such bourgeois values women, in particular, must to some extent de-sex and harden themselves. Thus, Anna Roylston and the other revolutionaries of the Fighting Groups must especially eschew the snares and sentiments engendered by family life.[52] In the case of Anna Roylston, this means eschewing any maternal role in favor of becoming "an executioner for the Fighting Groups" (168). While many critics have identified the character of Anna Roylston with the real life Jane Roylston, secretary of a local IWW chapter, Charles Watson has suggested that a clipping found along with notes for an article by London on anarchy and Louise Michel, heroine of the Paris Commune, provides better insight into the representation of the "Red Virgin": "Louise Michel, the Red Virgin. Describe her life, and, after pointing out how illogical, unscientific and impossible is anarchy, hold Louise Michel up as a better type of human than a woman of the bourgeoisie, fat and selfish and dead."[53]

If London had Louise Michel and the Paris Commune in mind as models for the cataclysmic conflict between revolutionaries of the

Fighting Groups and counterrevolutionaries of the Iron Heel, the location of the climax of the novel in the Chicago Commune is a testament to the iconic hold that the city of Chicago had for radicals of this time. From Haymarket (1886) to the Pullman strike (1894), Chicago was seen as a firestorm of radical activity and repression. As Avis notes in her journal: "There the revolutionary spirit was strong. Too many bitter strikes had been curbed there in the days of capitalism for the workers to forget and forgive. Even the labour castes of the city were alive with revolt" (197). The Everhard Manuscript goes on to point out that "Chicago had always been the storm-centre of the conflict between labour and capital, a city of street battles and violent death . . . [which would] become the storm-centre of the premature First Revolt" (197).

Why the "Chicago Commune" would produce a premature revolt has as much to do with resonances of apocalyptic utopian novels like Ignatius Donnelly's *Caesar's Column* (1890) as with London's own loss of faith in the redemptive and efficacious power of mass movements for radical change.[54] The climaxes in *Caesar's Column* and *The Iron Heel*, although taking place in different cities, see the massive lumpen and even proletarian elements of urban America as awash in seething rage that can only explode into mindless and vengeful violence.[55] For London, who prided himself on his superior intelligence and the need for disciplined understanding of the workings of nature and society, such an outburst would be doomed to failure precisely because it lacked a directing intelligence. Moreover, the "people of the abyss" that London wrote about and feared were themselves icons for the predispositions of naturalism. Such naturalist predispositions saw the proletariat as unthinking and lacking in all of the traits necessary to realize its own redemption.[56]

In the class war that engulfs the "Chicago Commune," echoes of primitive cries amid modern weaponry conclude in an abortive and futile effort at revolution. The final image in the chapter recalls not only an earlier century's failed utopian image of "Liberty Leading the People" but also a dystopian reminder of the difficulty of regeneration and redemption that London would come to recognize in the cause of socialism and in his own life.

> Turning a corner, we [Avis and a male comrade named appropriately Hartman] came upon a woman. She was lying on the pavement in a pool of blood. Hartman bent over and examined her. As for myself, I turned deathly sick. I was to see many dead that day, but the total carnage was not to affect me as did this first forlorn body lying there at my feet abandoned on the pavement. "Shot in the breast," was Hartman's report. Clasped in the hollow of her arm, as a child might be clasped, was a bundle of printed matter. Even in death she seemed

> loath to part with that which had caused her death; for when Hartman
> had succeeded in withdrawing the bundle, we found that it consisted
> of large printed sheets, the proclamations of the revolutionists. (205)

Just as Delacroix's 1831 painting featured the prominent fore-
grounding of the bare-breasted figure of "Liberty" waving the tricol-
ors while leading revolutionaries to the barricades, London's
emphasis on this anonymous dead woman's breast wound could be
read as the appropriate symbol of a stillborn revolution. While it is
also tempting to read this image of the bullet-shattered breast
through the lens of the psychobiography of London's own estrangement from his mother and frustration over his and Charmian's
inability to provide a male offspring from their union, the gender
and power dimension of the paragraph and, indeed, the whole
chapter suggest instead the difficulty of defending and sustaining
revolutionary socialism against the well-armed and ruthless min-
ions of the capitalists, or, in the case of Jack London, in sustaining
his own ideological fervor in the face of both personal and political
limitations.

The failure to give birth to a successful revolution and to render
any attempts to do so as abortive, as captured in the image above,
further reinforces the sense that *The Iron Heel* is more about
London's focus on dystopian realities than utopian possibilities and
more about emotional limitations than political liberation.[57] Yet,
perhaps, the final meaning of the novel is that the power and gender
relationships unveiled in *The Iron Heel* cannot persist if utopia and
political liberation are to be realized. In fact, in all of the references
to Meredith's annotations cited above it is evident that such power
and gender relationships have been superseded in the utopian
society of the future. The key to that supersession and to London's
own despondent hopes for the future is the Nietzschean idea of the
"transvaluation of values." Not only does Avis refer to the "passion-
less transvaluation of values" (208), but also much of London's later
literature and life contains both direct and indirect references to the
concept.[58] Moreover, the transfigurative politics that are integral to
the transvaluation of values are crucial to the utopian project and
those ideologies promoting such a politics and project.[59]

That London saw in revolutionary socialism an ideology that
promised a transvaluation of values is apparent in much of what he
wrote and lectured about until nearly the end of his life. However,
London's appropriation of the ideological discourse of revolutionary
socialism contained those contradictions that marked his life, the
socialist movement, and the era of the late nineteenth and early
twentieth centuries. As one critic of London's work points out: "His

Socialism was always interpenetrated by his individualism, a condition which explains how both he and his writings could at once combine racism, the glorification of the superior individual over the mass, a fascination with brute force, and a warm-hearted sense of the brotherhood of man."[60] Yet, London's individualism and his embrace of a kind of Nietzschean "will-to-power" are also a consequence of his striving for an individuation from those class and gender forces embedded in *The Iron Heel* and evident in his essay "How I Became a Socialist." Renouncing an "individualism . . . dominated by the orthodox bourgeois ethics," London recounts that his intellectual conversion to socialism resulted from his willpower to rise above the "Social Pit."[61] It was in the social pit than one's manly strength and one's security would be drowned in a sea of humanity tossed aside by the ever-churning waves of social and economic degradation. Thus, London's striving for separating himself from those class and gender forces that would pull him back into the social pit is a key to understanding London's socialism and its discontents.

On the other hand, London's socialism, at some level, replicated the contradictions within the socialist movement of the early twentieth century. While the socialist movement contained any number of tendencies and a variety of factions, it was riddled throughout with tensions over ethnicity and class and plagued by debates over evolution versus revolution, organizational alignments, and political versus direct action strategies and tactics.[62] In exposing those contradictions, tensions, and discontents of socialism through the ideological discourse of *The Iron Heel*, Jack London provides the reader with some insight into the icons, images, and language of socialism.

Because London was so clearly identified with the socialist movement during the period in which *The Iron Heel* was written, it is not surprising that the immediate response to the novel became an occasion to debate the meaning of socialism. By examining the responses to the novel in the socialist and nonsocialist newspapers and journals of the time, one can gain further insight into how such a text could mean different things to different readers struggling with their own definitions of and reactions to the ideological discourse of socialism in early twentieth-century America.

London manifested his own fear of the misunderstanding and misreading of *The Iron Heel* before the publication of the novel in 1907. He initially had considered sending a manuscript copy to *Appeal to Reason*, the leading socialist newspaper of its day, for serialization. In a letter dated December 15, 1906, London demonstrated his ambivalence about such a move. He noted: "The more I think about it, the more impossible it seems to me the story is, even for a socialist publication like *Appeal to Reason*. It runs such a strong liability of being misunderstood, and hence, instead of being a help, it would turn out a hurt to the propaganda."[63]

In fact, as far as the editors and socialist promoters of *Appeal to Reason* were concerned, *The Iron Heel* was "the best [socialist novel] we had seen."[64] Upton Sinclair, whose novel *The Jungle* had been serialized initially in *Appeal to Reason*, earning in the process high praise from London, reciprocated by lauding *The Iron Heel*. Sinclair wrote in a 1908 letter of endorsement to *Appeal to Reason* that *The Iron Heel* was "one of the best propaganda documents that has come along. . . . Every reader of *Appeal to Reason* ought to own a copy of this story and lend it to everybody he knows."[65]

Other socialist journals promoted *The Iron Heel* not for its truncated or marginalized vision of socialism, but for its vivid denunciation of capitalism. An Oakland, California, socialist publication noted in its April 1908 capitalized advertisement for *The Iron Heel*: "In All the Literature of the Modern Revolutionary Movement There is Not a Volume Which So Thoroughly and Convincingly Condemns the Capitalist System."[66] *Wilshire's Magazine*, one of the leading socialist journals of the time, reinforced London's sense that *The Iron Heel* was different from other utopian novels, especially because of its attention to the intricacies of capitalist rule. "*The Iron Heel* is not a utopian dream story," noted *Wilshire's*, "but a gripping drama of the overthrow of the capitalist oligarchy of the present time. . . . It never loses touch with the present conditions; it has the intense interest of a drama of real life."[67]

Beyond the socialist boosterism found in the above publications, *The Iron Heel* elicited commentary in some socialist newspapers highlighting the need to combat the capitalist oligarchy through education and organization. The *Chicago Socialist* contended:

> We must realize that today the working class is disorganized and can be twisted and turned and made anything of by the capitalist class with its newspapers, priests, schools, colleges, and power to reward those who are ready to be traitors.
> That the Iron Heel has begun its rule is apparent. If it is not rooted out before 1912, there is every reason to believe that the workers will be awakened too late and find themselves in a completely Russianized country.[68]

In effect, such commentary rearticulated the very analysis found in London's work. Accepting London's analysis and prognosis was seen by some socialist editorialists as putting tremendous pressure on socialists to organize even more effectively. As *The Socialist* of

Seattle averred: "If Jack London's idea in *The Iron Heel* that Social-ism may be deferred for three centuries by the rise of the oligarchy . . . because of the weakness of the American Proletariat, then the responsibility of the present generation of Socialists so to educate and stimulate the wage class as to prevent such dread event becomes enormous."[69]

For much of the nonsocialist press, the response to *The Iron Heel* provided an opportunity to demonize and dismiss socialism in particular and radicalism in general. The *Nashville Banner*'s Febru-ary 29, 1908, review asserted that the "book is one that will be much relished by the extreme radicals. It is really vicious in some aspects and very nearly advocates the diabolism of the anarchist."[70] No matter that London specifically criticizes anarchism in the novel: for this and other reviewers socialism is an ideology bent on stirring up class hatred, leading to violent destruction. The *San Francisco Chronicle* predictably denounced the socialism in the novel as a "creed of destruction." Noting that "class hatred is obviously one of the articles of his faith," the *Philadelphia Telegram* claimed that London "shrieks his hatred from every page, and exerts all of his undoubted descriptive powers and energy to blowing into a blood-red flame the passions of what . . . may be called the masses."[71]

A number of antagonistic reviewers take London to task for the violent passions presented in and aroused by the novel. William Morton Payne, writing in the refined *Chicago Dial*, expresses what surely is a condescendingly bourgeois opinion that "such books as this . . . have a mischievous influence upon unbalanced minds and we cannot but deplore their multiplication. . . . [O]ur civilization has no worse enemies than those who are engaged in the truly devilish work of fomenting social dissension and arraying class against class." In turn, the *Johnstown Democrat* intimates in its March 27, 1908, review that "men, like Mr. London, with their intemperate and inflammatory utterances, . . . may bring about a condition approxi-mating that drawn in *The Iron Heel*."[72]

Beyond attacking London for his "mischievous influence," other reviewers deny the credibility of *The Iron Heel*'s criticisms of the capitalist system and the socialist alternative. The Rochester *Post-Express* critic maintained in a March 21, 1908, review that under "the guise of a story this volume presents a distorted picture of present industrial conditions with a view of advancing socialistic ideas. The misrepresentation is so gross that few readers of mature years can be misled by it." The *Wall Street Journal* in its March 19, 1908 review dismissed London's "indictment of the present social system," noting that the "advocate of socialism must not only show the abuses of individualism, but they must also show convincing

proof that the substitution of socialism would be an adequate
remedy. This Mr. London has not been able to do."[73]

While other nonsocialist newspapers farther away from the east
coast also doubted the validity of London's claims about the vices
of capitalism and the virtues of socialism, a number of these reviews
grudgingly lauded the particular gendered vibrancy of *The Iron Heel*.
According to the review in the *Tacoma News*: "We recommend this
latest book on Socialism to any interested in the subject, not for its
accuracy, but for its inaccuracy, not for its convincing argument,
but for its vividness." On a more sympathetic note, the review in the
Duluth Herald asserted: "Though overwrought, the book is a stupen-
dous work of imagination, in all the vigor and virility of this young
champion of the proletariat from which he has so marvelously
sprung."[74] Clearly, out on the prairies and in the backwoods,
London's "red-blooded" realism and "virilist" writing struck a resonant note, superseding the socialist message by articulating a
masculinist realism.[75]

It was precisely that realism that convinced a number of reviewers
that *The Iron Heel* was not some utopian fantasy, but a sobering
wake-up call about the deplorable conditions of industrial capital.
As noted in the *Manchester Union*: "The disquieting thing about this
remarkable tale is, that it bases itself solidly and logically on things
as they actually exist today." Admiring the "daring" quality of the
book, a review in the Nashville *American* insisted: "It differs from
Looking Backward and other books of that character in that the
events narrated begin practically in the present, and the history
never loses touch with present conditions. In fact, it is the very
reverse of the usual Utopian story, for while the final conquest of
Socialist ideals is clearly indicated, the story deals directly with the
present system in an intensified form, and stops before ever the
remedy has been applied."[76]

It was precisely the remedy of London's socialism and, especially,
the violent manner of its birthing in *The Iron Heel* that repelled
sympathetic reformers. Acknowledging that among the "good things
and true" in the novel are the "condemnation of immense dividends
and the methods by which they are secured . . . and that the
conditions in which the laboring man works ought to be improved
vastly," the reformist *Religious Telescope* nonetheless condemned
London for undermining the genteel Christian socialism advocated
in its review. "Under the banner of socialism," asserted the reviewer,
"there have been grouped men from the rankest anarchy up to the
purest Christian principles, so that no one can say he approves or
condemns it without making proper distinctions. There are socialist
doctrines which ought to be promulgated, both for the good of man

and the nation. The advocates have our heartfelt sympathy and encouragement, but London's book, on the whole, will increase the bad and hinder the good."[77]

Another journal of middle class reform, *The Arena*, recognized *The Iron Heel* as a "powerful book, abounding in profoundly thoughtful suggestions, that should appeal to all patriots who love free government." Nevertheless, the review made clear that the novel was "precisely the opposite of the kind of literature that is needed to-day. We need literature that will strengthen . . . all reformers, no less the people who are under the wheel—literature that shall . . . lead all friends of justice to unite fearlessly and resolutely in a step-by-step plan of progress that by peaceable means will lead to a triumph of justice." Emphasizing peaceful progress and the power of the "ballot-box," the review concluded with a condemnation of *The Iron Heel*'s embrace of revolution. "All talk of forcible revolution," opined *The Arena*, "is not only foolish, but it is bound to injure the people's cause."[78]

Even among well-known socialists, London's vision of revolutionary socialism was found to be injurious to the cause. While admitting that the novel was "full of strength, vigor, and red blood," the *Chicago Socialist* lamented that *The Iron Heel* was "more apt to frighten than to educate."[79] Reiterating those sentiments and enunciating, more specifically, the ideological flaws of the novel, John Spargo, writing in the *International Socialist Review*, penned the following assessment of *The Iron Heel*:

> It is impossible to deny the literary skill which London displays in this ingenious and stirring romance. He has written nothing more powerful than this book. In some senses it is an unfortunate book, and I am by no means disposed to join those of our comrades who hail it as a great addition to the literature of Socialist propaganda. The picture he gives is well calculated, it seems to me, to repel many whose addition to our forces is sorely needed; it gives a new impetus to the old and generally discarded cataclysmic theory; it tends to weaken the political Socialist movement by discrediting the ballot and to encourage the chimerical and reactionary notion of physical forces, so alluring to a certain type of mind.[80]

It was probably Spargo's review more than any other that disappointed London and led him to conclude he got "nothing from knocks from the socialists." Yet, Spargo's position as a believer in gradualist socialism and evolutionary organicism reflected not only an antagonism to London's ideological discourse but also to the left tendencies within the socialist movement.[81] That left tendency was particularly evident in Joseph Wanhope's review of *The Iron Heel* in

The Worker. Noting that "Jack London has performed a valuable service for the Socialist movement," Wanhope goes on to "advise every Socialist to procure this striking volume and give it a careful perusal." Taking up the militant cudgel, he tendentiously avers that "there are few Socialists who believe that the social revolution can be consummated through the ballot alone. . . . If the point is ever reached when the ruling class refuse to abide by . . . [the ballot], nothing remains for Socialists but armed revolution—conquest by physical force of the powers of government."[82]

While London continued to participate in the debates about the course of socialist politics, ending with a rejection of the compromised timidity of the Socialist Party in his 1916 resignation letter, his pessimism over the viability of the socialist movement and personal estrangement from the circle of socialist friends he had made at the turn of the century help to explain both the cataclysmic tone and marginalized utopia in *The Iron Heel*.[83] In particular, London's despair about the prospects for revolutionary change and the transvaluation of values as a collective project of willed transformation led to locating utopia in *The Iron Heel* as marginal notes from a very distant future. Thus, the socialist postures adopted by his characters in the novel are more revealing of the ways in which his own class and gender identity were marked by the contradictions and discontents of his life and times. In effect, by responding to the ideological discourse in *The Iron Heel*, readers and reviewers identified their own sense of socialism and its discontents.

NOTES

1. Quoted in Carolyn Johnston, *Jack London—An American Radical?* (Westport, Conn.: Greenwood Press, 1984), p.140. n.49.

2. Quoted in ibid. p. 126.

3. Tom Moylan, *Demand the Impossible: Science Fiction and the Utopian Imagination* (New York: Methuen, 1986), p. 6; and Gorman Beauchamp, "Jack London's Utopia Dystopia and Dystopia Utopia," in *America as Utopia*, ed. Kenneth M. Roemer (New York: Burt Franklin, 1981), p. 91.

4. *The Letters of Jack London*, Vol. II, ed. Earle Labor, Robert C. Leitz, and Milo Shephard (Stanford: Stanford University Press, 1988), p. 676.

5. Jean Pfaelzer, "The Impact of Political Theory on Narrative Structures," in *America as Utopia*, pp. 119–20. On locating ideological discourses in literature, see Terry Eagleton, "Ideology, Fiction, Narrative," *Social Text* 2 (Summer 1979): 62–80.

6. Peter Ruppert, *Reader in a Strange Land: The Activity of Reading Literary Utopias* (Athens: University of Georgia Press, 1986), p. 19.

7. Tony Bennett, "Texts in History: The Determination of Readings and Their Texts," in *Post-Structuralism and the Question of History*, ed.

Derek Attridge, Geoff Bennington, and Robert Young (Cambridge: Cambridge University Press, 1987), p. 80.

8. Barbara Goodwin and Keith Taylor, *The Politics of Utopia: A Study in Theory and Practice* (New York: St. Martin's Press, 1982), p. 138.

9. On the millennial character of turn-of-the-century socialism, see James R. Green, *Grass-Roots Socialism: Radical Movements in the Southwest, 1895–1943* (Baton Rouge: Louisiana State University Press, 1978), pp. 12–52; and Howard H. Quint, *The Forging of American Socialism: Origins of the Modern Movement* (Columbia: University of South Carolina Press, 1953). On the fragmentation of working class life in America and the attendant splintering of turn-of-the-century socialism, see Mike Davis, *Prisoners of the American Dream: Politics and Economy in the History of the US Working Class* (London: Verso, 1990), pp. 3–51; and Richard J. Oestreicher, *Solidarity and Fragmentation: Working People and Class Consciousness in Detroit, 1872–1900* (Urbana: University of Illinois Press, 1986). On the introjection of marginalization in London's life and characters, see, for example, comments in the "Introduction," in *The Science Fiction of Jack London*, ed. Richard Gid Powers (Boston: Gregg Press, 1975), esp. p. x.

10. Joan London, *Jack London and His Times: An Unconventional Biography* (Seattle: University of Washington Press, 1968), p. 307.

11. On the theoretical connection between different forms of masculinity and power, see Arthur Brittan, *Masculinity and Power* (New York: Basil Blackwell, 1989). The connection between a discursive force field and power and gender is derived from the work of Michel Foucault. See Foucault, *The History of Sexuality, Volume I—An Introduction*, trans. Robert Harley (New York: Pantheon, 1978); and Foucault, "The Subject of Power," in *Michel Foucault: Beyond Structuralism and Hermeneutics*, ed. Hubert L. Dreyfus and Paul Rabinow (London: Harvester Press, 1982), pp. 208–26. For a discussion of Foucault's discursive force field and its link to power and gender in history, see Joan Wallach Scott, *Gender and the Politics of History* (New York: Columbia University Press, 1988), esp. p. 42. For an excellent overview of the social construction of gender and power, see R. W. Connell, *Gender and Power: Society, the Person and Sexual Politics* (Cambridge, Mass.: Polity Press, 1987). On Everhard and London's virilist connection to the historical and cultural characteristics of the age, see Richard Slotkin, *Gunfighter Nation: The Myth of the Frontier in Twentieth Century America* (New York: Harper Perennial, 1992), esp. pp. 164–66.

12. Andrew Sinclair, *Jack: A Biography of Jack London* (London: Weidenfeld and Nicolson, 1978), p. 129.

13. Joan Hedrick, *Solitary Comrade: Jack London and His Work* (Chapel Hill: University of North Carolina Press, 1982), p. 83.

14. Jack London, *The Iron Heel* (Westport, Conn.: Lawrence Hill, 1980), p. 1. All further references to this edition will be noted in the text.

15. In claiming that London's use of the utopian narrator "creates a Brechtian alienation effect," Carolyn Johnston proceeds to misconstrue the purpose for such an effect. See Johnston, *Jack London*, pp. 120–21. It is not to enlist the sympathies of the reader for the characters; rather,

Brecht sees this alienation or estrangement effect as a way to get his audience to consider fully the conditions which produce the characters. For an illuminating discussion of the role of this estrangement effect in utopian literature, see Darko Suvin, *Metamorphoses of Science Fiction: On the Poetics and History of a Literary Genre* (New Haven: Yale University Press, 1979), pp. 37–62.

16. Joan London, *Jack London and His Times*, p. 379.

17. Hayden White, *The Content of the Form: Narrative Discourse and Historical Representation* (Baltimore: Johns Hopkins University Press, 1987), pp. 185–213.

18. For a masterful biography of Debs that sets out this connection between American manhood and socialism, see Nick Salvatore, *Eugene V. Debs: Citizen and Socialist* (Urbana: University of Illinois Press, 1982). In a direct reference to Debs and his iconic significance in his short story "The Dream of Debs" (1909), London contrasts the resolve and masculine strength of the organized working class in a future general strike to the weakness and cowardice of the leisured men of the ruling class.

19. Hedrick, *Solitary Comrade*, p. 15.

20. Clarice Stasz, "Androgyny in the Novels of Jack London," *Western American Literature* 11 (May 1976): 122, 133.

21. June Howard, *Form and History in American Literary Naturalism* (Chapel Hill: University of North Carolina Press, 1985), p. 77.

22. Hedrick, *Solitary Comrade*, p. 28.

23. On the role of Jackson's arm in the education of Avis, see Charles N. Watson, Jr., *The Novels of Jack London: A Reappraisal* (Madison: University of Wisconsin Press, 1983), pp. 113–15.

24. On the reconstructive approach, see Dominick LaCapra, *Rethinking Intellectual History: Texts, Contexts, Language* (Ithaca: Cornell University Press, 1983), esp. pp. 23–71. On the deconstructive or semiological decoding method, see White, *The Content of the Form*, pp. 185–213.

25. Watson, *The Novels of Jack London*, p. 104.

26. Nell Irvin Painter, *Standing at Armageddon: The United States, 1877–1919* (New York: W. W. Norton, 1987), p. 206. For other historical references to the rates of industrial accidents, see James R. Green, *The World of the Worker: Labor in Twentieth Century America* (New York: Hill and Wang, 1980), p. 13.

27. See, for example, Peter N. Stearns, *Be a Man!: Males in Modern Society* (New York: Holmes and Meier, 1990). In arguing that the absence of Jackson's arm reflects the absence of the authentic working class in *The Iron Heel*, Alessandro Portrelli also asserts that the "loss of Jackson's arm, torn and chewed by the teeth of the machine, sums up London's strategy of loss, absence, void, fragmentation by which he indicates—by *not* describing them—the essential objects of *The Iron Heel*." See Alessandro Portrelli, "Jack London's Missing Revolution: Notes on *The Iron Heel*," *Science Fiction Studies* 27 (July 1982): 184.

28. Johnston, *Jack London*, p. 121.

29. For an incisive analysis of the sexual politics of *The Iron Heel*, see Hedrick, *Solitary Comrade*, pp. 188–99. For a discussion of patriarchal

politics as connected to the period, see Jeff Hearn, *Men in the Public Eye: The Construction and Deconstruction of Public Men and Public Patriarchies* (London: Routledge, 1992); and Michael S. Kimmel, "The Contemporary 'Crisis' of Masculinity in Historical Perspective," *The Making of Masculinities: The New Men's Studies*, ed. H. Brod (Boston: Allen and Unwin, 1987), pp. 121–53.

30. Paul Stein, "Jack London's *The Iron Heel*: Art as Manifesto," *Studies in American Fiction* 6 (Spring 1978): 80.

31. Howard, *Form and History in American Literary Naturalism*, p. 122.

32. On London's own brand of evangelical socialism, see Johnston, *Jack London*, pp. 109–45. On the social gospel and Christian Socialism, see Sidney Fine, *Laissez Faire and the General Welfare State* (Ann Arbor: University of Michigan Press, 1964), pp. 169–97; Robert M. Crunden, *Ministers of Reform: The Progressives Achievement in American Civilization, 1889–1920* (New York: Basic Books, 1982); and R. C. White and C. H. Hopkins, *The Social Gospel: Religion and Reform in Changing America* (Philadelphia: Temple University Press, 1976).

33. Watson, *The Novels of Jack London*, p. 119.

34. From "The Preacher and the Slave," in *Songs of the Workers*, 34th ed. (Chicago: IWW, 1974), p. 64. This Joe Hill song was first published in the 1911 edition of the Wobblies' "Little Red Song Book." On Hill's life and martyrdom, see Philip S. Foner, *The Case of Joe Hill* (New York: International Publishers, 1965).

35. Quoted in Melvyn Dubofsky, *We Shall Be All: A History of the Industrial Workers of the World* (New York: Quadrangle, 1973), p. 157. On the same page, Dubofsky alludes to this passage from *The Iron Heel* and attests to how the novel was "well known to Wobblies." On the ideological orientation and millennial fervor of the IWW, see ibid., pp. 146–70; and Donald E. Winters, Jr., *The Soul of the Wobblies: The IWW, Religion, and American Culture in the Progressive Era, 1905–1917* (Westport, Conn.: Greenwood Press, 1985). On the life and significance of "Big Bill" Haywood, see Peter Carlson, *Roughneck: The Life and Times of Big Bill Haywood* (New York: W. W. Norton, 1983). On London's emotional and ideological ties to the Wobblies, see Johnston, *Jack London*, pp. 115–16. It is not surprising that the "one-big union" which brings the ruling class to its knees in London's "The Dream of Debs" is referred to only as the ILW.

36. Portrelli, "Jack London's Missing Revolution," p. 186.

37. Quoted in Joan London, *Jack London and His Times*, pp. 333–34.

38. Antonio Gramsci, *Selections from the Prison Notebooks*, trans. and ed. Quentin Hoare and Geoffrey Nowell Smith (New York: International Publishers, 1971), p. 276.

39. Beauchamp, "Jack London's Utopia Dystopia," p. 91; Howard, *Form and History*, pp. 39, 41. See also Peter Conn, *The Divided Mind: Ideology and Imagination in America, 1898–1917* (Cambridge: Cambridge University Press, 1983), pp. 104–9, where the brief description of London's "ambiguous" socialism helps to situate any anomalies in the contradictory context of the times.

40. On the crisis and conflicts of the times in the United States, see Painter, *Standing at Armageddon*. On the sense of cataclysm in the United States, see Frederic C. Jaher, *Doubters and Dissenters: Cataclysmic Thought in America, 1885–1918* (New York: Free Press of Glencoe, 1964). On reform and repression in the Western World at this time, see E. J. Hobsbawm, *The Age of Empire, 1875–1914* (New York: Vintage, 1989).

41. On the historical context of masculine concerns, especially in the working class, during this period, see Stearns, *Be a Man!*. On the masculinist ethos of radical workers like the Wobblies, see my "Masculine Power and Virile Syndicalism: A Gendered Analysis of the IWW in Australia," *Labour History* 63 (November 1992); 83–99. On the masculine bias in naturalism, see Howard, *Form and History*, p. 140. Although, as a number of critics point out, the name Everhard came from a Michigan cousin of London's, the gender posturing of the character conveys a strong sense of phallocentric power. On the Everhard name and character, see, for example, Watson, *The Novels of Jack London*, pp. 102–3.

42. Jack London, *War of the Classes* (New York: Grosset and Dunlap, 1905), pp. 269–70. Although London claims this was an individualist phase, he retained part of that orientation. On Nietzsche's influence on London, see Johnston, *Jack London*, pp. 79–88.

43. For a discussion of the role of *Ubermensch* socialism in London's writings, see Geoffrey Harpham, "Jack London and the Tradition of Superman Socialism," *American Studies* 16 (Spring 1975): 23–33.

44. Quoted in *Johnston, Jack London*, p. 80.

45. On the tradition of authoritarian socialism rooted in Bellamy's thought and influence, see Arthur Lipow, *Authoritarian Socialism in America: Edward Bellamy and the Nationalist Movement* (Berkeley: University of California Press, 1982). On De Leon's role in socialist politics and thought in America, see Glen L. Seretan, *Daniel De Leon: The Odyssey of an American Marxist* (Cambridge, Mass.: Harvard University Press, 1979).

46. Quoted in Joan London, *Jack London and His Times*, p. 336.

47. On the influence of Coxey's army for London and *The Iron Heel*, see Robert Barltrop, *Jack London: The Man, the Writer, the Rebel* (London: Pluto Press, 1976), p. 41; and Johnston, *Jack London*, pp. 11–17. On Coxey's army and the repression of strikes and movements for social change during this period, see Painter, *Standing at Armageddon*, pp. 117–21 and *passim*.

48. On the impact of competition and ambition in undermining the lure of radical messages and movements during the late nineteenth and early twentieth centuries, see Aileen Kraditor, *The Radical Persuasion, 1890–1917* (Baton Rouge: Louisiana State University Press, 1981).

49. On the connections between Lenin's "What Is to Be Done?" and the Fighting Groups in *The Iron Heel*, see Stein, "Jack London's *The Iron Heel*," p. 89. On the implication of the Fighting Groups for the conception of the Leninist vanguard party, see Portrelli, "Jack London's Missing Revolution," pp. 185–86.

50. On Charmian Kittredge as the "new woman" and London's ideal mate, see Johnston, *Jack London*, p. 79; and Clarice Stasz, *American*

Dreamers: Charmian and Jack London (New York: St. Martin's Press, 1988). For a discussion of the development of the "new woman" and its impact on social and gender relations in early twentieth-century America, see Peter G. Filene, *Him/Her/Self: Sex Roles in Modern America*, 2d ed. (Baltimore: Johns Hopkins University Press, 1986), pp. 19–34.

51. Hedrick, *Solitary Comrade*, p. 15.

52. Portrelli, "Jack London's Missing Revolution," p.190.

53. Quoted in Watson, *The Novels of Jack London*, p. 105.

54. On the influence of Donnelly's *Caesar's Column*, see ibid., pp. 109–12. On the loss of faith in *The Iron Heel*, see Barltrop, *Jack London*, p. 127.

55. On the vengeful return of the repressed, see Portrelli, "Jack London's Missing Revolution," p.189.

56. On naturalist predispositions and proletarianization, see Howard, *Form and History*, p. 140. London's 1903 journalistic account of the poor of London's ghettos, entitled *The People of the Abyss* (thus the self-referential connection in the novel), contains not only the familiar tropes of naturalism but also features London undertaking a disguise in class transvestism that Avis and the Fighting Organizations take on in different form in *The Iron Heel*.

57. On the dystopian tone of *The Iron Heel*, see Beauchamp, "Jack London's Utopia Dystopia and Dystopia Utopia." On how *The Iron Heel* "reveals the radical disjunction between London's political insight and his emotional limitations," see Hedrick, *Solitary Comrade*, p. 189.

58. On the "transvaluation of values" in other London literary texts, see Johnston, *Jack London*, p. 88.

59. On the politics of transfiguration, the transvaluation of values, and utopia, see Seyla Benhabib, *Critique, Norm, and Utopia: A Study of the Foundations of Critical Theory* (New York: Columbia University Press, 1986), p. 13.

60. Walter B. Rideout, *The Radical Novel in the United States, 1900–1954* (New York: Hill and Wang, 1966), pp. 41–42. For the interconnections between London's contradictions and those of socialism, see Johnston, *Jack London*, pp. 183–84.

61. London, *War of the Classes,* pp. 272–75.

62. For a discussion of the contradictions, tensions, and divisions within the socialist movement during the early twentieth century, see, for example, the essays in *Failure of a Dream: Essays in the History of American Socialism*, rev. ed., ed. John H. M. Laslett and Seymour Martin Lipset (Berkeley: University of California Press, 1984); Robert Hyfler, *Prophets of the Left: American Socialist Thought in the Twentieth Century* (Westport, Conn.: Greenwood Press, 1984); and Milton Cantor, *The Divided Left: American Radicalism, 1900–1975* (New York: Hill and Wang, 1978). For a concise critical analysis of how those contradictions and divisions led to the splintering and eventual failure of American socialism during the first two decades of the twentieth century, see Davis, *Prisoners of the American Dream*, pp. 40–51.

63. London Collection, Box 266 (8), The Huntington Library, San Marino, California.

64. All reviews cited in the text are part of the London Collection, Box 517, The Huntington Library, San Marino, California, 1 February 1908. No page numbers were evident.

65. *Appeal to Reason*, 4 April 1908.

66. Ibid.

67. *Wilshires Magazine*, n.d.

68. *Chicago Socialist*, 23 April 1908.

69. *The Socialist* (Seattle), 25 April 1908.

70. *The Nashville Banner*, 29 February 1908.

71. *San Francisco Chronicle*, March 1908; and *Philadelphia Telegram*, 9 March 1908.

72. *Chicago Dial*, 16 April 1908; and *Johnstown Democrat*, 27 March 1908.

73. Rochester *Post-Express*, 21 March 1908; and *Wall Street Journal*, 19 March 1908.

74. *Tacoma News*, 28 March 1908; and Nashville *American*, 29 February 1908.

75. Slotkin, *Gunfighter Nation*, pp. 157, 164–66.

76. *Manchester Union*, 27 March 1908; and Nashville *American*, 22 March 1908.

77. *Religious Telescope*, April 1908.

78. *The Arena*, April 1908.

79. *Chicago Socialist*, 6 April 1908.

80. *International Socialist Review* 8 (1908): 629.

81. On Spargo's position, see Mark Pittenger, *American Socialists and Evolutionary Thought, 1870–1920* (Madison: University of Wisconsin Press, 1993), esp. pp. 164–65; also see pp. 202–11 for an overview of London's ideological discourse.

82. *The Worker*, 14 March 1908.

83. Eric Homberger, *American Writers and Radical Politics, 1900–1939: Equivocal Commitments* (London: Macmillan, 1986), pp. 1–33. On London's resignation letter, see Jaher, *Doubters and Dissenters*, p. 200. On the marginalized utopia of *The Iron Heel*, see Francis Shor, "*The Iron Heel*'s Marginal(ized) Utopia," *Extrapolation* 35 (Fall 1994): 211–29.

Part II

Utopianism and Radicalism in Political and Communal Projects

5

Journeying to Socialism: Utopian Communal Experiments in the 1890s

The emergence of American socialism as a self-conscious political formation grew out of the ferment in the late nineteenth century. Economic turbulence, social dislocation, and cultural conflict resulted in movements that sought to restore harmony in the social order and to renew the American dream for those marginalized by the transformation of American society. As Alan Trachtenberg has pointed out in *The Incorporation of America*, the very effort to define the meaning of America was fundamental to the social and political struggles in the late nineteenth century. Moreover, that definition included attempts to salvage America as a utopian experiment that guaranteed the continuing allegiance to life, liberty, and the pursuit of happiness.[1] Out of this context emerged an American version of socialism in the 1890s that embodied the contradictory tendencies of past promises and present realities.

Although socialism in the 1890s grew as a consequence of the economic, social, and political crises of the decade, the formation of a coherent socialist movement floundered because of the contradictory goals pursued by those who began to identify themselves as socialists. Nowhere was this contradiction as evident as in the proposals for and development of communal experiments. Whether these experiments were seen as central or peripheral to building socialism in America was at the core of the debates among socialists during the 1890s. In particular, two proposals for communal experiments, the Ruskin Colony in Tennessee and the Brotherhood of Cooperative Commonwealth's Equality Colony in the state of Washington, were the most prominent expressions of utopian socialist strategy. While these experiments were touted as practical solutions to the social and economic dislocations in the 1890s, they also reflected deep-rooted utopian impulses for cultural redemption through "journeying," a process whereby a "migration in both a physical and psychological sense could create community."[2] In exploring the journeying to socialism embodied in the construction of utopian communal experiments at Ruskin in Tennessee and Equality in Washington, this chapter will also consider the difficulties and contradictions in constructing socialist politics and culture in the 1890s and into the twentieth century.

Within this framework of the construction of socialist politics and culture, the utopian Ruskin Colony of Tennessee endeavored to enact a small scale socialist version of the cooperative commonwealth. From 1894 to 1899 a diverse group of native-born Americans sought refuge in an environment where they could "establish a new social pattern based on a vision of the ideal society."[3] Their efforts to construct a utopian colony, motivated by their understanding of socialism, reflected not only their desire to reject the competition and conflict of the late nineteenth century but also to blaze a trail as "cooperative colonizers." As cooperative colonizers, they "believed that secular salvation could be attained by establishing groups of people in new settlements and that, by collectively assuming responsibility for the financial future of their communities, the colonists would improve both their moral and economic conditions."[4] However, in seeking to improve their moral and economic conditions, the Ruskin colonists were constrained by the very contradictions that marked the development of American socialism. Their internal squabbles, in fact, mirrored the larger picture of the emergent socialist movement in the 1890s.

First and foremost among the contradictions in the formation of socialism in the 1890s was the resonance of utopian aspirations against the need to achieve pragmatic goals. The social dislocation caused by the economic crisis of the period gave rise to millenarian rhetoric and movements. From the proliferation of utopian literature to the frequency of populist/socialist sentiments, the discourse of apocalyptic change and redemption fueled desires to make a heaven on earth.[5] Certainly, such religiously invested utopianism can be traced to the early European settlers of America and can be seen as a constant in American reform.[6] On the other hand, while utopianism, as a cultural imperative, played a role in shaping

ideology in America, utopian aspirations and expectations influ-
enced the trajectory that American socialism would take in the
1890s.

Among the most important and influential utopian visionaries of
modern American socialism was Edward Bellamy. Bellamy's utopian novel *Looking Backward* fired the imagination of millions of
Americans seeking secular salvation. That salvation, however, was
more of a spiritual and utopian quest than the enactment of a
practical political program. As one recent study of Bellamy has
concluded: "His discussion [of socialism] thus had less to do with
programs and platforms than moral attitudes and the informed
conscience."[7] Bellamy's literary effort to salvage the conscience of
America in the face of the dilemmas of class conflict, the individual
and the state, urban and technological growth, and changes in
moral and sexual codes represented not only a moment in the life
of a novelist and his story line but also the convergence of contradictions of emergent socialism with the social conditions of late
nineteenth century America.

The middle class utopianism and socialism espoused by Bellamy
and his followers looked to the state as an active instrument in the
balancing of class forces and the facilitating of progress and prosperity. As Robert Hyfler contends: "While the dominant strains of
middle-class socialism viewed the state as either inherently progressive or easily adaptable to their ends, the working-class activist,
from Gompers to Haywood to Debs, looked upon the state with
ambivalence, suspicion and disdain."[8] Investing their faith in the
state actually led certain middle class reformers and socialists, like
Bellamy, to resist calls for self-activity on the part of the working
class and to reject attempts at founding utopian colonies, even
those, such as Ruskin, motivated by *Looking Backward*. "We do not
believe in the colony ideas as a help to the solution," wrote Bellamy,
"any more than we believe in the monastic ideas as an assistance
to the moral solution."[9] On the other hand, Eugene Debs, viewing
the devastating effects of the depression of 1893 and the blacklisting
of union men, threw in his lot with the utopian colonization plans
spawned by the short-lived socialist-sponsored Brotherhood of the
Cooperative Commonwealth. Such a socialist cooperative could help
workers to attain, in Debs's own words, "their own salvation, their
redemption and independence, . . . break every fetter, rise superior
to present environments, and produce a change such as shall
challenge the admiration of the world."[10]

While Bellamy and Debs, as representatives of middle class and
working class versions of American socialism, respectively, differed
about the role of the state and colonization schemes in the 1890s,

they nevertheless shared a common utopian desire to reconstitute the republican virtues of the past through a projection of their own idealization of small-town America. At a time of increasing urbanization and corruption in big-city life—uncovered by the muckraking journalists and social critics such as Henry George and Henry Demarest Lloyd—the belief in a restored republicanism animated both the middle class and working class constituents of the emerging socialist movement.[11] An attempt at the reconciliation of the republican and Christian ethic in modern life found its way into the vision of technological abundance in *Looking Backward*.[12] However, the contradictions inherent in such visions to protect traditional moral moorings against the tide of technological and social transformations often foundered on the utopian shores of emergent socialism. Believing in progress while preserving their visions of the past, newly converted socialists sought a variety of instruments to chart their course.

One of the most fascinating individuals among those newly converted to American socialism was the founder of the Ruskin Colony, Julius A. Wayland. Born to a poor Indiana family in 1854, Wayland made his way to socialism through a career as a Midwestern printer and Republican and Colorado real estate entrepreneur and Populist. It was in Colorado that Wayland saw the light of socialism with the help of populist agitation, socialist literature, and the depression of 1893. Anticipating that depression, Wayland sold his holdings and returned to Indiana to renew his role as owner-editor of a crusading newspaper. That weekly newspaper, the *Coming Nation*, became the vehicle for disseminating Wayland's curious mix of down-home socialism and encouraging the founding of the Ruskin Colony. Although Wayland left the colony one year after its inception in 1894, eventually selling the *Coming Nation* to a group of Ruskinites, his next newspaper, *Appeal to Reason*, became in a few short years the most successful and widely read socialist newspaper in America. His success with the paper and his widely acclaimed influence in socialist politics did not prevent Wayland from falling into despair after the death of his wife and the defeat of Debs in the 1912 presidential election. Wayland took his own life, leaving behind a note that ironically read: "The struggle against the capitalist system isn't worth it. Let it pass."[13]

Nevertheless, Wayland's participation in the struggle for a socialist America drew upon his ability as an archetypical propagandist of an indigenous radicalism whose eclecticism was both inspiring and insipid. Described as "a reincarnate Tom Paine" and called by a contemporary "the greatest propagandist of Socialism that has ever lived," Wayland saw himself in a folksy and self-deprecating manner as "The One Hoss Editor."[14] As editor of the *Coming Nation* and *Appeal to Reason*, Wayland offered a blend of socialism gleaned from the anti-modernist writings of English art and social critic John Ruskin and the utopian visions of Edward Bellamy. Above the masthead of the *Coming Nation*, Wayland placed the assertion that the paper favored a "government of, by, and for the people, as outlined in Bellamy's *Looking Backward*, abolishing the possibility of poverty."[15] Throughout the pages of the *Coming Nation*, Wayland scattered his own aphorisms about socialism as well as the indict-ments of the modern industrial world found in the work of Ruskin. Yet Wayland did not eschew modern sales techniques in pitching his platitudes and his socialist newspapers. Wayland's efforts to promote his papers led to amazingly successful campaigns that were carried out with evangelical and entrepreneurial fervor. While it may be true that Wayland "evangelized Socialism for his readership," he also offered his readers the opportunity to find secular salvation in their own little economic triumphs through sales of subscriptions to the newspaper.[16] Combining socialist salesmanship and politics, Wayland spread the gospel of an American socialism.

Wayland's socialism owed more to its utopian and American roots than to the influence of classic socialist thinkers. That utopian vision is contained in Wayland's rambling and optimistic projection of a Bellamy-like future for America: "When the public owned industry closes for the day it will be early in the afternoon. There will be public theaters, concerts, libraries, gymnasiums, lectures. There will be enjoyment, happiness, laughter and they will go to their wholesome, healthy supper in bright homes, a happy people, bright laughing children, and fathers and mothers no longer tor-mented with the fear of a poverty-stricken-future."[17] On the other hand, Wayland was not satisfied with mere utopian speculation about the future. Too much of a practical-minded and en-trepreneurial man, Wayland decided to use subscription sales to the *Coming Nation* as a vehicle to raise the capital for the establishment of a socialist communal experiment. In response to criticism that such a communal venture was too utopian and impractical, Way-land replied: "Do you think that better conditions can ever come about except by practical lessons? . . . One practical success, widely advertised, showing that men can live and love and have peace and plenty, will do more toward bringing the Brotherhood of Man than a thousand speakers."[18]

Wayland's practical socialist utopia was launched through the pages of the *Coming Nation*. In the July 21, 1894, edition Wayland issued his call for charter members to join him in publishing the next *Coming Nation* in Tennessee. After securing land some fifty miles west of Nashville, Wayland and his followers set up the Ruskin Cooperative Association. Immediately, disagreements ensued over how cooperative the Ruskin Colony would be. With Wayland unwilling to surrender control of the *Coming Nation* as his own investment property, the Ruskinites became embroiled in a divisiveness that led Wayland to resign as owner-editor of the *Coming Nation* and to leave the Ruskin Colony a year after its founding. The contradictions of his own role and the internal workings of the Ruskin Colony reflected those contradictions found both in his personality and in the emergent socialist movement.[19] It is to those contradictions that we must now turn.

Although the Ruskin Colony was envisioned as a small-scale utopian venture in the cooperative commonwealth revered by Wayland and American socialists, it quickly developed into something approximating a corporate business with administrative controls rather than egalitarian consensus as its operating procedures. The bylaws, encapsulating utopian aspirations, detailed the functions of the Ruskin Cooperative Association in the following manner: "The object of the Association shall be to own and operate manufactories, to acquire land, to build homes for its members, to insure members against want or the fear of want, to provide educational and recreative facilities of the highest order, and to promote and maintain harmonious social relations on the basis of cooperation."[20] However, since Tennessee laws precluded incorporating a cooperative community, Wayland convinced the other members to incorporate under the legal provisions governing business corporations. Wayland favored what he believed would be a transvalued corporate model that would invest each and every member with control over the business of the colony. Directors and other officers would be elected both at large and through special section representation. As Wayland argued in the *Coming Nation*, the colony would replicate the form of "a railroad or a land, or a mercantile corporation . . . [doing] all things necessary to make a success, financially and socially, of a co-operative colony."[21]

By conforming to capitalist and patriarchal rules, Ruskin was organized as a joint stock company that excluded women from the board of directors although wives of charter members were given equal shares. Wayland was elected the first president of the board of directors and others were elected as superintendents of departments such as education and recreation, agriculture, manufacturing, sanitation and medical care, public works, cuisine, and distribution. Eventually, the board of directors exercised an authority that diminished democratic control while elevating a bureaucratic and corporate ideal of governance. However, numerous colonists noted what appeared to be the irreconcilable differences between corporate and cooperative imperatives at Ruskin.[22]

In spite of the administrative corporate authority, Ruskin was organized at the base along cooperative and utopian socialist lines. Although there was a variety of manufacturing and agricultural occupations, all work was regarded as equal in value. There were no costs for basic necessities such as food, medical care, and housing. Paper certificates were issued in accordance with egalitarian principles for additional purchases from the community commissary. A common dining room was used for all meals and entertainment. The use of a communal dining hall underscored the cooperative commitment at Ruskin and the difficulties of overcoming the traditional gendered division of labor. The women at Ruskin were major boosters of such communal arrangements. Echoing the criticisms of Charlotte Perkins Gilman and other material feminists of the period concerning the drudgery built into the private home and women's work, the women at Ruskin moved to collectivized household tasks like cooking and cleaning. Yet women dominated the domestic duties at Ruskin, reaffirming at some level the separate spheres doctrine that socialist communalism attempted to overcome.[23]

On the other hand, strenuous efforts were made at the insistence of the women of Ruskin to overcome the invidious distinctions between male waged labor and female unwaged labor in order to achieve a form of communal egalitarianism. While rates of compensation took into account differences between married women with and without children, allowing fewer hours per day for full compensation to those women with children, all household jobs were rewarded with either a "maintenance fee" or "labor notes." In his elucidating study of Ruskin, historian W. Fitzhugh Brundage makes clear in his interpretation of this effort that "colonists, in matters of compensation, drew no distinction between an hour of sewing, childcare, or plowing. Although women may have performed the same dreary chores they had previously, to be paid for doing housework was certainly a small revolution that added immeasurably to their sense of self-worth."[24] Nevertheless, such cooperative communal activities and attempts at egalitarian gender relations did not restrain those more ambitious and capitalist-minded souls from setting up their own profit-oriented businesses within the colony (reselling produce purchased outside Ruskin) and dissenting from affixing equal wage scales. Thus, Ruskinites could organize along both cooperative and entrepreneurial lines in pursuing their utopian goals.

The entrepreneurial spirit, pervasive in the Ruskin Colony and the larger society, allowed the colony to prosper and expand even as it bogged down in internal bickering. Beyond the publication and printing business, the colony built several mills and machine shops that canned goods and manufactured such items as suspenders and sash and door fixtures. Instead of turning their backs on machine civilization, as the writings of their namesake suggested, the Ruskinites asserted that "[m]an must be made master of the machine," and "machines should be employed to relieve human brain, nerve, and muscle."[25] Holding more to Bellamy's vision of the machine-dominated future, Wayland envisioned farmers eventually being transported from "their fields of labor on rapid transits" that would return them to their cooperative villages after a brief period of work in the fields.[26] This utopian and Jeffersonian vision of a progressive small-town environment coincided with the labor-saving advantages of the machine age. For Wayland and the middle class former city dwellers who populated the growing Ruskin colony (it stood at one hundred residents in the fall of 1894), such contradictions of a Jeffersonian republic and Bellamy cooperative commonwealth could coexist in their nondoctrinaire socialism. What could not be contained, however, was the entrepreneurial spirit that guided Wayland and others and the class divisions that followed from that spirit and its articulation through the governance of the Ruskin Colony.

After Wayland left the colony, control remained with a middle class leadership still interested in pursuing hard work and genteel cooperative relationships. However, newcomers, imbued with more radical visions borne from their working class experiences as displaced farm and factory laborers, created dissension that went beyond criticizing the leadership for its corporate control and antidemocratic attitudes. At issue was the matter of how expansive the utopian socialist agenda should be. At the center of the dispute was a challenge to the traditional moral and sexual customs upheld by the middle class leadership and most of the Ruskinites. While revealing his own middle class biases in his account of the debate and divisions over manners and morals, especially those relating to sexuality, Isaac Broome, erstwhile Ruskin educator, ridiculed the newcomers and "anarchists" as motivated by "besotted sensualism." Issues around "free love," nude bathing, open marriages, contraception, and the open publication and expression of the aforementioned animated Broome's animus and provide an insight into the internal arguments that divided the Ruskin Colony in the last years of its existence (1897–1899).[27] While self-proclaimed anarchists were only a small minority of the approximately 250 residents in the expanded and relocated Ruskin Colony, the militant declamations by the anarchist wing and the intolerance for such radical rhetoric and "deviant" behavior resulted in further polarization and the adoption of a requirement for passing a test about socialism as an entrance exam to the Ruskin Colony.[28] Disagreements over adhering to the socialist principles of Ruskin thus became debates over the nature of the inclusiveness and exclusiveness of the meaning of socialism and its impact on moral, social, and cultural norms.

Nevertheless, political and cultural movements of the late nineteenth and early twentieth centuries that confronted dominant norms often ran counter to the "search for order" that characterized the age.[29] The desire for order even informed the work of middle class reformers and radicals like those socialists at Ruskin who sought some measure of control over the political, social, and economic forces that threatened their identity and ideology. Radical politics in late nineteenth- and early twentieth-century America could not escape projecting a moral vision of a harmonious society. Thus, radical politics and utopian visions in late nineteenth- and early twentieth-century America were infused with moral dimensions containing contradictory tendencies. These tendencies were at times in agreement with and at variance to the dominant norms of the age even when erecting a banner of oppositional politics and alternative social and cultural movements.[30]

In shaping educational and cultural practices at Ruskin, members of this communal experiment sought to create alternatives to what they considered the debased and competitive ventures in the dominant society. Especially in the realm of education, new pedagogical methods such as those of Friedriech Froebel were employed. Although its leaders had hoped to construct a counter cultural educational practice, schooling at Ruskin eventually succumbed to more conventional methods.[31] "In their attempts to create a new socialist culture," contends the most astute historian of the Ruskin Colony, "Ruskinites never overcame their indebtedness to inherited cultural and moral values. The colony's culture evidenced many of the contradictions so marked in its history. People who performed stereotypical racist blackface comedies for their weekly entertainment also listened to Mary 'Mother' Jones and other reformers denounce industrial capitalism and the incipient imperialism it spawned."[32]

While struggling with residual cultural and moral values, Ruskinites tried to fashion a commitment to their own understanding of socialism. The debates and dissension within the Ruskin Colony over their journey to socialism were an inevitable consequence of the contradictory tendencies and shifting social and political allegiances during the period. Moreover, frenetic experiences and changing allegiances marked both the inhabitants of the

1890s in America and the heterogeneous population at Ruskin. The high turnover of Ruskinites (nearly 20 percent annually) represented not only the instability within Ruskin but also the fluidity in the decade.[33] As a socialist utopian experiment in the 1890s, Ruskin failed to develop the kind of commitment mechanisms critical to the survival of any intentional community. The problem of retention and group cohesiveness was directly related to the lack of instrumental and affective commitment mechanisms built into the daily activities at Ruskin. Although the adoption of a socialist entrance examination was an effort to establish ideological control over newcomers, there were no consistent efforts to establish definitive practices that could bind together the socially diverse colonists. Without the binding power of traditional religious beliefs, charismatic leadership, or the inculcation of distinctive social or cultural instructions, the Ruskin Colony could not sustain its utopian experiment beyond temporary relief and retreat from the social and economic dislocations of the decade.[34]

While Ruskin began as a socialist utopian experiment, it never succeeded in establishing itself as the self-contained and socially significant example envisioned by its founder, Julius Wayland, and its most active members. In fact, on one level Ruskin became quickly integrated into the rural Tennessee environment. Trading and socializing with its neighbors, Ruskin was soon tagged by the *Nashville Banner* as "a commendable and harmless enterprise."[35] Ruskin's connections to its cultural environment, expressed most poignantly in its annual public July 4th celebration, led one local newspaper to claim that the Ruskin colonists were "not anarchists and revolutionaries, but good, lawabiding citizens who any county would be glad to claim."[36] While such neighborly relations diminished local hostility to the socialist colony and exemplified the values of virtuous republicanism that motivated socialists and nonsocialists alike during this period, those same relations and values reflected what Rosabeth Moss Kanter has labelled as "isomorphism"—"the structural similarity between the community and its environment." As she points out: "While isomorphism may aid environmental and exchange goals, . . . it may also interfere with the maintenance of communal systems, whose purpose in existing may be their expression of unique and different values."[37]

The contradictory tendencies in the emergence of American socialism and the utopian Ruskin Colony of Tennessee were too overwhelming for building a viable movement or community. Trying to construct organizational and ideological commitments in an age marked by explosive class and cultural issues proved particularly difficult for those seeking a socialist utopia. Struggling with the strategic dilemmas that plagued the larger socialist movement, the efforts by the Ruskin colonists to reconcile utopian and pragmatic, modernist and anti-modernist, democratic and authoritarian, traditional and nontraditional, and middle class and working class sentiments and sensibilities were sometimes valiant, but ultimately divisive and self-defeating. In his concluding assessment of the Ruskin communal experiment, Fitzhugh Brundage contends: "Their commitment to an inclusive radical synthesis sharply circumscribed their understanding of how much, how quickly, and by what means American society could be changed. Absorbed in the reform debates of the day and hostile to the most radical critiques of their society, the Ruskinites were too much a part of the world they wanted to change."[38]

At the same time that Ruskin was struggling to survive, another utopian effort of journeying to socialism was taking shape in the swirl of radical and reform politics in Maine. Disenchanted with the flaws of populism, Norman W. Lermond developed an organization in 1895 that set the stage for the emergence of the Brotherhood of the Cooperative Commonwealth (BCC) in 1896. As prominently reported in the pages of the *Coming Nation*, the BCC intended "to educate the people in the principles of Socialism, to unite all Socialists in one fraternal organization," and "to establish cooperative colonies and industries, and so far as possible, concentrate these colonies and industries in one State until said state is socialized."[39] Lermond begin to propagandize his colonization ideas to the leading reformers and radicals of the age. In a letter to the muckraking journalist and populist booster Henry Demarest Lloyd, Lermond wrote: "The people must be aroused from their present lethargy, indifference, and dispondency [sic]. The country must be stirred from centre to circumference. And the quickest and best way to do this is by colonizing a state such as Kansas was colonized prior to the Civil War. The example thus set would be contagious and neighboring states would not be slow to follow in the same road."[40]

Not content to enlist the support of individual reformers of repute, Lermond sought to capture organized political forces. When his call to meet at the Populist Party Convention in St. Louis in 1896 failed to elicit any significant response, Lermond and his fledgling BCC turned to Eugene V. Debs and the American Railway Union. Involved with establishment of a new political organization, the Social Democracy of America, Debs endorsed the colonization scheme of the BCC as much out of a practical concern with relief efforts for displaced railroad workers as out of a utopian commitment to the Cooperative Commonwealth. Nonetheless, while attracting support of socialist leaders like Debs, the colonization plans of the BCC were to create constant divisions and factional fighting in the fledgling socialist parties that emerged in this period, from the Social Democracy of America to the Social Democratic Party.[41]

Against this background of factional infighting, Lermond and his associates, especially fellow Mainer Ed Pelton, went about looking for a propitious site to begin their colonizing. After meeting with socialists in Seattle and Tacoma, Pelton decided that a spot in Washington's Puget Sound area would be particularly hospitable to a socialist communal venture. Purchasing land in Skagit county with money from the BCC treasury, Pelton set in motion the founding of the Equality Colony in 1897. On November 1, 1897, fifteen colonists took over a pre-existing home as temporary headquarters for the colony they named after the new Edward Bellamy novel. The first new building, constructed entirely of logs harvested from the surroundings, was named Fort Bellamy. Thus, grounded in the frontier surroundings of the northwest and imbued with the utopian socialist visions of Lermond and Bellamy, Equality began to confront those very contradictions that were beginning to tear apart the Ruskin Colony in Tennessee.[42]

At the heart of Lermond's vision for the BCC and the spiritual impetus for Equaltiy, one he shared with Bellamy, Wayland, and other radical intellectuals of the period, was a form of evangelical socialism. At the conclusion of one of his first declarations about the BCC, Lermond penned the following poem filled with the resonances of Protestant millenialism (and gender-privileged universalism):

> How bright, how sweet, this world would be
> If men could live for others.
> How sweet, how bright, how full of light,
> This life, if justice, truth and right
> Were once enthroned; if men were free;
> If men would all be brothers!
>
> And is this nothing but a dream?
> Must wrong go on forever?
> Must poverty forever be?
> And selfish greed and tyranny?
> Must hate and strife be still supreme,
> And love and peace come never?
>
> No, I will not believe it. No.
> God still reigns somewhere, brother;
> Somewhere, sometime the race will climb
> Above its selfishness and crime:
> Will gentler, nobler, happier grow
> And men will love each other.

The morn is rising soft and bright,
The way grows light before us.
Cheer, brothers, cheer! through doubts, through fear,
The world grows brighter year by year;
And fast and bright a day of light
Will spread its white wings o'er us.[43]

Reiterating these sentiments, another organizer of the BCC, Reverend George Candee, articulated the sensibility that socialism should "dethrone mammon and enthrone man."[44]

Beyond the sentiments of evangelical socialism, there was considerable practical work to undertake at the Equality Colony. Infused with a pioneer spirit, one colonist at Equality wrote in 1898: "The TALKING stage of Socialism has passed, . . . but now ACTION is the live word."[45] Settlers began to arrive from around the country, especially after Lermond moved the BCC headquarters to Edison, Washington, a short two miles southwest of Equality. Membership in the BCC, surpassing three thousand in 1898, helped to spread the word about Equality. Aiding in disseminating the gospel of communitarian socialism at Equality was the establishment of the BCC weekly newspaper *Industrial Freedom*. However, the relationship between the relocated BCC and Equality soon soured as a consequence over debates about funding for and the role of Equality. With the demands for increased autonomy by Equality colonists and the sudden departure of Lermond in August of 1898, the headquarters at Edison essentially dissolved. By February 1899 the BCC had been absorbed into the Equality Colony. Without an independent BCC headed by Lermond, the determination to spread the colonization within the state of Washington died and the focus of building communitarian socialism in one colony, Equality, commenced.[46]

Industrial Freedom remained the primary propaganda organ for Equality and also its leading vehicle for recruitment. (It ceased publication in 1902.) Periodic calls for a variety of workers telegraphed the practical needs of the colony and its internal problems. One such notice read: "Wanted! Men and women who are willing to work, and are not jealous for fear they will do more than their associates; who are willing to go ahead and set a good example, instead of waiting for the other fellow to do it; who believe thoroughly in co-operation whether they are working inside or outside the Colony."[47] Such a notice revealed one of the real stresses within Equality and one that plagued other communal experiments, that of voluntary or directed labor. This issue was debated during the first summer and then over the course of Equality's demise and transformation in 1905 into an anarchist colony, renamed Freeland by the anarchist colonist Alexander Horr. In fact, according to historian Charles LeWarne, the stress over voluntary versus regimented labor was at the core of the ultimate failure of Equality.[48]

On the other hand, LeWarne and other historians of the Equality Colony have acknowledged the extensive development of its communitarian social practices. Similar to Ruskin, Equality emphasized education and recreation as critical elements in cultural improvement and renewal. With dynamic leadership by Kate Halladay and Harry Ault, still in their teens, the children at Equality were inducted into a form of socialist schooling. Nonetheless, the socialist component of that schooling often, as in the case with Ruskin, floundered. What was most cultivated at Equality, as well as at Ruskin, was the sense of self-improvement and cultural renewal. Seemingly isolated at the margins of society, Equality and Ruskin were atypical rural communities because of their heroic efforts at communal existence.[49] On the other hand, in the case of Equality, what had started out as the premier socialist experiment in colonizing a whole state had shrunk to a minor and marginalized community by the time of the official founding of the Socialist Party in 1901.

The journey to American socialism in the 1890s embodied in the efforts at Ruskin and Equality to create community in both a physical and psychological sense was weighted down by all of the social and cultural baggage that nineteenth-century America bequeathed to its reformers and radicals. Striving to resolve difficult questions concerning class and gender divisions, and with that peculiarly American blind spot about race, Ruskin and Equality did, at least, demonstrate the fervor of the utopian longing for communal redemption. As historian Paul Buhle has noted in his description of the legacy of nineteenth-century American socialism: "[I]n seeking to cut through the webs of non-class reform and radicalism, the Socialists created impossible expectations for their own small movement. Their political descendants would have to begin again after 1900, in the construction of a Socialist movement and the recuperation of a legacy larger than themselves."[50]

NOTES

1. Alan Trachtenberg, *The Incorporation of America: Culture and Society in the Gilded Age* (New York: Hill and Wang, 1982), esp. pp. 33–34, 180–81.

2. Robert S. Fogarty, *All Things New: American Communes and Utopian Movements, 1860–1914* (Chicago: University of Chicago Press, 1990), p. 19. For the most complete discussion of Ruskin, see W. Fitzhugh Brundage, *A Socialist Utopia in the New South: The Ruskin Colonies in Tennessee and Georgia, 1894–1901* (Urbana: University of Illinois Press, 1996). The most detailed presentation of the Equality Colony can be found

in Charles Pierce LeWarne, *Utopians on Puget Sound, 1885–1915* (Seattle: University of Washington Press, 1975), pp. 55–113. For a concise overview of Ruskin and Equality, see Yaacov Oved, *Two Hundred Years of American Communes* (New Brunswick, N.J.: Transaction Books, 1988), pp. 247–56, 262–67.

3. This is Robert V. Hine's definition of a "utopian colony." See Hine, *California's Utopian Colonies* (San Marino, Calif.: Huntington Library, 1953), p. 5.

4. Fogarty, *All Things New*, p. 16.

5. For an analysis of the connection of economic crises to millenarian and utopian movements and literature, see Michael Barkun, "Communal Societies and Cyclical Phenomena," *Communal Societies* 4 (1984): pp. 35–48; and Edgar Kiser and Kriss A.Drass, "Changes in the Core of the World System and Production of Utopian Literature in Great Britain and the United States, 1883–1975," *American Sociological Review* 52 (April 1987): 286–93. On the proliferation of utopian literature and its relationship to the social conditions of the late nineteenth century, see Jean Pfaelzer, *The Utopian Novel in America, 1886–1896: The Politics of Form* (Pittsburgh: University of Pittsburgh Press, 1984); Kenneth M. Roemer, *The Obsolete Necessity: America in Utopian Writings, 1888–1900* (Kent, Ohio: Kent State University Press, 1976); and Charles J. Rooney, Jr., *Dreams and Visions: A Study of American Utopias, 1865–1917* (Westport, Conn.: Greenwood Press, 1985). On the continuity of populist and socialist ideology and its relationship to the millenarian and utopian expressions of the period, see James R. Green, *Grass-Roots Socialism: Radical Movements in the Southwest, 1895–1943* (Baton Rouge: Louisiana State University Press, 1978), pp. 12–52, 163–75.

6. For a discussion of the links between utopianism and reform in America, see *American Utopianism*, ed. Robert S. Fogarty (Itasca, Ill.: F. E. Peacock, 1972); and Robert H. Walker, *Reform in America: The Continuing Frontier* (Lexington: University Press of Kentucky, 1985). For overviews of the persistence and pervasiveness of utopianism in America, see Vernon Louis Parrington, Jr., *American Dreams: A Study of American Utopias* (Providence: Brown University Press, 1947); *America as Utopia*, ed. Kenneth M. Roemer (New York: Burt Franklin, 1981); and Edward K. Spann, *Brotherly Tomorrows: Movements for a Cooperative Society in America, 1820–1920* (New York: Columbia University Press, 1989).

7. John L. Thomas, *Alternative America: Henry George, Edward Bellamy, Henry Demarest Lloyd and the Adversary Tradition* (Cambridge, Mass.: Belknap Press of Harvard University Press, 1983), p. 56. Contrasting views of the influence of Bellamy and *Looking Backward* can be found in Arthur Lipow, *Authoritarian Socialism in America: Edward Bellamy and the Nationalist Movement* (Berkeley: University of California Press, 1982); and Daphine Patai, ed., *Looking Backward, 1988–1888: Essays on Edward Bellamy* (Amherst: University of Massachusetts Press, 1988).

8. Robert Hyfler, *Prophets of the Left: American Socialist Thought in the Twentieth Century* (Westport, Conn.: Greenwood Press, 1984), p. 6.

9. Quoted in Krishan Kumar, *Utopia and Anti-Utopia in Modern Times* (New York: Basil Blackwell, 1987), p. 137.

10. Quoted in Nick Salvatore, *Eugene V. Debs: Citizen and Socialist* (Urbana: University of Illinois Press, 1982), pp. 162–63.

11. Thomas, *Alternative America*, pp. 119–20; and Salvatore, *Eugene V. Debs*, p. 24.

12. Pfaelzer, *The Utopian Novel in America*, p. 32; and Thomas, *Alternative America*, pp. 242–43.

13. Quoted in John Egerton, *Visions of Utopia: Nashoba, Rugby, and the "New Communities" in Tennessee's Past* (Knoxville: University of Tennessee Press, 1977), p. 86. For biographical portraits of Wayland, see ibid., pp. 64-86; Brundage, *A Socialist Utopia in the New South*, pp. 20–40; Howard H. Quint, *The Forging of American Socialism: Origins of the Modern Movement* (Columbia: University of South Carolina, 1953), pp. 175-209; and Elliott Shore, *Talkin' Socialism: J. A. Wayland and the Role of the Press in American Radicalism, 1890–1912* (Lawrence: University Press of Kansas, 1988).

14. Cited in Quint, *The Forging of American Socialism, p. 175.*

15. Ibid., p. 183.

16. Paul Buhle, *Marxism in the United States: Remapping the History of the American Left* (London: Verso: 1987), p. 82.

17. J. A. Wayland, *Leaves of Life: A Story of Twenty Years of Socialist Agitation* (Girard, Kan.: Appeal to Reason, 1912), p. 134. Brundage suggests that Wayland's utopian vision, revealed in this and other representations of the idealized community, "most closely resembled an ongoing socialist chautauqua." See Brundage, *A Socialist Utopia in the New South*, p. 33.

18. Quoted in Quint, *The Forging of American Socialism*, p. 190. Wayland combined the tendency of a "cooperative colonizer" with that of the "political pragmatist." For a discussion of these categories in the context of communitarian ventures in the late nineteenth century, see Fogarty, *All Things New*, pp. 16–19.

19. See Brundage, *A Socialist Utopia in the New South*, pp. 20–40. According to Egerton: "Wayland was a man of many contradictions: a believer in colonization schemes, a soft-hearted man with a hot temper, and finally, an eternal optimist who committed suicide" (*Visions of Utopia*, p. 86).

20. Quoted in Eltweed Pomeroy, "A Sketch of the Socialist Colony in Tennessee," *The American Fabian* 3 (April 1897): 1.

21. *Coming Nation*, 3 February 1894, p. 1.

22. A critique of the authoritarian executive board can be found in an exceedingly critical account of life in Ruskin by Isaac Broome, *The Last Days of the Ruskin Cooperative Association* (Chicago: Charles H. Kerr, 1902), pp. 27–29. For a discussion of the contradictions of the corporate structure at Ruskin, see Brundage, *A Socialist Utopia in the New South*, pp. 35–36 and *passim.*

23. On the material feminism of the age, see Dolores Hayden, *The Grand Domestic Revolution* (Cambridge: MIT Press, 1981). For differing

views of the women of Ruskin, see Brundage, *A Socialist Utopia in the New South*, pp. 69–97; and Yvonne Belanger Johnson, "The Ruskin Colony: A Paradox in the Communitarian Movement," Ph. D. diss., University of Oklahoma, 1992, pp. 74–111.

24. Brundage, *A Socialist Utopia in the New South*, p. 85.

25. Quoted in Charles H. Kegal, "Ruskin's St. George in America," *American Quarterly* 9 (Winter 1957): 417.

26. Wayland, *Leaves of Life*, p. 218.

27. Broome, *The Last Days of the Ruskin Cooperative Association*, pp. 98–128. On the impact of this debate around anarchism and "free love," see Brundage, *A Socialist Utopia in the New South*, pp. 138–39.

28. Egerton, *Visions of Utopia*, pp. 76–78.

29. Robert H. Wiebe, *The Search for Order, 1877–1920* (New York: Hill and Wang, 1967).

30. On the moral dimensions of reform and radical movements in the late nineteenth and early twentieth centuries and contradictory concerns over power and control, see Peter Conn, *The Divided Mind: Ideology and Imagination in America, 1898–1917* (Cambridge: Cambridge University Press, 1983); Robert M. Crunden, *Ministers of Reform: The Progressives' Achievement in American Civilization, 1889–1920* (New York: Basic Books, 1982); Aileen Kraditor, *The Radical Persuasion, 1880–1917* (Baton Rouge: Louisiana State University Press, 1981); Christopher Lasch, *The New Radicalism in America, 1889–1965: The Intellectual as Social Type* (New York: Vintage, 1967); and T .J. Jackson Lears, *No Place of Grace: Antimodernism and the Transformation of Americn Culture, 1880–1920* (New York: Pantheon, 1981).

31. On the educational practices at Ruskin, see Brundage, *A Socialist Utopia in the New South*, pp. 117–24.

32. Ibid., pp. 125–26.

33. On the fluidity and freneticism of the decade, see John Higham, "The Reorientation of American Culture in the 1890's," in *The Origins of Modern Consciousness*, ed. John Weiss (Detroit: Wayne State University Press, 1965), pp. 25–48. On the contradictory meanings of socialism at Ruskin, see Brundage, *A Socialist Utopia in the New South*, esp. pp. 98–131, 166–94.

34. On the problem of commitment mechanisms for utopian communities, see Rosabeth Moss Kanter, *Commitment and Community: Communes and Utopias in Sociological Perspective* (Cambridge: Mass. Harvard University Press, 1977), esp. pp. 64–74. For an excellent explication of Kanter, see Barbara Goodwin and Keith Taylor, *The Politics of Utopia: A Study in Theory and Practice* (New York: St. Martin's Press, 1982), pp. 187–96.

35. Quoted in Egerton, *Visions of Utopia*, p. 75.

36. Ibid., p. 78.

37. Kanter, *Commitment and Community*, pp. 153–54.

38. Brundage, *A Socialist Utopia in the New South*, p. 167.

39. *Coming Nation*, 25 April 1896, p. 4.

40. Quoted in LeWarne, *Utopias on Puget Sound*, p. 57. On Lermond's background and role in the development of the BCC, see Brundage, *A*

Socialist Utopia in the New South, pp. 181–82; Fogarty, *All Things New*, pp. 136–38; Quint, *The Forging of American Socialism*, pp. 282–85; and Le-Warne, *Utopias on Puget Sound*, pp. 57–60.

41. LeWarne, *Utopias on Puget Sound*, pp. 60–61. For a discussion of the development of Debs's politics, see Salvatore, *Eugene V. Debs*. On the factionalism within the fledgling socialist parties over colonization schemes, see Ira Kipnis, *The American Socialist Movement, 1897–1912* (New York: Columbia University Press, 1952), pp. 50–61; and Quint, *The Forging of American Socialism*, pp. 280–318.

42. For discussions of the Equality Colony and its utopia socialist dilemmas, see LeWarne, *Utopias on Puget Sound*, pp. 62–113; Oved, *Two Hundred Years of American Communes*, pp. 262–67; and Axel Rolf Schaefer, "The Intellectual Dilemma of Socialist Communitarian Thought: The Communal Settlements of Equality and Burley in Washington," *Communal Societies* 10 (1990): 24–38.

43. Quoted in Fogarty, *All Things New*, p. 138.

44. Quoted in Schaefer, "The Intellectual Dilemma of Socialist Communitarian Thought," p. 33.

45. Quoted in LeWarne, *Utopias on Puget Sound*, p. 65.

46. On the debate between BCC and Equality and the demise of BCC, see LeWarne, *Utopias on Puget Sound*, pp. 65–72; and Oved, *Two Hundred Years of American Communes*, pp. 263–64.

47. Quoted in LeWarne, *Utopias on Puget Sound*, p. 79.

48. Ibid., pp. 79–80, 101–2.

49. On education, self-improvement, and cultural renewal at Ruskin, see Brundage, *A Socialist Utopia in the New South*, esp. p. 116. At Equality, see LeWarne, *Utopias on Puget Sound*, pp. 94–102.

50. Buhle, *Marxism in the United States*, p. 24.

6

Anarchist Utopianism in the Progressive Era

Proponents and interpreters of anarchism have often dismissed utopianism with the same sort of disdain found in mainstream political thought. From charges of impracticality and mental rigidity to resistance to projections into an idealized future, anarchists as wide-ranging as Bakunin, Kropotkin, Thoreau, and Paul Goodman have distanced themselves from the specter of utopianism while incorporating a body of utopian principles into their own perspectives.[1] In order to prove the relevance and creative capacities of anarchist thought, Daniel Guerin, a contemporary interpreter and advocate of anarchism, contends: "Because anarchism is constructive, anarchist theory rejects the charge of utopianism."[2] In spite of the disavowals and defensiveness of such anarchist commentators, anarchism and utopianism share certain common ground in their attempts to transform society and its inhabitants. Trying to define where anarchism and utopianism intersect requires clarifying those theoretical components of each and then reconstituting their isomorphic moments.

While the theory and practice of anarchism have numerous variations, there are several essential points which can be seen to link anarchism to utopianism. As succinctly asserted by George Woodcock: "Historically, anarchism is a doctrine which poses a criticism of existing society, a view of a desirable future, and a means of

passing from one to the other."[3] Although such a definition captures
the critical form of anarchism, it neglects the specific strategic
content which animates anarchist thought and practice. That content is represented by the emphasis on alternatives to those coercive, authoritarian, and centralist structures embedded in both
modern states and social relationships.[4] Thus, anarchist discourse,
with its calls for freedom and self-determination, challenges not only
the political order but the basic fabric of social reality that each
individual confronts.

It is this challenge by anarchism to social reality that also
connects it to utopianism. However, it is this common point that
often leads critics of anarchism and utopianism to derisively dismiss
both systems of thought. Even sympathetic social theorists such as
Karl Mannheim perpetuate a positivist reading of anarchism and
utopianism that maligns and misunderstands their interconnected
discursive dynamics. In particular, Mannheim's insistence that
utopian thinking "hides certain aspects of reality" serves to sever
the dialectical tensions that are part of the utopian and anarchist
challenge to social reality.[5] As one critic of Mannheim's method
points out: "With his scientific attitude Mannheim does not see that
two kinds of rationality and reality must be distinguished but not
separated, viz., on the one hand scientific rationality and empirical
reality in the narrow sense, and on the other hermeneutic reality
and the reality of life in the broad sense. This 'enlarged reason' or
'context-dependent rationality' as the recognition and understanding of certain collective values precisely offers the interpretive
framework within which alone facts can appear and receive their
character of reality."[6] Instead of situating utopianism outside of
reality, an interpretive framework is needed which distinguishes
how the context influences conflicting norms and values that constitute a political and cultural field where contending thought
systems, such as utopianism and anarchism, compete.

Crucial to identifying the context within which utopianism and
anarchism operate is the concept of hegemony. Most helpful to the
interpretive framework for this chapter is the reformulation of
Gramsci's work on hegemony by the British literary and social
historian Raymond Williams. According to Williams: "[Hegemony] is
a whole body of practices and expectations, over the whole of living:
our senses and assignments of energy, our shaping perceptions of
ourselves and our world. It is a lived system of meanings and
values—constitutive and constituting—which as they are experienced as practices appear as reciprocally confirming. It thus constitutes a sense of reality for most people in the society. . . . It is,
that is to say, in the strongest sense a 'culture,' but a culture which

has also to be seen as the lived dominance and subordination of particular classes."7 As Williams goes on to suggest, while hegemony may establish a dominant discursive context, it is never "total" or "exclusive." "At any time," Williams contends, "forms of alternative or directly oppositional politics and culture exist as significant elements in the society."8 This distinction between alternative and oppositional forms further highlights the dialectics of utopianism and anarchism in a specific historical context since the oppositional form necessitates transforming society in light of living out a different reality. Moreover, from Williams's perspective specific political formations develop within a hegemonic context and constantly test the boundaries of that context.9 Since these political formations have ideological and utopian components in a constitutive and constituting sense, hegemony is in a continual process of reformulation and reformation.

By posing this dynamic of hegemony against the static classifications of the "utopian mentality" discussed by Mannheim, one can begin to discern the clear connections between anarchism and utopianism and other discursive systems and political formations. While one can affirm the validity of Mannheim's categories of socialism, anarchism, liberalism, and conservatism as basic modern political formations which contain their own distinctive utopian tendencies, one must also insist that such categories are only static when viewed through the theoretical approaches of positivism. In reality, the hegemonic context out of which these political formations operate is contested terrain where strategic conflicts over specific norms and values constantly charge and change that context.10 Thus, anarchist utopianism, as a political and cultural formation, opposes the coercive, authoritarian, and centralist tendencies within a given society in order to transform that society along the lines of a non-coercive, non-authoritarian and decentralist social reality.

Before situating anarchist utopianism in the specific context of America, it is necessary to identify two separate but overlapping dimensions that will provide an additional frame of reference for more clearly defining the isomorphic qualities of anarchism and utopianism and for measuring the meaning of anarchist utopianism in the Progressive Era. The first dimension is a social-psychological one. It is within this dimension that matters of will, passion, and sentiment obtain. Daniel Guerin's contention that anarchism is a "visceral revolt" echoes throughout anarchist thought and practice.11 In particular, it animates the theory and practice of one of the focal points of this study: Emma Goldman. The emphasis on will and passion is also central to the history of utopian thinking.12

When Harry Kelly, writing in the anarchist journal *Mother Earth*, described anarchism as "in its essence an ethical idea," he joined a host of anarchists, including his comrade and editor of *Mother Earth*, Emma Goldman, who raised the question of what constitutes a moral society.[13] The assertion of this ethical dimension continues to run through contemporary interpretations of anarchism with discussions of an anarchist "moral urge" and "ethical capital."[14] While the moral component of utopianism may raise transhistorical demands, the philosophical perspectives of Martin Buber and Paul Tillich suggest the convergence of history and morality in utopian thinking.[15] Thus, this chapter will consider how the ethical and social-psychological dimensions informed the specific historical thought and practice of anarchist utopianism in the Progressive Era.

In summation, the crystallization of anarchist utopianism contains a theoretical and/or action critique of the dominant norms and values, reflecting an ideal of and commitment to transfigurative practices of non-coercion, non-authoritarianism, and decentralism.[16] Thus, anarchist utopianism can be seen as contesting the dominant political culture through a counter hegemonic movement or counterculture that stresses liberty, self-determination, and self-expression. As one study of utopianism suggests: "To be a counter-culture, a system of beliefs and postulates must engage in a significant polemic with the dominant culture, must question it, so to speak, in its own words."[17] Through the words of Emma Goldman and the anarchist founders and members of utopian communal experiments at Home and Stelton, the discursive contexts and hegemonic boundaries of the Progressive Era in America will be examined. Such an examination should reveal the meaning of anarchist utopianism as a countercultural critique of the dominant political culture and a movement for expanding and transforming the boundaries of hegemony in modern America. With this in mind, we must now turn to placing anarchism and utopianism in a cultural and historical context and locating the dimensions of the hegemonic conflict in the Progressive Era.

ANARCHIST UTOPIANISM IN AN AMERICAN CONTEXT

For historian David DeLeon, the continuous radical thread in America is anarchism. DeLeon asserts that "the black flag has been the most appropriate banner of the American insurgent."[18] While ably portraying the terrain of the political culture in America, DeLeon nonetheless elevates a visceral anti-institutionalism, anti-authoritarianism, and fragmented political consciousness to the level of a hegemonic force. By emphasizing exceptionalist features in American society and radical movements, DeLeon's analysis neglects the ideological and structural commonalties inherent in the development of capitalist culture from possessive individualism to the institutional state. The conflating of categories that follows from this obfuscation of the dynamics and contradictions in American political culture prevents DeLeon from separating anarchism as a self-conscious political formation from individualism as a constituent component of the cultural hegemony of capitalism. Although some light is thrown on anarchist attitudes in American political thought, there is little rigorous analysis of the political-cultural trajectory of these attitudes. This chapter will attempt to locate that trajectory more accurately within a specific historical context.

On the other hand, identifying how anarchism operates as a theoretical and action critique of dominant norms and values cannot compartmentalize either anarchist ideas or the anarchist movement. Given the earlier conceptualization of the dialectics of the hegemonic process, anarchism must be seen as part of the dynamic of modern political culture. In fact, as one of the foremost scholars of anarchism has suggested: "American anarchism is essential to an understanding of such subjects as labor and immigration, pacifism and war, birth control and sexual freedom, civil liberties and political repression, prison reform and capital punishment, avant garde culture and art. In a larger sense a study of American anarchism will shed interesting light on the nature of American democracy, American capitalism, and American government."[19] As a touchstone for the strategic value conflicts arising in a particular historical period, the focus on anarchism can help to identify the constituent parts of both modern American political culture and the efforts to construct an oppositional, alternative, or counter culture.[20] Yet the particular conditions out of which anarchist utopianism emerged in the Progressive Era require a clear analysis of not just an amorphous American ideology but also of the concrete struggle of the fashioning of a hegemonic field where discursive practices and political formations, such as anarchist utopianism, have developed.

Two historical studies that deal with political formations and cultural movements within the Progressive Era help to clarify the particular constitution of the hegemonic field in modern America. Aileen Kraditor's *The Radical Persuasion* and Jackson Lears's *No Place of Grace* both recognize that movements for social change during the Progressive Era were charged with cultural, sociopsychological, and moral preoccupations. Moreover, both authors analyze these movements against the backdrop of a hegemonic reordering of American life. However, where Kraditor's conceptualization of hegemony leads to a static and "compartmentalized" reading of the conflictual field, Lears's more dynamic application of hegemony provides a more inclusive sense of the dialectical struggle in modern America.[21] Both studies, nevertheless, expand our understanding of the relationship of hegemony to the public and private sectors and of how political formations and cultural movements contested for legitimacy during the Progressive Era.

Kraditor's analysis of the Progressive Era as a "shake-up" period where fluidity marks the hegemonic field is helpful in understanding why anarchism and utopianism could gain a hearing in the strategic conflict over values. Her insight that political discourse in shake-up periods "tends to be more moralistic than usual," with more appeals to "transcendent principles," elucidates why these dimensions invest anarchism and utopianism with a particular historical currency.[22] Moreover, her comprehension of the role of privatization and segmentation in modern American culture helps to explain the waning of oppositional political formations and cultural movements. However, her inability to distinguish between the hegemonic absorption of oppositional and alternative political formations and cultures, her consistent undervaluing of the intrusive and repressive role of the state in the public and private sectors, and her overvaluation of the democratic constancy of corporate liberalism militate against her interpretation of the general irrelevance and marginality of radical political formations in the Progressive Era.[23]

On the other hand, Lears situates the anti-modernist and utopian thrust of much of the radical critique within a shifting hegemonic order in a way that apprehends both the flourishing and withering away of alternative and oppositional political formations and cultural movements during the Progressive Era. As he points out in his preface: "Writing this book helped me to understand (at least partially) why so much twentieth century American dissent has been so easily re-assimilated to the mainstream. Preoccupied with authentic experience as a means of revitalizing a fragmented personal identity, dissenters have often been unable to sustain larger loyalties outside the self. Their criticism has frequently dissolved into therapeutic quests for self-realization, easily accommodated to the dominant culture of our bureaucratic corporate state."[24] His ability to demonstrate how the Progressive ethos transmuted calls for social change and social justice into seeking authentic personal fulfillment aids in the location of how radical political ideals contained within anarchist utopianism were absorbed into the larger hegemonic ordering of society.[25]

However, that absorption should not be seen as the total obliteration or failure to sustain the vision and longings contained in radical and dissenting political formations and cultural movements. As we will see with anarchist utopianism in the thinking and social praxis of Emma Goldman and the communal experiences in Home and Stelton, the construction of oppositional political formations and cultural movements during the Progressive Era interacted with the hegemonic process in ways that led to increasing personal self-expression and liberties at the expense of the actual institutionalization of the specific formations and movements. Thus, analyzing the theory and practice of anarchist utopianism in the Progressive Era becomes a means by which we recognize the political and cultural traces of those formations and movements in a reconstituted American hegemonic context.

ANARCHIST UTOPIANISM IN THE POLITICAL DISCOURSE OF EMMA GOLDMAN

For Emma Goldman, one of the foremost and best-known advocates of anarchism in America, anarchism was rooted in passion and "sentiment." Even though she did more to promote anarchism through her speeches and writings than any other single radical during the Progressive Era, perhaps reaching more Americans than any other radical of her day, she recognized that the animating force behind her own anarchist conversion and convictions lay beyond grasping "our ideas," but in feeling those convictions "in every fiber like a flame, a consuming fever, an elemental passion."[26] As she argued in one of her definitive statements on anarchism: "It [anarchism] stands for the spirit of revolt in whatever form, against everything that hinders human growth."[27] Embedded in that "spirit of revolt" was a recognition that the social-psychological and moral dimensions of anarchism were essential to the realization of free and autonomous individuals and the utopian future that such individuals could usher in. Emma Goldman's contributions to the anarchist utopian discourse in the Progressive Era lay in challenging those norms and values that constrained the birth of a new libertarian world. "More than any other idea," she would argue, "[anarchism] is helping to do away with the wrong, and foolish, more than any other idea, it is building and sustaining new life."[28]

The birth of that "new life" was the prime political task that Emma Goldman saw for anarchism and for herself. As midwife to the new individual, Emma Goldman participated in the struggle against the shibboleths and dying traditions of a patriarchal and repressive past and for the new assertiveness and independence of a liberated future. It was the call of anarchy, as articulated by Goldman, that rallied many who sought release from middle class conventions and culture and those psychological traps that were part of a dominant, albeit shifting, order. Thus, Goldman's anarchist message became the catalyst for self-expression and self-determination that marked both the contradictions within and the furthest limits of reform in the Progressive Era.[29] When she talked and wrote about "human nature caged in a narrow space, whipped daily into submission," she not only captured Weber's insight about the "iron cage" of modern bureaucratic life and Freud's sense of civilization's inexorable instinctual repression, but she also awakened those who felt bound to a sterile and psychologically degrading world.[30] For her, anarchism was part of "nature's forces," which "destroys, not healthful tissue, but parasitic growths that feed on life's essence of society. It is merely clearing the soil from weeds and sagebrush that it may bear healthy fruit."[31] This organic metaphor that is repeated throughout her work, anarchist discourse (especially the writings of Kropotkin), and vitalist attitudes in the modern world reflects her anarchist utopian desire to nurture that which will be born anew.[32]

The emphasis on being born anew or reborn represents in Goldman both a commitment to the will-to-power (à la Nietzsche) and a "displaced religious discourse," attributable in no small part to her Jewish roots.[33] On the other hand, the anarchist utopian elements of Goldman's thought contain a voluntaristic ideal grounded in libertarian and romantic traditions that she incorporated into her discourse. Quoting Emerson on the "active soul" she points toward the "reborn social soul."[34] This secular liberation theology, however, is not aimed at reconstituting a new dogma but is advanced to destroy repressive forces—"government and statutory laws"—in order "to rescue the self-respect and independence of the individual from all restraint and invasion by authority."[35] "Anarchism is not," she contends, "a theory of the future to be realized through divine inspiration. It is a living force in the affairs of our life, constantly creating new conditions."[36] The utopian vision embodied in such anarchist utopianism is that of a concrete utopia where the future is a "free human task."[37] As Goldman wrote in validating her own politics against the charge of utopianism: "Every daring attempt to make a great change in existing conditions, every lofty vision of new possibilities for the human race, has been labeled Utopian."[38] With this utopian will to transform the world and her anarchist "moral urge," Emma Goldman took to heart what her comrade Max Baginski argued in *Mother Earth*: "What is most necessary nowadays, when it is so urgent to wake the people from their stupor and to inspire them with confidence in their own strength and initiative, is the example of men and women who with high idealism combined the will to act."[39]

Emma Goldman's will to act was directed not only against those institutions that stifled the free development of the individual, but also for a cultural rebellion that offered freedom from coercion and authority. While she aimed to replace a hegemonic order through a revolution in values, those values were changing in a way that would open up additional personal space for liberty and justice while closing down that public space within which a counterhegemonic political formation attempted to emerge. While Goldman reviled those "stronghold[s] of . . . enslavement"—"Religion, the dominion of the human mind; Property, the dominion of human needs; and Government, the dominion of human conduct"—those strongholds were to be transformed through the combined efforts of elite forces seeking a restored and rationalized order and of insurgent forces (women, labor, immigrants, etc.) seeking a wider enfranchisement and empowerment during the Progressive Era.[40] On the other hand, the anarchist utopian ideal of "a society based on voluntary coop-eration of productive groups, communities, and societies loosely federated together" was a yearning for an idealized past that many anarchists, and some socialists, like William Morris, and the arts and crafts movement touted.[41] Instead of attributing this to an ahistorical nostalgia, however, one can better locate it within the strategic conflict over values where residual longings for communal bonds represented the ongoing struggle over contested political and cultural terrain. Nevertheless, the hyperbolic quality of Goldman's attack on "machine subserviency" and "centralization" as the "death-knell of liberty, . . . health and beauty, of art and science" indicated profound ambivalence about the modern age that infected not only anarchists, but many reformers and radicals in the Pro-gressive Era.[42]

Goldman's greatest contribution to the transformation of values in the modern age was her emphasis on sexual liberation as a form of self-determination and self-expression both in the erotic and aesthetic sense. Her essays and agitation around the right of women to control their own bodies extended from the anarchist commit-ment to "free love" (a much misunderstood concept that had nothing to do with promiscuity) to the feminist commitment to birth con-trol.[43] Her anarchist commitment to direct action on these "women's" issues and her other anarchist ideals brought her into constant confrontation with the repressive apparatus of the state, from the Comstock Commission to various police and vigilante forces. "Direct action against the authority in the shop, direct action against the authority of the law, direct action against the invasive, meddlesome authority of our moral code," she argued, "is the logical, consistent method of anarchism."[44] Direct action in the public sphere through various free speech and other issue campaigns had its analogue in freeing up the private sphere for the extension of liberty. The transfiguring power of free love envisioned by Goldman went beyond the legal and cultural constraints embedded in statutes and customs. For Goldman, sexual liberation meant not only extending freedom to women but also eliminating the repressive bonds that shackled both the body and the mind of the individual.[45] Her efforts in this area of sexual liberation were the opening rounds in the fight of the "party of eros" that was to find its mature theoretical development in the work of later critics of repressive civilization such as Wilhelm Reich, Herbert Marcuse, and Norman O. Brown.[46] While Goldman's own erotic longings were buffeted by her stormy relationship with Ben Reitman, she nonetheless offered a theoretical and action critique of the dominant norms and values in this area that would find its way into a future liberated zone of personal liberty even as that zone would become assimilated into a transformed hegemonic order.[47]

In leading the struggle for sexual liberation in the Progressive Era Emma Goldman became a lightning rod for women and disaffected intellectuals whom Christopher Lasch has called the "new radicals."[48] Many of these middle class rebels were attracted by Goldman's deliberate and self-conscious attack on Victorian standards and morality. Those middle class followers were praised by Goldman as individuals, motivated by "spiritual hunger and unrest," who "live Anarchism" in a manner that would have a "moral influence . . . [of] lasting values."[49] Yet, that "spiritual hunger and unrest" was difficult to sustain as a movement for transformation of hegemonic power in the public sphere. When Emma Goldman rallied women for emancipation around "inner regeneration" and conceptualized wealth in aesthetic terms as things of "utility and beauty . . . that help to create strong, beautiful bodies," the anarchist utopianism articulated in such appeals could easily be relegated to a quest for mere self-expression.[50] Although Goldman's erstwhile anarchist followers would find ways to fit into a reconstituted hegemonic order, she never retreated from her own political engagement with institutionalized power. "In the battle for freedom," she would write referring to Ibsen, "it is the struggle for, not so much the attainment of, liberty, that develops all that is strongest, sturdiest and finest in human character."[51] Certainly, Goldman's struggle for liberty in the Progressive Era expanded the public arena for liberty, albeit one still constrained by the capriciousness of state power and fair-weather radicalism.

ANARCHIST UTOPIANISM IN THE COMMUNAL
EXPERIENCE OF HOME AND STELTON

If political engagement is confrontation with institutionalized power for the purposes of the transformation of that power, then the effort to construct utopian communal experiments is a form of political disengagement. That disengagement, however, is not a retreat from any form of engagement. What it represents is a form of cultural engagement where the withdrawal from the confrontation with institutionalized power is for purposes of the transcendence of power. This distinction between political and cultural engagement is similar to Laurence Veysey's distinction between political and cultural radicalism. The hallmark of political radicalism, Veysey contends, "is that it engages directly in the immediate struggle for power, relegating all other considerations to a distinctly secondary role, or, at its most extreme, insisting they be abandoned entirely. . . . Cultural radicalism, on the other hand, is usually related to a communitarian impulse. . . . The self-directed living of life rather than the contest for power is the primary aim of cultural radicals."[52] In this section we will turn to exploring how the cultural radicalism of the anarchist utopian colonies at Home, Washington, and Stelton, New Jersey, reflected a form of strategic conflict over values enacted through the social-psychological and moral dimensions of a shifting political culture in the Progressive Era.

While it may be true, as Rosabeth Moss Kanter argues, that "utopian communities are society's dreams," they are often unrealized dreams.[53] Partly that unfulfilled quality is based on the utopian expectation that ideals are easily realizable; but, more significantly, the lack of fulfillment can be attributed to an isomorphism that overwhelms the utopian colony with the larger environmental or hegemonic forces.[54] The maintenance of oppositional culture in the form of a utopian colony can quickly fade into an alternative and even complementary environment, as we will see in the situation with Home and Stelton. However, in the beginning both Home and Stelton represented significant anarchist attempts "to establish a new social and cultural living arrangement based upon a vision of the ideal society."[55] How that anarchist utopianism fared at Home and Stelton during the Progressive Era will be the focus of the remainder of this chapter.

The anarchist community at Home, near Tacoma, Washington, was founded in 1896. Coming in the midst of a decade of profound changes, Home seemed to be caught on the end of a dying century and its exhausted culture. A number of colonists at Home were veterans of previous utopian colonies that had been generated by the enthusiasm over Edward Bellamy's novel *Looking Backward*, the short-lived Nationalist movement that grew out of Bellamy's visions, and the efforts of socialists in the late nineteenth century to colonize a state as a means of instituting social democracy in America. The anarchism represented at Home was clearly part of the individualist anarchism that had flourished in the laissez faire ethos of the nineteenth century but was being transformed into the anarcho-communism, anarcho-syndicalism, and bohemian anarchism of the early twentieth century. While Home was on the edge of a frontier settlement at its inception, the urbanization that occurred over the next few decades turned Home into a less remote rural outpost. Although isolated and a haven for nonconformists, Home became a beacon for anarchy, gaining a reputation among anarchists and facing the outrage of the mainstream community at various points of national hysteria over anarchism and radicalism—for example, McKinley's assassination and World War I. By the end of World War I, Home's radical edge had been blunted by internal feuding, a weakening commitment to an oppositional culture, and the increasing ability of the hegemonic order to tolerate certain forms of private cultural deviance.[56]

Nonetheless, during its heyday Home represented a version of anarchist utopianism that combined a spirit of revolt and idealism in a deliberately out-of-the-mainstream approach. One sympathetic contemporary assessment, written in 1903, saw the purpose of Home as a "living example of perfect liberty of thought and action and the coincident existence of happiness and prosperity." Colonists did not believe that the general society was ready to live out its ideals until a "higher development of personal morality and self-control is attained."[57] While the emphasis on morality and self-control was also fundamental to the dominant ideology in the Progressive Era, Home residents attempted to redefine that morality through their commitment to a radical critique of the dominant culture and to an alternative lifestyle. As remembered by Macie Pope, the daughter of founder Oliver A. Verity, "[the colonists] were dreamers who wanted to reform the world. . . . They always seemed to want something beyond or better than the way it was. That's why they named the paper, *Discontent*. They weren't satisfied with the world as it was, and without discontent they said there would be no progress."[58] In one of its earliest definitions of anarchism, *Discontent* maintained that it would "battle for the freedom of the human race from tyranny and superstition of all kinds and sorts . . . [and] for the full freedom of all to enjoy life untrammeled by statutory enactments and deep-rooted prejudices fossilized by time."[59]

While articulating well-worn anarchist critiques of the dominant order, *Discontent* neither spoke as the official organ of the Home colony nor expressed the primary political ideology of all the colonists. As one of the original settlers at Home, George Allen, noted: "We had heard and read many isms and had tried some of them with varying success. We wished to give each ism a chance to prove its usefulness to humanity."[60] When David Dadisman arrived with his father, Martin, at Home in 1899, his father had already tried communal living at the nearby socialist colony of Equality. According to David, his father "was not an anarchist."[61] On the other hand, he and the other colonists did share with Oliver Verity the belief that they had "the personal liberty to follow their own line of action no matter how much it may differ from the custom of the past or present, without censure or ostracism from their neighbor."[62]

In following their personal liberty at Home, colonists advocated "free love," sexual liberation, nudity, communal land-holding, and radical politics which, in turn, challenged the dominant norms and values of their neighbors and the wider society. Because of these challenges, colonists were at times subjected to scorn, slander, suppression, prosecution, and the threat of vigilante action in response to their ideas and activities.[63] In the aftermath of the McKinley assassination, David Dadisman recollected that "the townsfolk of Tacoma threatened to come out here and destroy the place. The only thing that prevented them from doing it was that the captain of the steamer [the one connecting Home to Tacoma] knew what kind of people were living here and dissuaded them from coming here and raising the devil."[64] Another example of political hysteria over what transpired at Home, prior to the McKinley assassination, involved the mailing out of feminist and free love articles authored by Home colonist Lois Waisbrooker (who had moved from California to Home in 1901) and inflammatory issues of *Discontent*. After shutting down Home's local post office in 1902, the state of Washington passed a repressive anti-anarchist statute in 1903 that curtailed the dissemination of anarchist literature from Home.[65] Finally, on a more cultural and comical note, another young member of the Home Colony remembered the following incident that raised problems with Home's neighbors: "We colony kids all bathed nude. One fellow at the colony—not an anarchist—took pictures and sold them to the Tacoma papers. That created a scandal and 'free love' accusations."[66]

While facing intolerance from the outside world, the internal tolerance that reigned at Home was so bound to the individualist idiosyncrasies of Home colonists that the colony itself lacked coherent and cohesive mechanisms of commitment necessary for the maintenance of utopian colonies.[67] Rather than enacting the "de-individuating mechanisms" that remove "the individual's sense of isolation and privacy," thus achieving a communal as opposed to personal sense of the world, Home was a place where individuals could be re-individuated.[68] In the words of one colonist concerning what enticed colonists to come to Home: "They come here to live normal lives, away from the maddening crowd's ignoble strife; away from the dictatorship of church and state, away from the study of duties they impose upon their subjects, their obligations, restrictions, persecutions, etc."[69] Although the anarchist utopianism at Home may be seen as an expression of the fringe eccentricities of an age in transition, Home did not shy away from issues that would resonate in later strategic value conflicts over personal freedoms.

Home's eventual transformation into a "conventional rural community" after World War I stands in stark contrast to the charged environment that led to the creation of the Stelton, New Jersey, colony in 1915.[70] Stelton grew out of the Ferrer Center and Modern School established in 1911 in New York City. The Ferrer Modern School was a forum for more than anarchist education; it was a cultural magnet that attracted a diverse group of reformers, free thinkers, and revolutionaries in politics and the arts. From Emma Goldman to Margaret Sanger, from Hutchins Hapgood to Alexander Berkman, from Robert Henri to Man Ray, the Ferrer Center represented not only the intellectual ferment of the times but also the desires of an alienated intelligentsia to develop oppositional and alternative institutions and culture. As historian Paul Avrich contends, the Ferrer Center in "its structure and operations, in the behavior of its participants to one another, . . . provided a foretaste of the libertarian future, of what life could be like once the restraints imposed by authority had been removed. For some it was also a vehicle for rebellion, a means of altering social foundations by removing the fetters of ignorance, dogmatism, and convention. Its central aim, however, was to free the child. From this the rest would follow."[71]

While the Modern School's emphasis on freeing the child provided the impetus for alternative educational practices at the Ferrer Center and Stelton, it also replicated at some level the emerging ideas on progressive education, especially those emphasized in more instrumentalist fashion by John Dewey.[72] On the other hand, while sharing certain ideas on the radical nature of progressive education, there was implicit in the anarchist conception of education adopted by the Ferrer Modern School a belief that social control, under any guise, was a coercive mechanism tied, ultimately, to the repressive state. According to Joseph Cohen, one of leaders of the Ferrer School and colony at Stelton, "The intrinsic value of the School could best be described in negative terms: it did not teach any dogmatism; it did not stuff the heads of the children with superficial cramming; it did not attempt to make good patriots of them to any particular nation."[73] The "main thing" remembered by Cohen's daughter, Emma Gilbert, about "the Ferrer School in New York and at Stelton was that the children were told that they were absolutely free to do anything they wanted, so long as it did not hurt anyone else."[74]

The Ferrer School moved to Stelton, New Jersey, in 1915 in order to escape the growing anti-radical hysteria and to develop a more extensive communal experiment. Most of the colony members were anarchists from Philadelphia and New York with immigrant backgrounds, eastern European Jews predominating. In fact, as recalled by Emma Gilbert, Stelton "was essentially a Jewish community with a traditional Jewish feeling about education, but with a libertarian slant."[75] While receiving support from a number of Jewish related labor and fraternal organizations, the Stelton Colony did not become the spark for cultural revolution in America as some had hoped. With the outbreak of the Russian Revolution and the attendant Red Scare in America, the Colony experienced a brief outburst of revolutionary rapture, followed by a sobering sense of their vulnerability to repression. Although the colony survived the Red Scare and continued until after World War II, its vital moment had passed by the beginning of the 1920s.

However, in the first flush of the move to Stelton and in the general excitement of the cresting of radicalism in the Progressive Era, Stelton could be seen as a beacon for radical social change. Mike Gold, novelist and later communist partisan, wrote after his four months at Stelton that the colony was "a strange exotic Jewel of radicalism placed in this dull setting, a scarlet role of revolution blooming in the cabbage patch, a Thought, an Idea, a Hope, balancing its existence in the great Jersey void."[76] In more prosaic, but nonetheless utopian terms, another colonist could state: "One by one, we are discarding our old habits and superstitions. We are beginning to live, naturally and fully."[77] The spirit of anarchist utopianism infused Stelton with a sense of political and cultural purpose. "Members here," according to a Stelton booster, "do not discuss questions of solidarity, brotherhood, and mutual aid—they go right ahead and practice them."[78]

Yet, Stelton was not without its doubters about the realization of the perfect anarchist utopia or about Stelton's centrality to the efforts to challenge the dominant norms and values of society at large. One of the primary movers of anarchism during this period, Harry Kelly, wrote about the difficulties faced at Stelton: "Anarchism is an ideal to strive for but it requires patience and fortitude in an uncanny degree to live it."[79] Questions, moreover, were raised about whether living anarchism in a rural retreat, as difficult as that might be, was a withdrawal from the battle to transform society. Debate at the Ferrer Modern School raged over this issue before the move. Much of that debate centered on whether a rural environment would be conducive to the kind of cosmopolitan anarchism and politically engaged utopianism evidenced at the Ferrer Center in New York City. Between a growing concern about the safety and future of the Ferrer Modern School in the city and fears of "de-politicizing the movement," the move was made. Harry Kelly later defended the "escape" to Stelton in the following manner: "We were not then and are not now neutral where liberty is violated and economic injustice prevails, but where children are concerned, less passion and calmer Judgment should prevail, if we would have them grow into rational and liberty loving men and women."[80]

The children and their schooling thus became the key to the communal effort at Stelton and to the anarchist utopian longings for a different future. One colonist saw the school at Stelton as "a training ground for a new world, for a society in which, as we hope, human beings will ultimately live their own lives in their own way, without coercion and without intolerance."[81] For others engaged in building the school as the core of a countercultural movement at Stelton, the children's future as individuals uncorrupted by the "evil influences and temptations of our artificial life" in the urban centers was of primary importance.[82] Yet, in preparing the children for the future, the Stelton colonists, many of whom were immigrants or children of immigrants, could not avoid the dominant norms in the modern world: the privatization of family and individualization of the future. As a number of interpreters of utopian experiments in the modern world have argued, communal and countercultural norms and values have a difficult time withstanding the self-enclosure of family life and the attendant values surrounding such privatization and individualization.[83] As Harry Kelly would ironically observe in 1921: "Stelton has ceased to be considered, by radicals at least, as a place for freaks where people expect to escape the laws of economic determinism and inaugurate a Utopia by raising children and chickens."[84]

The difficulty of sustaining a counterculture at Stelton cannot be attributed solely to the lack of moral resolve, anarchist will, or utopian vision of the colonists. The fact that most worked outside the colony certainly had an impact on the communal commitment and ability to build an integral and oppositional political culture. In many respects the Kropotkin-like mutual aid and self-help generated at Stelton combined the spirit of anarchist utopianism with forms of living not dissimilar, in Laurence Veysey's analysis, from "a large section of the English working class, and to a lesser degree, that of the traditional small town."[85] Yet the absorption of those anarchist utopian norms and values into the hegemonic reordering of the cultural environment in modern America was consistent with what one interpreter of British working class life in the nineteenth and twentieth centuries saw as the "transmutation of working class values and institutions." "This transmutation," argues Francis Hearn, "involved a shifting of working class values from the communal to the individual level. Emancipation became redefined as social mobility. . . . The self-help institutions, created along communal principles by the workers at the turn of the century, were reorganized into institutions which provided workers with the social and technical education necessary to become members of the middle class."[86] Thus, oppositional politics and culture became assimilated to a redefined hegemonic order.

Although anarchist utopianism did offer oppositional and alternative politics and culture during the Progressive Era, the disfigurement of such practices through integration into hegemonic structures of consumerism and non-solidaristic individualism eroded efforts at constructing countercultural norms and values. Nonetheless, the foreclosure of anarchist utopianism in America was only temporary, since the dreams and demands for non-coercive, non-authoritarian, and decentralist modes of living reemerged in a later decade, continuing their resonance even today.

NOTES

1. Kingsley Widmer, "Thinking About Libertarian Good Places: Some Notes on Anarchism and Utopia," *Social Anarchism* 3 (1983): 4; and George Woodcock, *Anarchism: A History of Libertarian Ideas and Movements* (Cleveland: Meridian, 1970), pp. 23–24.

2. Daniel Guerin, *Anarchism: From Theory to Practice*, trans. Mary Klopper (New York: Monthly Review Press, 1970), p. 41.

3. Woodcock, *Anarchism*, p. 9. Another formulation of the links between anarchism and utopianism can be found in Richard Sonn's description of how the anarchist "alternative fused elements of a remembered past with a vision of a utopian future" (Richard D. Sonn, *Anarchism* [New York: Twayne, 1992], p. 3).

4. For similar definitions of the strategic components of anarchism, see James J. Martin, *Men Against the State: The Expositors of Individualist Anarchism in America, 1827–1908* (DeKalb, Ill.: Adrian Allen Associates, 1953), p. 4; and John P. Clark, "What Is Anarchism" in *Anarchism*, ed. J. Roland Pennock and John W. Chapman (New York: New York University Press, 1978), p. 13.

5. Karl Mannheim, *Ideology and Utopia*, trans. Louis Wirth and Edward Shils (New York: Harvest, 1936), p. 40. For a critique of Mannheim's

sociology of knowledge method "which translates dialectical concepts into classificatory ones," see Theodor W. Adorno, "The Sociology of Knowledge and Its Consciousness," in *The Essential Frankfurt School Reader*, ed. Andrew Arato and Eike Gebhardt (New York: Urizen Books, 1978), p. 458.

6. Martin G. Plattel, *Utopian and Critical Thinking* (Pittsburgh: Duquesne University Press, 1972), p. 71. Other points of criticism along these lines can be found in Barbara Goodwin and Keith Taylor, *The Politics of Utopia: A Study in Theory and Practice* (New York: St. Martin's Press, 1982), pp. 77–80.

7. Raymond Williams, *Marxism and Literature* (Oxford: Oxford University Press, 1977), p. 110. Additional insightful elaboration of Gramsci's concept of hegemony can be found in T.J. Jackson Lears, "The Concept of Cultural Hegemony: Problems and Possibilities," *The American Historical Review* 90 (June 1985): 567–93.

8. Ibid., p. 113.

9. Ibid., pp. 118–19. For a brilliant use of Williams's distinction between oppositional and alternative formations, see Roy Rosenzweig, *Eight Hours for What We Will: Workers and Leisure in an Industrial City, 1870–1920* (Cambridge: Cambridge University Press, 1983), pp. 64, 189, 293–94, and *passim*.

10. For Mannheim's discussion of the "utopian mentality" and political classifications, see Mannheim, *Ideology and Utopia*, pp. 192–263. For an example of strategic value conflicts within socialist utopianism, see Goodwin and Taylor, *The Politics of Utopia*, pp. 129–37.

11. Guerin, *Anarchism*, p. 13.

12. See, for example, Frank E. Manuel, "Towards a Psychological History of Utopias," in *Utopias and Utopian Thought*, ed. Frank E. Manuel (Boston: Houghton Mifflin Co., 1965), pp. 69–98.

13. Quoted in Blaine McKinley, "A Religion of the New Time: Anarchist Memorials to the Haymarket Martyrs, 1888–1917," *Labor History* 28 (Summer 1987): 394.

14. On the "morai urge" of anarchism, see Woodcock, *Anarchism*, p. 15. On "ethical capital," see Giovanni Baldelli, *Social Anarchism* (Chicago: Aldine, 1971), pp. 13–65.

15. Martin Buber, *Paths in Utopia*, trans. R.F.C. Hull (Boston: Beacon Press, 1966), esp. pp. 7–15, and Paul Tillich, "Critique and Justification of Utopia," in Manuel, *Utopias and Utopian Thought*, pp. 296–309.

16. In addition to the works previously cited, the following have been instrumental in developing a definition of anarchist utopianism: Seyla Benhabib, *Critique, Norm, and Utopia: A Study of the Foundations of Critical Theory* (New York: Columbia University Press, 1986); Charles Erasmus, *In Search of the Common Good* (New York: Free Press, 1977); Richard K. Fenn, *The Spirit of Revolt: Anarchism and the Cult of Authority* (Totowa, N.J.: Rowman and Littlefield, 1986); Rosabeth Moss Kanter, *Commitment and Community: Communes and Utopias in Sociological Perspective* (Cambridge, Mass.: Harvard University Press, 1977); Melvin J. Lasky, *Utopia and Revolution* (Chicago: University of Chicago Press, 1976); and Frank E.

Manuel and Fritzie P. Manuel, *Utopian Thought in the Western World* (Cambridge, Mass.: Belknap Press of Harvard University Press, 1979).

17. Zygmunt Bauman, *Socialism: The Active Utopia* (New York: Holmes and Meier, 1976), p. 47. For a discussion of utopianism, anarchism, and the counterculture in an American context, see Laurence Veysey, *The Communal Experience: Anarchist and Mystical Communities in Twentieth Century America* (Chicago: University of Chicago Press, 1973).

18. David DeLeon, *The American as Anarchist: Reflections on Indigenous Radicalism* (Baltimore: Johns Hopkins University Press, 1978), p. 114.

19. Paul Avrich, *An American Anarchist: The Life of Voltairine de Cleyre* (Princeton: Princeton University Press, 1978), p. xviii.

20. Studies of the anarchist movement in America and individual American anarchists that illuminate these efforts to construct an opposition, alternative, or counter culture, in addition to those previously cited, can be found in the following: Paul Avrich, *The Modern School Movement: Anarchism and Education in the United States* (Princeton: Princeton University Press, 1980); Richard Drinnon, *Rebel in Paradise: A Biography of Emma Goldman* (New York: Bantam, 1973); Margaret S. Marsh, *Anarchist Women, 1870–1920* (Philadelphia: Temple University Press, 1981); William O. Reichert, *Partisans of Freedom: A Study of American Anarchism* (Bowling Green: Bowling Green University Press, 1976); and Blaine McKinley, " 'The Quagmires of Necessity': American Anarchists and Dilemmas of Vocation," *American Quarterly* 34 (Winter 1982): 503–23.

21. Kraditor's misreading of Gramsci locks hegemony into an "essentialist" mold. See Aileen Kraditor, *The Radical Persuasion, 1890–1917* (Baton Rouge: Louisiana State University Press, 1981), pp 64–69. For Lears's synthesis of Gramsci through Williams with Freud and Weber, see T.J. Jackson Lears, *No Place of Grace: Antimodernism and the Transformation of American Culture, 1880–1920* (New York: Pantheon, 1981), pp. xvii–xviii. For Lears's critique of Kraditor's compartmentalized and rationalist analysis of the public and private sphere, see Lears, "The Concept of Cultural Hegemony," pp. 582–83.

22. Kraditor, *The Radical Persuasion*, pp. 64, 91–92.

23. Ibid. pp. 78, 86–110. For an incisive understanding of how alternative and oppositional cultures contend with a reconstituting hegemony, see Rosenzweig, *Eight Hours for What We Will*, pp. 27–32, 64, 89, 293–94. While Kraditor rightly criticizes certain historians' use of repression as a monocausal factor for the failure of radicalism (see esp. pp. 14–15), she too readily dismisses the role of state repression in containing radicalism. See William Preston, Jr., *Aliens and Dissenters: Federal Suppression of Radicals. 1903–33* (New York: Harper Torchbooks, 1966).

24. Lears, *No Place of Grace*, P. xix. For a similar point about the progressives' belief that "personal regeneration would achieve social regeneration," see Robert M. Crunden, *Ministers of Reform: The Progressives' Achievement in American Civilization, 1889–1920* (New York: Basic Books, 1982), p. 51. For an opposing view of how self-involvement has enlarged

the social agenda in contemporary America, see Peter Clecak, *America's Quest for the Ideal Self* (New York: Oxford University Press, 1983).

25. Lears, *No Place of Grace*, pp. 73, 80, and *passim*.

26. Quoted in Alice Wexler, *Emma Goldman: An Intimate Life* (New York: Pantheon Books, 1984), p. 38. On her own "emotional" conversion to anarchism, see Emma Goldman, *Living My Life*, Vol. 1 (New York: Dover Publications, 1970), pp. 9–10. On her early involvement with anarchism, see Drinnon, *Rebel in Paradise*, pp. 21–32; and Marian J. Morton, *Emma Goldman and the American Left: "Nowhere at Home"* (New York: Twayne, 1992), pp. 15–35.

27. Emma Goldman, "Anarchism: What It Really Stands For," in *Red Emma Speaks*, ed. Alix Kates Shulman (New York: Schocken, 1983), p. 75.

28. Ibid., p. 63.

29. On Goldman's anarchist message for self-expression and self-determination related to women and cultural radicals, see Drinnon, *Rebel in Paradise*, pp. 105–213; Marsh, *Anarchist Women*, pp. 20–21 105; Morton, *Emma Goldman and the American Left*, pp. 36–80; and Wexler, *Emma Goldman*, pp. 88–89, 205–6.

30. Goldman, "Anarchism," p. 73.

31. Ibid., p. 63.

32. On vitalism and its contradictions, see Lears, *No Place of Grace*, esp. pp. 143, 159–67.

33. Peter Conn, *The Divided Mind: Ideology and Imagination in America, 1898–1917* (Cambridge: Cambridge University Press, 1983), p. 313. Goldman herself recounts an incident when a rabbi claimed that "in spite of all Miss Goldman has said against religion, she is the most religious person I know" (*Living My Life*, Vol. II, p. 561). Although Goldman and other Jewish anarchists were reluctant to claim their Jewishness as a source for their radicalism, it nonetheless provided an important prophetic base for their sense of persecution and justice. On this point, see Gerald Sorrin, *The Prophetic Minority: American Jewish Immigrant Radicals, 1880-1920* (Bloomington: Indiana University Press, 1985); and Francis Shor, "Cultural Identity and Americanization: The Life History of a Jewish Anarchist," *biography* 9 (Fall 1986): 332–35. For the influence of prophetic Judaism and Jewish life on Goldman, see Drinnon, *Rebel in Paradise*, pp. 28–29; and Morton, *Emma Goldman and the American Left*, p. 14.

34. Goldman, "Anarchism," p. 65. On the libertarian and romantic connections to anarchism, see DeLeon, *The American as Anarchist*, esp. pp. 85–101; Reichert, *Partisans of Freedom*; and Blaine McKinley, "Anarchist Jeremiads: American Anarchists and American History," *Journal of American Culture* 6 (Summer 1983): 75–84.

35. Goldman, "Anarchism," p. 72.

36. Ibid., p. 74.

37. Plattel, *Utopian and Critical Thinking*, p. 59. Plattel relies on Ernst Bloch's monumental work on utopia from which the concept "concrete utopia" comes.

38. Goldman, "Socialism: Caught in the Political Trap," in Goldman, *Red Emma Speaks*, p. 105.

39. Quoted in McKinley, "Anarchist Jeremiads," p. 83.

40. Goldman, "Anarchism," p. 64. On elite forces and the reform movement during the Progressive Era, see Gabriel Kolko, *The Triumph of Conservatism* (Chicago: Quadrangle Books, 1963); and Robert H. Wiebe, *The Search for Order, 1877–1920* (New York: Hill and Wang, 1967). On insurgent forces and the reform movement during the Progressive Era, see Bruno Ramirez, *When Workers Fight: The Politics of Industrial Relations in the Progressive Era, 1898-1916* (Westport, Conn.: Greenwood Press, 1978); and Meredith Tax, *The Rising of the Women: Feminist Solidarity and Class Conflict, 1880-1917* (New York: Monthly Review Press, 1980). For a balanced and incisive view of the role of the state and reform forces in the Progressive Era, see Alan Dawley, *Struggles for Justice: Social Responsibility and the Liberal State* (Cambridge, Mass.: The Belknap Press of Harvard University Press, 1991), pp. 63–171.

41. Goldman, "What I Believe," in Goldman, *Red Emma Speaks*, p. 50. On the arts and crafts movement and utopian and "nostalgic" progressivism, see Lears, *No Place of Grace*, pp. 60–97.

42. Goldman, "Anarchism," pp. 67–68. The specific charge of nostalgia in Goldman's discourse can be found in Conn, *The Divided Mind*, p. 314. On nostalgia and ambivalence in the Progressive Era, see Crunden, *Ministers of Reform*, pp. 144–57; and Lears, *No Place of Grace*, pp. 64–65, and *passim*.

43. See Goldman's essays on feminist issues collected in *Red Emma Speaks*, pp. 150–222. For Goldman's work on issues such as birth control, see Drinnon, *Rebel in Paradise*, pp. 205–12: Bonnie Haaland, *Emma Goldman: Sexuality and the Impurity of the State* (Montreal: Black Rose, 1993), pp. 71–82; Marsh, *Anarchist Women*, pp. 111–12; Morton, *Emma Goldman and the American Left*, pp. 75–79; and Wexler, *Emma Goldman*, pp. 209–15.

44. Goldman, "Anarchism," pp. 76–77.

45. Wexler, *Emma Goldman*, pp. 93–94. On Goldman's free speech fights and her struggle for women's rights and sexual liberation, see Drinnon, *Rebel in Paradise*, pp. 149–75 183–90; and Morton, *Emma Goldman and the American Left*, pp. 59–80.

46. Richard King, *The Party of Eros: Radical Social Thought and the Realm of Freedom* (Chapel Hill: University of North Carolina Press, 1972). Like the later male proponents of the "party of eros," Goldman, according to Bonnie Haaland and other contemporary feminists, "neatly categorized sexuality as positive and liberatory for both men and women, without attending to the ways in which so-called 'sexual liberation' could be unequally experienced according to one's gender" (Haaland, *Emma Goldman*, p. 120).

47. On Goldman's relationship with Reitman, see Drinnon, *Rebel in Paradise*, pp. 154–54; and Wexler, *Emma Goldman*, pp. 157–58, and *passim*. On the hegemonic control of sexual liberation, see Herbert Marcuse's analysis of "repressive de-sublimation" in his *One Dimensional Man* (Boston: Beacon Press, 1968), pp. 72–74. For Marcuse's more optimistic

reading of sexual liberation, see his *Eros and Civilization* (New York: Vintage, 1962).

48. Christopher Lasch, *The New Radicalism in America, 1889-1963: The Intellectual as a Social Type* (New York: Vintage, 1967).

49. Quoted in Wexler, *Emma Goldman*, pp. 206–7. When Goldman was attacked by some of her anarchist allies for her appeals to the middle class, she responded in the pages of *Mother Earth*: "The men and women who first take up the banner of a new liberating idea generally emanate from the so-called respectable classes." Quoted in Morton, *Emma Goldman and the American Left*, p. 47.

50. Goldman, "The Tragedy of Women's Emancipation," p. 167 in *Red Emma Speaks*; and "Anarchism," p. 67.

51. Goldman, "What I Believe," p. 49.

52. Veysey, *The Communal Experience*, p. 52.

53. Kanter, *Commitment and Community*, p. 237. Kanter's separation of utopian categories into the "religious, political-economic, and psychosocial" tends to reify the historical complexity and contradictions of utopian motivations and overprivilege religious factors.

54. Ibid., pp. 153–54. Kanter doesn't explicitly deal with hegemonic forces, although her analysis does implicitly recognize them.

55. This definition of the utopian colony can be found in Robert V. Hine, *California's Utopian Colonies* (San Marino, Calif.: Huntington Library, 1953), p. 5.

56. The most complete discussion of Home can be found in LeWarne, *Utopias on Puget Sound*, pp. 168–226. A brief mention of Home and the anarcho-feminist connection can be found in Marsh, *Anarchist Women*, pp 117–18. On Home and its relation to the anarchist communal tradition, see Veysey, *The Communal Experience*, pp. 178–79.

57. Quoted in Marsh, *Anarchist Women*, p. 117.

58. Quoted in Paul Avrich, *Anarchist Voices: An Oral History of Anarchism in America* (Princeton: Princeton University Press, 1995), p. 292.

59. *Discontent*, 18 September 1901, n.p.

60. Quoted in LeWarne, *Utopias on Puget Sound*, p. 171.

61. Avrich, *Anarchist Voices*, p. 293.

62. LeWarne, *Utopias on Puget Sound*, p. 171. Although Verity's ideal of personal liberty fit easily into individualist anarchist tradition, his daughter, Macie Pope, disputed labelling him an anarchist. See Avrich, *Anarchist Voices*, p. 291.

63. For a discussion of the official harassment of the Home Colony, see Lewarne, *Utopias on Puget Sound*, pp. 178–86.

64. Quoted in Avrich, *Anarchist Voices*, p. 293.

65. LeWarne, *Utopias on Puget Sound*, pp. 182–86.

66. Avrich, *Anarchist Voices*, p. 296.

67. One colonist in Home suggested that the "watchword of this place is 'Mind Your Own Business.'" Quoted in LeWarne, *Utopias on Puget Sound*, p. 187. On the difficulties encountered in developing commitment in utopian colonies, see Kanter, *Commitment and Community*, esp. pp. 64–74. On the application of commitment mechanisms in the Washington

utopian colonies like Home, see LeWarne, *Utopias on Puget Sound*, pp. 237–38.

68. Kanter, *Commitment and Community*, p. 110.

69. LeWarne, *Utopias on Puget Sound*, p. 194.

70. Home's ending as a "conventional rural community" is discussed in ibid., p. 224. On Stelton's creation and development, see Avrich, *The Modern School Movement*, pp. 219–55; and Veysey, *The Communal Experience*, pp. 77–177. On Stelton's connection to the anarcho-feminist movement, see Marsh, *Anarchist Women*, pp. 118–22.

71. Avrich, *Anarchist Voices*, p. 193. On the Ferrer Modern School, see Avrich, *The Modern School Movement*, pp. 111–64.

72. On the Ferrer Center's connection to Dewey, see Avrich, *The Modern School Movement*, pp. 38, 162. On Dewey's instrumentalism and its link to the politics of social control during the Progressive Era, see Lasch, *The New Radicalism in America*, pp. 159–63.

73. Quoted in Avrich, *The Modern School Movement*, pp. 228–29.

74. Quoted in Avrich, *Anarchist Voices*, p. 227. For one of the first teachers at Stelton, Nellie Dick, this emphasis on freedom often meant to the kids "that they could make a mess of the place." Ibid., p. 286.

75. Ibid., p. 228.

76. Quoted in Avrich, *The Modern School Movement*, p. 220.

77. Quoted in Veysey, *The Communal Experience*, pp. 122–23.

78. Quoted in ibid., p. 119.

79. Quoted in Avrich, *The Modern School Movement*, p. 221.

80. Quoted in Veysey, *The Communal Experience*, p. 107; on the debate and charges of retreat, see pp. 108–12.

81. Quoted in ibid., p. 173.

82. Quoted in ibid., p. 111.

83. On the erosion of countercultural schooling at Stelton, see ibid., p. 175. On the conforming of immigrants to the privatization of family life in America, see Kraditor, *The Radical Persuasion*, p. 78. On the undermining of utopianism by familistic individualization, see Erasmus, *In Search of the Common Good*, esp. pp. 190–91, and Yonina Talmon, *Family and Community in the Kibbutz* (Cambridge, Mass.: Harvard University Press, 1972), pp. 1–50.

84. Quoted in Veysey, *The Communal Experience*, pp. 133–34.

85. Ibid., p. 196.

86. Francis Hearn, *Domination, Legitimation and Resistance: The Incorporation of the Nineteenth Century English Working Class* (Westport, Conn.: Greenwood Press, 1978), pp. 154–55.

7

Oppositional Utopianizing and the Political/Cultural Project: The Paterson and Star of Ethiopia Pageants

While the forms of utopianism presented in previous chapters fit into recognizable boundaries, this chapter intends to explore another utopian moment often unaccounted for. In a recent article Lyman Tower Sargent once again draws our attention to what he construes as the three fundamental forms of utopianism: utopian literature; communitarianism; and utopian social theory.[1] While delineating these forms in the larger context of Ruth Levitas's definition of utopia, he nonetheless occludes her emphasis on the function of utopia—a function that Levitas links to the expression and education of desire.[2] By separating form from function, Sargent short-circuits the historical process in which a social imaginary finds concrete representation. It is within that historical process that particular social groups articulate specific visions intended to mobilize sentiments for social fulfillment. That historical process of articulation underscores both the dialectical relationship between form and function and what Ernst Bloch understood to be the inherent utopianizing underlying the social desire for fulfillment.[3]

In determining the historical contours of utopianizing, it is important to recognize how such utopianizing articulates what I regard as another form of utopianism: the political/cultural project. The political/cultural project can range from the utopian moments of such social revolutions as the Russian and the Chinese to the emancipatory movements of anarchist women during the Spanish civil war and the black power struggles in America during the 1960s.[4] Common to the utopianizing of all political/cultural projects is the articulation of certain concerns and hopes and the anticipation that those concerns and hopes can be translated into a better life.

The mechanism by which such hopes and concerns are translated into a better life demarcates how utopianizing encapsulates a "dialectical tension" between ideology and utopia.[5] Such a tension not only indicates how ideology and utopia are part of either an integrative or subversive social imaginary, but also how utopianizing can reflect either an integrative or oppositional tendency within the political/cultural project. Thus, in articulating an integrative or oppositional tendency, the political/cultural project is part of the struggle over a hegemonic structuring of social practices and social expectations.[6] To the extent that the political/cultural project reinforces the dominant ordering of society, it performs an integrative or hegemonic utopianizing function. On the other hand, to the extent that the political/cultural project challenges the dominant order, it performs an oppositional or counter-hegemonic utopianizing function.[7]

In order to understand what constitutes oppositional utopianizing and the cultural moment of a political project, I want to examine the impact of the Paterson and *Star of Ethiopia* Pageants. On the eve of World War I and in the face of patriotic pageantry that attempted to instill in a multicultural population a sense of national identity, these two pageants were mounted in New York City in 1913. They both challenged the dominant ideology and form of pageantry produced in the United States during the Progressive Era. Against such ideology and pageantry that suppressed class distinctions and trivialized racial/ethnic differences, the Paterson and *Star of Ethiopia* Pageants enacted class and racial dramas, respectively, that promoted oppositional utopianizing and alternative cultural identities. Translating the "social dramas" that marked the everyday world of the mass immigrant worker and of African-Americans into a staged drama in stadium settings, the Paterson and *Star of Ethiopia* Pageants provided an opportunity for participants and viewers to appropriate history as self-determining actors in a society where they were mostly despised and marginalized.[8]

The Paterson Pageant took place in Madison Square Garden on June 7, 1913. It grew out of the massive strike by silk workers in Paterson, New Jersey, that began in February 1913. Pulled together by the radical leaders of that strike, organizers of the Industrial Workers of the World like "Big Bill" Haywood and their intellectual allies among the New York bohemians, Mabel Dodge Luhan and John Reed, the Paterson Pageant featured a thousand Paterson strikers re-enacting the critical moments of the strike for a mostly working class audience of over fifteen thousand. Enthusiastically received by those in attendance, the Paterson Pageant represented not only "a potent instrument in raising political consciousness and forging a sense of working-class solidarity" but also the merging of "politics and art, a strike tactic and a cultural revolution."[9]

In the fall of 1913 another pageant was presented in New York City (to be repeated in Washington, D.C., in 1915 and Philadelphia in 1916). The *Star of Ethiopia* Pageant, presented before an audience of fourteen thousand at the 12th Regiment Armory as part of New York's commemoration of the fiftieth anniversary of the Emancipation Proclamation, was the brainchild of W.E.B. Du Bois. Featuring a cast of thousands, the *Star of Ethiopia* Pageant was a three-hour enactment of Du Bois's 1911 book of the same title. Blending "Afrocentric aesthetics and historiography," this African-American pageant promoted a racial pride and oppositional utopianizing that tried to counter the virulent racial discrimination and violence that plagued the country at the turn of the century.[10]

In reconstructing the impact these two pageants had on the participants and their target audiences, I want to consider whether white and African-American intellectuals of pre–World War I America could translate such political/cultural projects represented by these pageants into the construction of a counter-hegemonic identity and politics. During the Progressive Era there was a struggle over the hegemonic ordering of a society undergoing profound changes, especially as a consequence of the changing social background and composition of a rapidly expanding population. One arena of contested terrain during this period was the pageantry movement, a movement that attempted to foster a definitive sense of cultural identity and an integrative/hegemonic utopianizing. Those social forces who most feared the immigrant waves constructed their nativist pageantry and hegemonic utopianizing to mirror their commitment to a form of Anglo-conformity that "projected an overarching civic identity, modeled on an imagined deferential consensus and social hierarchy of the past, that the elite claimed could transcend neighborhood, class, and ethnic conflicts and differences."[11] Such hegemonic utopianizing lay behind much of the "genteel pageantry" of the period. On the other hand, a form of "new historical pageantry," promoted by progressive educators and leaders in the settlement house and playground movements of the early twentieth century, attempted to make the pageant a vehicle for the melting pot ideal of civic virtue and democratic citizenship.

While recognizing the various cultural identities of the new immigrants, such pageantry, promoted by the American Pageant Association, founded in 1913, required the kind of professional expertise for purposes of order and control that were part of progressivist hegemonic restructuring of American society.[12] In contradistinction to such progressivist utopianizing attached to dominant ideologies, the Paterson and *Star of Ethiopia* Pageants attempted to promote oppositional and counter-hegemonic utopianizing.

In reconstructing the impact that the Paterson Pageant had on immigrant workers, radical intellectuals, and middle-class sympathizers, one must first consider how this particular pageant differed from the pageantry of the period in articulating its oppositional utopianizing. Secondly, one must identify how the concerns and hopes of disenfranchised workers mobilized by the IWW reflected a social movement and political project intended to "fan the flames of discontent" and to bring about a social transformation through the general strike. Finally, one must trace how the intersection of workers and intellectuals on a cultural project like the Paterson Pageant offered the possibility for the realization of a new and revolutionary form of what one of the radical intellectuals of the period, Hutchins Hapgood, called "self-expression in industry and art."[13] In effect, I want to consider in this chapter to what extent oppositional utopianizing could translate a political/cultural project into a counter-hegemonic social praxis.

Hapgood's glowing review of the Paterson Pageant, recounted in his autobiography, *A Victorian in the Modern World*, asserted that such pageantry might be a "hope for real democracy . . . spreading a human glow over the whole of humanity."[14] Such utopian sentiments were not at all foreign to the cultural movement for pageantry which emerged in the early twentieth century. In fact, as one historian of pageantry has noted: "In a sense, historical pageantry flourished at the intersection of progressivism and anti-modernism and placed nostalgic imagery in a dynamic, future oriented reform context."[15] While such nostalgic imagery reflected a conservative, traditional, and hegemonic utopianizing, the cultural politics of pageantry were contested terrain for a variety of promoters and a mix of ideological and utopian functions.

In contradistinction to such hegemonic restructuring that tried to suppress or smooth over class and ethnic conflicts, the Paterson Pageant chose to confront head-on those class and ethnic conflicts that were at the forefront of the labor strife in Paterson, New Jersey.[16] As social critic Randolph Bourne observed: "Who that saw the Paterson Strike Pageant in 1913 can ever forget the thrilling evening when an entire labor community dramatized its wrongs in one supreme outburst of group-emotion."[17] As another observer of the Paterson Pageant, Bernadine Kielty, remarked: "No one who saw the Paterson strike pageant was likely ever again to think of the working class as an indefinable mass."[18] In effect, for all the participants, whether performers or members of the audience, the Paterson Pageant, enacting a moving articulation of grievances and the hopeful stirring for a better future by class-conscious workers, clearly cast the Pageant as oppositional utopianizing.

Central to the oppositional political/cultural project of the Paterson Pageant was the role of the Industrial Workers of the World. Although the IWW did not initiate the 1913 Paterson silk strike, it quickly became the leading organization behind the mobilization of workers. Bringing together the talents of organizers like Haywood, Elizabeth Gurley Flynn, and Carlo Tresca, the IWW forged the disparate and disenfranchised immigrant silk workers of Paterson into a militant social force. Coming off a successful 1912 strike in the textile mills of Lawrence, Massachusetts, the IWW sought to put its experience into operation at Paterson.

It is important to stress that the IWW always saw itself as more than a mere labor organization; rather, IWW leaders emphasized that the Wobblies were a revolutionary social movement. For Haywood, the historical mission of the IWW, enunciated in his opening address to the 1905 founding organization, was "to confederate the workers of this country into a working class movement that shall have for its purpose the emancipation of the working class from the slave bondage of capitalism."[19] While various historians have tried to identify the nature of that revolutionary social movement by defining the IWW along the lines of a religious sect or cadre organization, it is clear that at the heart of the IWW movement was an "oppositional culture" that mobilized "diverse and relatively transient loci of working-class subcultures."[20]

One means of uniting the diverse and relatively transient loci of working-class subcultures was to articulate a vision of social solidarity at the point of production that would empower those who were exploited and oppressed by industrial capitalism. Such revolutionary industrial unionism was central to the oppositional utopianizing of the IWW. According to Haywood in a 1911 speech: "By organizing the workers industrially you at once enfranchise the women in the shops, you at once give the black men who are disfranchised politically a voice in the operation of the industries."[21] Both the means and the end for the ultimate transformation of disenfranchised and dishonored workers were the general strike, an almost mystical and religious concept of utopian redemption for the IWW, best represented in the IWW's version of the last stanza of the

"Internationale": "Tis the final conflict!/Let each stand in his place/The Industrial Union/Shall be the Human Race."[22]

It should come as no surprise to note the significant role that the singing of the "Internationale" and the representation of the general strike played in the Paterson Pageant. In the fourth scene of the Pageant, both performers and the audience sang out the Wobbly version of the "Internationale," along with other musical numbers. Part of the 31-page program for the Pageant included an essay on "The General Strike in the Silk Industry" which avowed that the "pageant represents a battle between the working class and the capitalist class, conducted by the IWW. . . . It is a conflict between two social forces."[23] Moreover, the final scene of the Pageant turned the whole affair into a giant general strike where strikers and the audience heard the appeals of the IWW leaders for social emancipation. Noting that "actors and audience were of one class and one hope," one review thus captured the expressive solidarity and oppositional utopianizing of a cultural moment of the political project of the IWW.[24]

The reaction in the Wobbly press confirmed, on one hand, the IWW's perception of the Pageant as an instance of expressive solidarity and as a vehicle for agitation. In reporting on the event, under the heading of "Two Thousand in Huge Show for Labor's Sake," the Spokane *Industrial Worker* asserted that the "pageant promises to be one of labor's publicity weapons when even peaceful picketing is stopped by the police."[25] Less concerned with the immediate tactical advantage that the pageant as propaganda might offer, the official IWW newspaper *Solidarity* provided a review of the pageant under the heading of "The Paterson Mass Play." Commenting on the mass nature of the pageant as one "born of mass actors," *Solidarity* further noted that "it was like the old morality play, a play with a purpose that marked the beginning of a new epoch in play writing and play acting."[26] Pronouncing the pageant "tremendously successful in the suggestion of the immense power and possibilities of solidarity" and "an inspiration," the journalistic voice of the IWW highlighted the cultural moment of oppositional utopianizing evident to promoters and supporters of the Paterson strike and its pageant.[27]

On the other hand, while even the most establishment newspapers acknowledged the impact of the Paterson Pageant, their evaluation of the role of the IWW continued to be prejudiced by their antagonism to the IWW's image as a militant revolutionary organization. *The New York Times*, which had assiduously disregarded the several-months-long strike in Paterson, fulminated against the IWW's subversive intentions at the Pageant:

Under the direction of a destructive organization opposed in spirit and antagonistic in action to all the forces which have upbuilded this republic, a series of pictures in action were shown with the design of stimulating mad passion against law and order and promulgating a gospel of discontent. The sordid and cruel incidents of an industrial strike were depicted by many of the poor strikers themselves, but with dominating and vociferous assistance from members of the I.W.W., who have at heart no more sympathy with laborers than they have with Judges and Government officers. . . . The motive was to inspire hatred, to induce violence which may lead to the tearing down of the civil state and the institution of anarchy.[28]

The more charitable coverage of the Pageant by the *New York Tribune* elicited the following commentary about the role of the IWW: "The I.W.W. has not been highly regarded hereabouts as an organization endowed with brains or imagination. Yet the very effective appeal to public interest made by the spectacle at the Garden stamps the I.W.W. leaders as agitators of large resources and original talent."[29]

Although the recognition of the IWW's leadership role was decidedly mixed in the establishment press, the organization and the strike became a major attraction for the community of radical intellectuals in New York. Especially prominent among this group and first to report on the Paterson strike was the young John Reed.[30] Convinced by Haywood at a Greenwich Village meeting to go to Paterson to help publicize the strike, Reed was arrested shortly after his arrival. Released after a few days, Reed wrote a story about Paterson for the *Masses* which denounced the violence of the Paterson establishment. Embracing the cause of the strikers and endorsing the leadership of the IWW, Reed commented in another article that he was impressed with the IWW's "understanding of the workers, their revolutionary thought, the boldness of their dreams, . . . Here was a drama, change, democracy on the march made visible—a war of the people."[31]

Despite Reed's enthusiasm for the strike and the increasing involvement of the New York radical intelligentsia, the drama of Paterson remained invisible to the community at large. Only after another Greenwich Village meeting between Haywood and several prominent New York bohemians did the idea emerge to translate the social drama at Paterson into a staged drama in New York. Mabel Dodge Luhan, one of the participants in that meeting and the guiding spirit of one of the most vital salons in New York, responded to Haywood's lament about the continuing news blackout: "Why don't you bring the strike to New York and show it to the workers? . . . Why don't you hire a great hall and re-enact the strike over here? Show the whole thing: the closed mills, the gunmen, the murder of the striker, the funeral. And have the strike leaders make their speeches at the grave as you did in Paterson."[32] Reed leaped upon the opportunity of putting together such a show, and with the help of a committee that included Mabel Dodge Luhan he gathered together his artist friends from Harvard (Bobby Jones for stage setting) and the *Masses* (John Sloan to paint scenery) to mount a pageant at Madison Square Garden in June.

The logistics of mounting such a pageant inspired in Reed and the radical community of New York a commitment not only to building support for the strike but also to staging "a political event whose goal was revolutionary."[33] As one historian of the Paterson Pageant notes, "the choice of significant moments—the walkout, the martyrdom, the funeral of the martyr, the May Day Parade, the sending away of the children, the strike vote—the repetition of the speeches of the strike leaders and the dramatic simplification and compression of events which may have been unclear when experienced in actuality, all made the striking workers conscious of their experiences as self-determining members of a class that shaped history."[34] In effect, the Pageant's plot replicated a condition articulated by one of the women strikers and participant in the Pageant: "We were frightened when we went in, but we were singing when we came out."[35]

The power of such singing, orchestrated by Reed, gave voice to the striving and utopian aspirations of the immigrant workers who were the backbone of the Paterson strike and made up the bulk of the thousand performers who merged with an audience of fifteen thousand at Madison Square Garden on the evening of June 7, 1913. In describing the opening scene, Grace Potter, a member of the audience, caught the spirit of oppositional utopianizing that motivated both the radical intelligentsia and immigrant workers who put on the Pageant:

First we saw the mill, stretching its black stoves menacingly to the sky. Its windows were lit, its whistles blowing. We watched the still sleepy men, women and children, with their coat collars turned up to keep out the chill of the early morning—it was in February the strike began—we watched them swallowed, one by one, through the mill's hungry door. Then the unending whir of iron-hearted machinery began. It seemed to us, waiting out there in the audience, that the machinery was grinding those workers to pieces. We thought of industrial accidents and diseases, of how terrible toil sucked all life, all initiative out of the workers. They were dying, and it was the same all over the world. We held our breath. And then—something happened. The machinery stopped grinding. A faint cry rises slowly, to deafening hosannas from a thousand throats as the workers rush from the mill. They wave their hands, they shout, they dance, they embrace each other in a social passion that pales individual feeling to nothing. They are a mad mob, glad and beautiful in their madness. They sing the Marseillaise. The strike is on! . . . Here and there, from the balcony, the boxes and the great main floor, the sound of sobbing that was drowned in singing proved that the audience had "got" Paterson.[36]

As Mable Dodge Luhan later noted in her memoirs, "I have never felt such a high pulsing vibration in any gathering before or since."[37]

While the event itself was an extraordinary experience for those involved, its meaning as a cultural moment for those radical intellectuals and revolutionary workers who came together in the Paterson Pageant was multifold. First of all, as a form of oppositional utopianizing, the Paterson Pageant was able to dramatize the class condition of immigrant workers in a way that challenged the genteel and melting-pot ideology of the patriotic pageantry of the period. In opposition to the those pageants that "were all too often merely spectacular rationalization of the status quo . . . it was made dramatically clear that the 'new citizens' were contributing more than their dances, their songs and their folk traditions to this country: they were being forced to contribute their health, their hopes, their honor and their children."[38] As one of those who participated in bringing the Paterson Pageant to life, Rose Pastor Stokes exclaimed: "Hail the new pageantry! Hail the red pageant—the pageant with red blood in its veins."[39]

The color red certainly captured the sense of vitality and political orientation of the Paterson Pageant. Both Madison Square Garden and the ushers were bedecked with red—red Wobbly banners surrounding the Garden and red carnations and red sashes on the ushers. On the other hand, the translation of red imagery into red ideology which the Paterson Pageant promised as a political project of oppositional utopianizing was overwhelmed by the difficulties in both sustaining the strike and building a Gramscian "historic bloc" that could go beyond mounting the staged and transitory barricades into institutionalizing a counter-hegemonic social praxis.[40] Although the "fragile bridge" erected during the Paterson Pageant between workers, intellectuals, and the middle class had a shaky foundation, the loss of the strike and the eventual state repression of the IWW undermined the strongest component of that bridge. Moreover, the outbreak of World War I split the ranks of the intellectuals and middle class supporters of social change.[41] As a consequence, the bright hopes and red-blooded desires raised by the oppositional utopianizing of the Paterson Pageant were swept aside by a form of hegemonic utopianizing that promised to make the world safe for democracy even while stanching the utopian aspirations of fervent advocates of radical democracy at home.

Against the patriotism of the national state with its politics of exclusion, one towering intellectual of an excluded minority, W.E.B. Du Bois, attempted through his writings and political agitation to transcode nationalist and racial categories to redeem African-Americans from their despised social position in American culture. As Du Bois conceptualized the social drama of race in America, blacks were "denied control over their identity" because of "white American cultural hegemony."[42] According to one interpreter of Du Bois's work, "[a]ppropriating theories of race nationalism available to him as a student at Fisk, Harvard, and Berlin, Du Bois. . . . struggled to institutionalize the world-spirit of Africa."[43] This world-spirit of Africa would play a central role not only in oppositional utopianizing articulated in the *Star of Ethiopia* Pageant but also throughout the long history of Du Bois's political/cultural projects.

In particular, the contested ideology of race becomes infused with historical and political meaning for Du Bois precisely to the extent that races can realize a Hegelian world-spirit. Thus, Du Bois conceives of races as "striving, each in its own way, to develop for civilization its particular message, its particular ideal, which shall help guide the world nearer and nearer that perfection of human life for which we all long, that 'one far off Divine event.' "[44] Du Bois's vision of the redemptive power of a race ideal conforms not only to the spiritual strivings of African-Americans but also to the connections between desire and hope embedded in utopianizing.[45] Moreover, the particularity of Du Bois's racial creed—"that the Negro people, as a race, have a contribution to make to civilization and humanity, which no other race can make"—promotes a critical universal role for African-Americans precisely at a time when they were being brutally marginalized by the hegemonic order in America.[46]

In developing a counter-hegemonic political/cultural project for African-Americans, Du Bois not only valorizes the contribution of Africans to America, as in *The Souls of Black Folk* (1903), but also inscribes Pan-Africanism in the cultural life of black America.[47] One utopianizing image of Africa that becomes crucial for Du Bois, as well as for a number of other African-American intellectuals in the early twentieth century, is that of Ethiopia. "For [Du Bois]," Eric Sundquist contends, " 'Ethiopia' was to become an uncolonized territory of the spirit, the black soul that had not been extinguished by slavery or colonial rule and that could never be fully assimilated to European American culture."[48] Thus, while Du Bois incorporates the historical Ethiopia into his work, the *Star of Ethiopia*, as a place in Africa that contributed to the development of civilization, the metaphorical Ethiopia conveys the double meaning of utopia as "no place" and the "good place."

Du Bois's literary efforts to articulate what Wilson Jeremiah Moses calls the "poetics of Ethiopianism," a messianic and millennial form of black nationalism with roots reaching back into the nineteenth century, is evident throughout Du Bois's writings in the first decades of the twentieth century.[49] In *The Souls of Black Folk*, Du Bois attempts to connect African-Americans to the past glories of Africa. Noting the "shadow of a mighty Negro flits through the tale of Ethiopia the Shadowy and of Egypt the Sphinx," Du Bois reminds his reader that the presently despised and debased "Negro" has been a significant contributor to the "kingdom of culture."[50] In *The Quest of the Silver Fleece*, Du Bois's first novel published in 1911, he merges classical Greek mythology with an aesthetic of black culture to render a heroine, Zora, who emerges as a representative of the genius of Ethiopianism (not unlike Reuel Briggs in *Of One Blood*). As part of the transfiguration of her genius, Du Bois notes that Zora's library contains Plato's *Republic*, thus underscoring the utopian aspirations in the novel and Du Bois's own elitist and anti-Booker T. Washington belief "that the good society must be led by the broadly educated."[51] While committed to such platonic leadership of the "talented tenth," Du Bois, nonetheless, nurtured a poetic and political longing for a revitalized Pan-Africanism embedded in the utopian aspirations of Ethiopianism.

In translating an original 1911 draft from a drama to the 1913 *Star of Ethiopia* Pageant, Du Bois offered a political/cultural project to his fellow African-Americans that embodied a clear sense of oppositional utopianizing. In order to realize such a project, Du Bois enlisted thousands of individuals and organizations—like the NAACP for whom he was the editor of its journal, *The Crisis*—to mount the Pageant in New York, Washington, and Philadelphia. Focusing on the centrality of the gifts bequeathed by Africa to the world, audiences were awakened to the voice of a herald in the Pageant to "learn the ancient Glory of Ethiopia, All-Mother of men, whose wonders men forgot. See how beneath the Mountains of the Moon, alike in the Valley of Father Nile and in ancient Negro-land and Atlantis, the Black Race ruled and strove and fought and sought the Star of Faith and Freedom, even as other races did and do."[52] While resurrecting a mythopoetical past for utopian purposes, Du Bois attempted to project a Pan-Africanist ideology that would counter the white supremacist dismissal of Africa as a critical component of civilization and culture.

Du Bois also intended to dramatize the historical significance of the African-American experience in the *Star of Ethiopia* for its redemptive and utopian promise. Thus, beyond the first three scenes which revel in the wonders and gifts that Africa contributes to civilization and culture from iron to religion, the Pageant's final scenes review the "humiliation" of and triumph over slavery. The Pageant ends with heralds announcing: "Hear ye, hear ye, men of all the Americas, ye who have listened to the tale of the eldest and strongest of the races of mankind, whose faces be black. Hear ye, hear ye, and forget not the gift of black men to this world—the Iron Gift and Gift of Faith, the Pain of Humility and Sorrow Song of Pain, the Gift of Freedom and Laughter and the undying Gift of Hope."[53] Clearly, Du Bois and his cohorts hoped to lift the spirits of a besieged African-American community through such a political/cultural project. Nonetheless, the expense of repeating such a pageant after its initial success in New York in 1913 led Du Bois to reinforce the message of hope embedded in the *Star of Ethiopia* in a 1915 report to the NAACP on the Pageant's costs. Du Bois noted: "I sympathized with the attitude of the Association in hesitating to make this venture, but I knew on the other hand the great educational value of pageantry for the colored people and I was convinced that the development of the dramatic talent and taste for the drama on the part of colored people lay the greatest present chance for education and social uplift in general lines."[54]

The *Star of Ethiopia* Pageant certainly had a profound impact on black members of the audience as well as on those whites who attended the various productions. One African-American viewer of the Washington 1915 presentation commented on how "intensely interesting, instructive and inspiring" the pageant was, further noting that "[a]ll colored Washington and thousands of white people are thinking and talking about 'The Pageant.' "[55] Among the white audience members in Washington was Louis Post, then Assistant Secretary of the Department of Labor in the Woodrow Wilson administration. Post contended that he "was profoundly impressed with the pageant for both its dramatic qualities and as an educational force."[56] Ironically, at almost the exact time that the *Star of Ethiopia* Pageant was being mounted in Washington to the praise of one of the most liberal members of the Wilson administration, President Wilson and his conservative southern allies in the White House were promulgating additional segregation measures in the nation's capital and lauding the premiere of the racist D. W. Griffith film *The Birth of a Nation*.[57] In effect, the drama and pageantry of the *Star of Ethiopia* could be assimilated by well-meaning whites without any consideration of its oppositional utopianizing for blacks.

On the other hand, Du Bois and many of his African-American allies were conflicted about the ultimate meaning of such oppositional utopianizing, especially in terms of the effect of the ideology of race nationalism as a counter-hegemonic project. Wanting to effectuate the transvaluation of race from a vertical to a horizontal axis, thus eliminating the hierarchical arrangement of races that dominated the cultural hegemony of the white Western World during this period, Du Bois could not escape the very contradictions of race that assigned inferior and superior categories.[58] Eventually siding with the Wilson administration in its utopian mission to "make the world safe for democracy," Du Bois saw his efforts at constructing a counter-hegemonic political/cultural project swallowed up by the war effort and then surpassed in the 1920s by the exclusivist nationalist ideology of Marcus Garvey and the Universal Negro Improvement Association.[59] Thus, the elitist and internationalist elements of Du Bois's Pan-African and reformist politics, combined with the patriotic fervor in wartime America, undermined the efforts to construct such a counter-hegemonic political/cultural project.

While *The Star of Ethiopia* and Paterson Pageants had a shining moment as oppositional utopianizing in pre–World War I America, that moment faded into the awful political pageantry of the war and its reactionary aftermath in America. In effect, the difficulties encountered in translating the oppositional utopianizing of a political/cultural project into a counter-hegemonic social praxis were overwhelmed by the ability of the hegemonic order to either mobilize integrative utopianizing or suppress oppositional utopianizing in World War I.[60]

Beyond the transitory historical moment of oppositional utopianizing represented in the Paterson and *Star of Ethiopia* Pageants lies the larger question of the difficulties inherent in institutionalizing a counter-hegemonic political/cultural project. Even as oppositional utopianizing strains to free itself in its transcendent moments from the bonds of the hegemonic order, it can never escape completely the taint of that order. However imaginative the social dreaming of utopianism is, it must always contend with the nightmare of history. In effect, along with Raymond Williams, one must acknowledge "that all or nearly all initiatives and contributions, even when they take on manifestly alternative or oppositional forms, are in practice tied to the hegemonic: that the dominant culture, so to say, at once produces and limits its own forms of counter-culture."[61] Yet, in giving fundamental expression to the social desire for a better life, the hope embodied in the oppositional utopianizing of political/cultural projects like the Paterson and *Star of Ethiopia* Pageants forever raises the specter of alternative and oppositional ideals and practices.

NOTES

1. Lyman Tower Sargent, "The Three Faces of Utopianism Revisited," *Utopian Studies* 5 (1994): 1–37.

2. Ruth Levitas, *The Concept of Utopia* (Syracuse: Syracuse University Press, 1990).

3. Ernst Bloch, *The Principle of Hope*, trans. Neville Plaice, Stephen Plaice, and Paul Knight (Oxford: Basil Blackwell, 1986). My understanding of Bloch and the function of utopianizing comes from Michael Gardiner, "Bakhtin's Carnival: Utopia as Critique," *Utopian Studies* 3 (1992): pp. 22–28, 35–37.

4. On the utopian moments of the Russian and Chinese revolutions see Richard Stites, *Revolutionary Dreams: Utopian Vision and the Experimental Life in the Russian Revolution* (New York: Oxford University Press, 1989); and Maurice Meisner, *Marxism, Maoism, and Utopianism* (Madison: University of Wisconsin Press, 1982). On the emancipatory moments for women during the Spanish Civil War and African-Americans during the black power struggle, see Martha A. Ackelsberg, *Free Women of Spain: Anarchism and the Struggle for the Emancipation of Women* (Bloomington: Indiana University Press, 1991); and William L. Van Deburg, *New Day in Babylon: The Black Power Movement and American Culture 1965-1975* (Chicago: University of Chicago Press, 1992).

5. Gardiner, "Bakhtin's Carnival," p. 27. For further explorations of that dialectical tension between ideology and utopia, see Paul Ricoeur, *Lectures on Ideology and Utopia*, ed. G. Taylor (New York: Columbia University Press, 1986); and Fredric Jameson, *The Political Unconscious: Narrative as a Socially Symbolic Act* (Ithaca: Cornell University Press, 1981).

6. While the primary theoretical work on hegemony comes from Gramsci, my understanding of hegemonic structuring derives from two critical interpretations of Gramsci's concept. See Raymond Williams, *Marxism and Literature* (Oxford: Oxford University Press, 1977), esp. 110, 118–19; and T. J. Jackson Lears, "The Concept of Cultural Hegemony: Problems and Possibilities," *The American Historical Review* 90 (June 1985): 567–93.

7. My understanding of oppositional and normative functions owes much to Gardiner, "Bakhtin's Carnival," pp. 23–24, and Williams, *Marxism and Literature*, esp. p. 113.

8. On the ritualization and performance of social dramas, see Victor Turner, *Dramas, Fields, and Metaphors: Symbolic Interaction in Human Society* (Ithaca, N.Y.: Cornell University Press, 1974), and Turner, *The Anthropology of Performance* (New York: PAJ Publications, 1986). On the emergence of pageantry during the Progressive Era, see David Glassberg,

American Historical Pageantry: The Uses of Tradition in the Early Twentieth Century (Chapel Hill: University of North Carolina Press, 1990).

9. Steve Golin, *The Fragile Bridge: Paterson Silk Strike, 1913* (Philadelphia: Temple University Press, 1988), p. 177.

10. David Levering Lewis, *W.E.B. Du Bois: Biography of a Race, 1868–1919* (New York: Henry Holt, 1993), p. 461. On the levels of virulent racism at the turn of the century, especially in the South, see, for example, Joel Williamson, *A Rage for Order: Black-White Relations in the American South Since Emancipation* (New York: Oxford University Press, 1986).

11. Glassberg, *American Historical Pageantry*, p. 52. On Anglo-conformity, see Milton Gordon, *Assimilation in America* (New York: Oxford University Press, 1964), pp. 88–114.

12. Ibid., pp. 63–64, 107–13. Also see Martin Green, *New York 1913: The Armory Show and the Paterson Strike Pageant* (New York: Charles Scribner's, 1988), esp. pp. 162–64.

13. Hapgood quoted in Golin, *The Fragile Bridge*, p. 164.

14. Hapgood, *A Victorian in the Modern World* (New York: Harcourt, Brace, 1939), pp. 351–52.

15. Glassberg, *American Historical Pageantry*, p. 5.

16. For a complete overview of the class and ethnic forces in Paterson and the resultant silk strike of 1913, see Golin, *The Fragile Bridge*; on the Paterson Pageant's connection to the labor strife in Paterson, see pp. 157–78. Also see Glassberg, *American Historical Pageantry*, esp. p. 128; and Green, *New York 1913*, esp. pp. 195–215.

17. Quoted in Golin, *The Fragile Bridge*, p. 175.

18. Ibid.

19. Quoted in Melvyn Dubofsky, *We Shall Be All: A History of the IWW* (New York: Quadrangle, 1973), p. 81.

20. Salvatore Salerno, *Red November/Black November: Culture and Community in the Industrial Workers of the World* (Albany: State University of New York Press, 1989), p. 41. On the relationship between the IWW and religious sects, see Donald E. Winters, Jr., *The Soul of the Wobblies: The IWW, Religion, and American Culture in the Progressive Era, 1905-1917* (Westport, Conn.: Greenwood Press, 1985), esp. pp. 90–91. On the IWW as a cadre organization, see William Preston, Jr., *Aliens and Dissenters: Federal Suppression of Radicals, 1903–1933* (New York: Harper Torchbooks, 1966), p. 43; and Robert L. Tyler, *Rebels of the Woods: The IWW in the Pacific Northwest* (Eugene: University of Oregon Press, 1967), p. 32. Dubofsky's attempt to interpret the IWW through the problematic application of Oscar Lewis's concept of the "culture of poverty" (which Dubofsky repudiated in his 1973 preface to the new edition of *We Shall Be All*, pp. v-vi) at least tried to understand the Wobblies as a collective response along the lines of a social movement. On the IWW as a social movement in opposition to the First World War, see Francis Shor, "The IWW and Oppositional Politics in WWI: Pushing the System Beyond Its Limits," *Radical History Review* 64 (Winter 1996): 74–94.

21. Haywood quoted in *Rebel Voices: An IWW Anthology*, ed. Joyce L. Kornbluh (Ann Arbor: University of Michigan Press, 1972), p. 50.

22. For a discussion of the mystical and redemptive qualities of the general strike, see Dubofsky, *We Shall Be All*, pp. 165–66; and Winters, *The Soul of the Wobblies*, p. 30. Salerno, *Red November/Black November*, pp. 101–105 and *passim*, emphasizes the connections to French syndicalist traditions in discussing the IWW idea of the general strike.

23. Quoted in Martin Green, *New York 1913*, p. 199.

24. Golin, *The Fragile Bridge*, p. 169; and Green, *New York 1913*, p. 203.

25. *Industrial Worker*, 12 June 1913, p. 1.

26. *Solidarity*, 14 June 1913, p. 3.

27. Ibid.

28. Quoted in *Rebel Voices*, p. 212.

29. Quoted in Golin, *The Fragile Bridge*, p. 169.

30. For an overview of Reed's role in the Paterson strike and Pageant, see Robert A. Rosenstone, *Romantic Revolutionary: A Biography of John Reed* (New York: Alfred A. Knopf, 1975), pp. 117–32.

31. Quoted in Arthur Frank Wertheim, *The New York Little Renaissance: Iconoclasm, Modernism, and Nationalism in American Culture, 1908–1917* (New York: New York University Press, 1976), p. 50.

32. Mable Dodge Luhan, *Movers and Shakers* (Albuquerque: University of New Mexico Press, 1985), p. 188. For an overview of Mabel Dodge Luhan and her role as a "new radical," see Christopher Lasch, *The New Radicalism in America, 1889–1963: The Intellectual as a Social Type* (New York: Vintage, 1967), pp. 104–40.

33. Golin, *The Fragile Bridge*, p. 161.

34. Linda Nochlin quoted in ibid., p. 163.

35. Quoted in Martin Green, *New York 1913*, p. 201.

36. Quoted in Golin, *The Fragile Bridge*, p. 166.

37. Luhan, *Movers and Shakers*, p. 204.

38. Nochlin quoted in Golin, *The Fragile Bridge*, p. 165.

39. Quoted in ibid.

40. Gramsci's discussion of the historic bloc and hegemony can be found scattered throughout his prison notebooks. See Antonio Gramsci, *Selections from the Prison Notebooks*, trans. and ed. Quintin Hoare and Geoffrey Nowell Smith (New York: International Publishers, 1971). For a relevant interpretation of Gramsci, see Walter L. Adamson, *Hegemony and Revolution: A Study of Antonio Gramsci's Political and Social Theory* (Berkeley: University of California Press, 1980). On the application of Gramsci's concepts to movements for radical change, see Ernesto Laclau and Chantal Mouffe, *Hegemony and Socialist Strategy: Towards a Radical Democratic Politics*, trans. Winston Moore and Paul Cammack (London: Verso, 1985).

41. On the impact of World War I on American society and dissident thought, see Walter Karp, *The Politics of War* (New York: Harper and Row, 1979); David M. Kennedy, *Over Here: The First World War and American Society* (New York: Oxford University Press, 1980); and H. C. Peterson and Gilbert C. Fite, *Opponents of War, 1917–1918* (Seattle: University of Washington Press, 1957). On state repression against the IWW, see Dubofsky,

We Shall Be All, pp. 349–444; Preston, *Aliens and Dissenters*, pp. 88–151; and Shor, "The IWW and Oppositional Politics in World War I."

42. Keith E. Byerman, *Seizing the Word: History, Art, and Self in the Work of W.E.B. Du Bois* (Athens: University of Georgia Press, 1994), p. 15.

43. Eric Sundquist, *To Wake the Nations: Race in the Making of American Literature* (Cambridge, Mass.: Belknap Press of Harvard University Press, 1993), p. 463.

44. Quoted in Kwame Anthony Appiah, *In My Father's House: Africa in the Philosophy of Culture* (New York: Oxford University Press, 1992), p. 29.

45. On the role of desire in utopia, see Levitas, *The Concept of Utopia*. On the connections of hope to utopia, see Bloch, *The Principle of Hope*. On Du Bois's conception of race as "a mystical cosmic force," see Wilson Jeremiah Moses, *The Golden Age of Black Nationalism, 1850–1925* (New York: Oxford University Press, 1978), p. 133.

46. Appiah, *In My Father's House*, p. 30.

47. On *The Souls of Black Folk*, see Byerman, *Seizing the Word*, pp. 10–35; Lewis, *W.E.B. Du Bois*, pp. 277–96; and Sundquist, *To Wake the Nations*, pp. 457–539. On inscribing Africa in black culture, see Byerman, *Seizing the Word*, esp. pp. 81–99; and Sundquist, *To Wake the Nations*, pp. 540–625.

48. Sundquist, *To Wake the Nations*, pp. 559–60.

49. Moses, *The Golden Age of Black Nationalism*, pp. 156–69.

50. W.E.B. Du Bois, *The Souls of Black Folk* (Greenwich, Conn.: Fawcett Premier, 1961), p. 17.

51. Lewis, *W.E.B. Du Bois*, p. 450.

52. Quoted in Sundquist, *To Wake the Nations*, pp. 578–79.

53. *Creative Writings of W. E. B. Du Bois: A Pageant, Poems, Short Stories, and Playlets*, comp. and ed. Herbert Aptheker (White Plains, N.Y.: Kraus-Thomson Organization, 1985), pp. 4–5.

54. Du Bois, *Pamphlets and Leaflets by W.E.B. Du Bois*, comp. and ed. Herbert Aptheker (White Plains, N.Y.: Kraus-Thompson Organization, 1986), p. 151.

55. Ibid., p. 104.

56. Ibid.

57. Lewis, *W.E.B. Du Bois*, pp. 506–10.

58. Appiah, *In My Father's House*, p. 46.

59. On Garvey's nationalism and its impact among African-Americans, see, for example, Tony Martin, *Race First: The Ideology and Organizational Struggles of Marcus Garvey and the Universal Negro Improvement Association* (Westport, Conn.: Greenwood Press, 1976); and Moses, *The Golden Age of Black Nationalism*, esp. pp. 262–69.

60. See, for example, Karp, *The Politics of War*; and Kennedy, *Over Here*.

61. Williams, *Marxism and Literature*, p. 114.

8

From Socialist Colony to Socialist City: The Llano del Rio Utopian Experiment in California

In the "Prologue" to *City of Quartz*, Mike Davis's brilliant excavation of the social and political geography of contemporary Los Angeles, he situates the analysis of the present in one of the shards of the past. Positioning himself on the "ruins of [Los Angeles's] alternative future," he describes the founding and development of the Llano del Rio utopian experiment, a socialist colony some fifty miles away from Los Angeles in the Antelope Valley northeast of the San Gabriel mountains that managed to attract much attention in its brief existence from 1914 to 1918.[1] Traveling to the ruins of the Llano del Rio colony on May Day, a day celebrated for three exuberant years at Llano, he discovers two young Salvadorean laborers camping out on the former site of a "*ciudad socialista.*" When he is queried by one of them whether "rich people had come with planes and bombed them out," he responds by saying that "the colony's credit had failed." To which, Davis notes, "[they] looked baffled and changed the subject."[2]

Coming from a country that had recently suffered horrendous violence mostly imposed from above by a military dictatorship and wealthy elite, these young men from El Salvador would naturally be confused about the peaceful demise of a socialist colony. Yet, Davis's simple explanation conceals a more complicated story about internal divisions and institutional constraints. To tell the complete story

of the Llano del Rio utopian experiment in California requires not
only reconstructing the conditions that led to the development of
this particular socialist colony but also interrogating the multiple
meanings of socialism and utopianism as oppositional or alternative
practices, especially in the California and Los Angeles contexts.

It should comes as no surprise that the white settlement of
California in the late nineteenth century was intimately bound up
with utopian dreams and aspirations, whether in the form of
get-rich-quick schemes or seeking refuge from the cold and dark
climes of the midwest. In fact, according to California historian
Kevin Starr, "Southern California developed in the 1870–1890
period as a confederation of transitional colonies, each with a
quasi-utopian impulse."[3] On the other hand, the degree to which
such utopian ventures were actual alternatives to the dominant
society, embodying oppositional politics and culture, is a measure
of the framing of counter-hegemonic practices.[4] While California did
have an inordinate number of utopian colonies in the late nineteenth
and early twentieth centuries, how those colonies attempted to
fashion their collective identities and activities says much about the
difficulty of separating from hegemonic ideologies and institutions.[5]
The focus of this chapter will be to determine the nature and degree
of oppositional politics and culture embodied in the Llano del Rio
utopian experiment in Southern California, especially in the socialism represented by Llano and its colonists.

The roots of Llano's and Southern California's socialism go back
to the 1880s and the curious blend of Protestant millenialism, racial
exclusionism, particularly vis-à-vis Asians, and populism that took
hold first in Northern California in the San Francisco Bay area. One
of the leading firebrands behind the emergence of this brand of
California socialism was Burnette Haskell, a founder also of a
utopian colony called the Kaweah Co-operative Commonwealth.[6] It
was the idea of the "co-operative commonwealth" in both a populist
and a hazy socialist aura that attracted middle class intellectuals
like Haskell and working class activists.

Haskell would also become instrumental in establishing one of
the first of many Nationalist Clubs in California, anticipating in
many respects the early trajectory of numerous California socialists,
including the founder of Llano, Job Harriman. "Nationalism," according to Kevin Starr, "followed by Populism, created an ambi-
ence—in Southern California especially—in which a middle class
Protestant community which had come to California out of incipi-
ently utopian motivations in the first place found it perfectly natural,
once there, to dream of shaping a public polity that would more
completely express its collective desire for a better life."[7] In many

respects, Nationalism in California demonstrated that middle class native-born Americans could be won over to a form of socialism as long as it did not conjure up class conflict. As the California journal *Overland Monthly*, commented in 1890, the Nationalist movement "put a silk hat on socialism."[8]

Nationalism also put a fancy bonnet on socialism because of the role of women activists in California in the establishment of the large numbers of Nationalist clubs, including the first Los Angeles chapter. From there such women activists as Caroline Severance brought other ideological strands, for example, Christian Socialism, into the heady mix that became the springboard into the more self-conscious socialism represented by the founding of the Women's Socialist League in 1901 in Los Angeles.[9] One well-to-do Southern California matron was drawn to socialism in the early twentieth century because, as she explained, "I brooded over the tragic contrast of the sorrows of the poor and the luxuries of the rich. Those who had created everything had nothing while those who had everything created nothing."[10]

This moral outrage against the extremes of poverty and wealth in the late nineteenth and the early twentieth century fueled the admixture of native-born American radicalism with Marxism that resulted in the socialism of this period. Representative of this mix was an Indiana born ex-minister named Job Harriman. Moving to San Francisco in 1886, Harriman began a career in law and socialist politics that would gain him national prominence as well as a loyal California following.[11] Starting out in the Nationalist movement in San Francisco, Harriman soon moved to Los Angeles in 1895 and to the Socialist Labor Party where, in the words of one contemporary commentator, "he made the party a dynamic reform movement during the years 1895–1900."[12] As the Socialist Labor Party candidate for governor of California in 1898, he garnered only 5,143 votes of 287,064 cast. This poor showing may have convinced Harriman that the SLP antagonism to the mainstream trade union movement should be reconsidered. So, in league with the New York SLPer Morris Hillquit, Harriman took part in the faction of the party that promoted closer ties to the labor movement and bolted to help form the Socialist Party. Becoming the vice-presidential candidate in the 1900 election with Eugene Debs at the head of the ticket, Harriman undertook a role as a leading articulator of the political vision of socialism.[13]

For Harriman that political vision of socialism was rooted in a "constructive" socialist politics that opposed the "impossibilism" of immediate revolution by fighting for immediate reforms.[14] In effect, Harriman shared with Hillquit and Victor Berger of the center-right of the Socialist Party a belief in finding ways to transform and thus transcend capitalism.[15] For Harriman, one of the key components in transforming capitalism was to build bridges to the mainstream trade-union movement and, at certain critical junctures, to fuse with the efforts of labor in formulating its own party. With the emergence of a Union Labor Party in California in 1902, Harriman found himself at odds with the National Executive element of the Socialist Party and local left members of the party. (This would have later repercussions at Llano.) Expelled from the Socialist Party in 1903, Harriman wrote in the *Los Angeles Socialist*: "Many members of the Socialist party seem to think that the labor movement with all its economic and political tendencies, is the outgrowth of the science of Socialism, but the fact is that the outgrowth of the science of Socialism is merely the expression of and a deduction from the labor movement and the present economic development."[16]

After this failure of labor-socialist fusion and his subsequent early retirement from the Socialist Party, Harriman, along with his wife and son, sought refuge in rural California. Reminiscent of a later personal and political defeat in the mayoral race of Los Angeles, Harriman moved first to a farm at the margin of the Imperial Valley. Increasingly ill with the tuberculosis that plagued him throughout his life, Harriman uprooted his family and headed to Arizona and then Colorado to recover. Barely able to survive economically, Harriman eventually returned to Los Angeles at the beginning of 1905. Again plunging into the labor and socialist politics of Los Angeles, Harriman once more reiterated his belief in a fusion of labor and socialism. As a consequence of a metal workers' strike and the fight against a corporate-sponsored anti-picketing ordinance in 1910, Harriman saw the realization of this fusion and it catapulted him into a historic mayoral race.[17]

In the midst of labor-management battles in Los Angeles and the emergent labor-socialist political campaign, an explosion ripped through the *Los Angeles Times* building, killing twenty and injuring scores of others and sending the conservative owner and publisher of the *Times*, Harrison Gray Otis, into an even more vitriolic tirade against unions and their radical allies. When James B. and John J. McNamara, iron worker unionists from the midwest, were charged with the bombing of the *Times* building in April 1911 (after their arrest and kidnapping by the notorious detective William J. Burns), their case became the defining issue of the mayoral campaign. Although Harriman was their initial attorney, Clarence Darrow was soon enlisted by the AFL to defend two of its staunch members. After Harriman's victory in the fall 1911 primary (along with the passage of amendments for woman suffrage and referendum and recall), the hysteria from Otis and the business community in Los Angeles over a prospective socialist mayor reached new heights of paranoid viciousness. Desperate to stop a Harriman victory, an election-eve guilty confession by the McNamara brothers was engineered that effectively derailed what appeared to be the certainty of a socialist mayor for Los Angeles.[18]

While Harriman was obviously shattered by the last-minute machinations in the mayoral campaign of 1911, he did not absent himself from the ongoing electoral struggle. Returning as the Socialist Party standard bearer in the 1913 Los Angeles mayoral election, Harriman just narrowly failed to make it through the primary, although three socialists, including a woman, were elected to the city council. Nevertheless, Harriman's focus for the realization of socialism was turning from the electoral arena to a colonization plan. As he later wrote: "A wide difference of opinion had heretofore existed among Socialists concerning the feasibility of all colonization enterprises. . . . Some Socialists have insisted that the powers of government must be captured before any far-reaching, practical steps could be taken in the economic field, while others were equally confident that cooperative, economic development must be conducted by the workers within the capitalist system."[19] In notes that he prepared in 1924 concerning the Llano experiment in California, Harriman asserted: "I was so impressed with the fact that the movement must have an economic foundation that I turned my attention to the study of means by which we could lay some foundation, even tho [sic] it be a small one as well as an experimental one. . . . I assumed that if a co-operative colony could be established in which an environment were created that would afford each individual an equal and social advantage, that they would, in a comparatively short time, react harmoniously to this environment."[20]

During 1913 and early 1914, Harriman recruited a number of his closest comrades in Los Angeles involved in the trade union movement, Bert Engle of the Central Labor Council and Frank McMahon of the Bricklayers Union, and labor journalist Frank E. Wolfe, to solicit financial backing and logistical support for a socialist colony. According to the stenographer later hired for the Llano Colony office in Los Angeles, Mellie Calvert, "[Harriman] thought that a cooperative colony could build socialism within capitalism."[21] Harriman also knew that he needed capitalist backing to underwrite the purchase of essential land and water rights. Seeking out a Christian Socialist banker in Corona, California, whose letter in the *Appeal to Reason* had attracted his attention, Harriman appealed to Gentry P. McCorkle for financial support. While helpful to the initial efforts at starting up the Llano Colony in 1914, McCorkle's financial dealings led to financial disaster for Llano near its end.[22]

With McCorkle's financial aid and the help of his socialist associates, Harriman took over the Mescal Water and Land Company with its extensive water and land holdings in the Antelope Valley near the headwaters of Big Rock Creek and turned it into the Llano del Rio Company, a joint stock corporation. Incorporated under the laws of California, this socialist venture was opened for business to anyone who could purchase up to, but no more than, two thousand shares, the initial purchase being five hundred shares at $500. Announcing the venture in *The Western Comrade*, a monthly socialist journal acquired in June 1914 by Harriman and Wolfe, Harriman laid out the business rationale and utopian goals as "incorporat[ing] in such a way as to insure to the stockholders and their families all the freedom, independence, character building influences, and other natural advantages of country life, combined with the most modern facilities for their education, entertainment, comfort and care."[23] Stressing that Llano was not a "co-operative colony, but a corporation, conducted upon the lines of ordinary private corporations,"[24] Harriman obviously took pains to protect the experiment from being hounded to death by his corporate enemies in the business community of Los Angeles. Nonetheless, Harriman's insistence on the nonsocialist aspects of Llano protected the colony neither from the scrutiny and opprobrium of the *Los Angeles Times* nor from internal divisions that developed over the lack of socialist democracy in the colony.

Harriman's attempts to frame the Llano experiment as a modest business venture that would allow for the comfort and care of stockholders and their families were countered in the very same issue of *The Western Comrade* by Bert Engle's boosterism. Under the heading of "Co-operative Colony Plans in Action," Engle enthusiastically noted that beyond the egalitarian wages, Llano would soon be home to "the greatest vocational school in America." Furthermore, Engle cited plans that "contemplate a city of greater beauty than any on the American continent."[25] Further elaborating on Engle's vision of the future socialist city, Frank Wolfe avowed: "There, on the upper table of the grand mesa, will grow a co-operative city of marvelous beauty, if the dreams of strong men and women, who are pioneering this enterprise, can be made to unfold into reality."[26]

Transforming a joint stock venture into a socialist colony and eventually into a socialist city was, indeed, a compelling vision shared by the founders of Llano del Rio. The difficulties in that transformation were apparent not only in the kind of overreaching optimism and boosterism promulgated by Engle and Wolfe and shared by socialists and capitalists alike, especially in the ever-expanding settlements of Southern California, but also in the hardship of sustaining a socialist community in the midst of the limit-situations of water rights, democratic and productive work and living arrangements, and wartime boom and repression. In tracing the developments within and outside the Llano del Rio experiment in California, one is invariably confronted with the contradictions between the rhetoric and the reality and the hopes and the fears of the colonists. From the recruitment of members to the political dissent within the colony, Llano wrestled with the meaning of its socialism. From the enactment of social and cultural practices to the vision of the future city, Llano presented an experiment in practical and wishful utopianism that was ultimately overwhelmed by both internal contradictions and external constraints.

On the other hand, Llano was able to attract willing and eager members as a consequence of Harriman's following, boosterism and sales pitches, and inviting promises of good wages and living conditions. The first few colonists to arrive when Llano opened for business on May Day in 1914 were dedicated socialists from the Young People's Socialist League. Finding little beyond a single standing building, which became the hub of Llano activities from General Assembly Meetings to evening dances, canvas tents were pitched as temporary housing. With the promise of $4-a-day wages (of which $1 went toward purchasing the remaining shares and the rest went into supplies), Llano lured workers whose daily wage in the open-shop atmosphere of Los Angeles was well below that standard. By the end of the year, Llano had around 150 resident colonists and many other interested buyers.[27]

One reason for the swelling numbers and the increasing amount of buyers was the employment by the Llano Company of a stock agent, C. V. Eggleston. Eggleston's sales techniques were part and parcel of getting money for capitalization of the colony, and he pursued his task more as a salesman than a socialist ideologue. According to one of the members of Llano, Walter Millsap, Eggleston's short-lived role as stock agent created an atmosphere of unwarranted expectations by those who bought the sales pitch. Calling Eggleston's brief tenure a "colossal blunder," Millsap further noted that the "agent promised everything under the sun and heaven on earth if they'd sign on the dotted line and give him $500, why they could just live in paradise from then on."[28]

Although it might appear from such practices that Llano del Rio was open to anybody who could come up with $500, there were a number of application procedures that were intended to screen out potential problems. One application for membership averred: "Only men and women whose high ideals, industrious inclinations and record for sobriety are such as to qualify them as co-operators on principle are wanted in the Llano del Rio Colony." This membership form also asked for three good references, preferably from a union local president or secretary.[29] Apparently, another application form requested information that attempted to apply a socialist test for entrance. Such questions as "Do you believe in the profit system?" and "Will solving the economic problem ultimately lead to solving the social problem?" suggested that there may have been at one time an attempt to elicit a level of ideological commitment before admission to the colony.[30]

While ideology played a part in the recruitment and admission process, membership in this socialist colony was limited to "Caucasians." As a revised "Gateway to Freedom" proclaimed in a 1916 edition of *The Western Comrade*: "Only Caucasians are admitted. We have had applications from Negroes, Hindus, Mongolians and Malays. The rejection of these applications are [sic] not due to race prejudice but because it is not deemed expedient to mix the races in these communities."[31] Whether Llano del Rio Colony was being disingenuous about the racial exclusivity or merely reflecting the white supremacist biases that informed much of social practices of white Californians, irrespective of their political orientation, is unclear. While the Socialist Party of Southern California made overtures to African-Americans and other minorities, the general policy and attitudes of most white socialists, including those at Llano, manifested deep-rooted racist biases.[32]

If Llano succumbed to the ideological hegemony of racism, it tried mightily to overcome the individualism and competition that were integral components of that ideological hegemony. Harriman's socialist vision of Llano as dedicated to "equal ownership, equal wage, and equal social opportunities" was touted constantly in publications about the colony.[33] Moreover, Llano adopted a "Declaration of Principles" that stressed community rights over individual ones.[34] Yet the institutionalization of community prerogatives over individual ones caused friction within Llano and led to the most extensive split in the colony. Auguring that split was the following letter from George Heffner, one of several members of the first community commission, to Frank Wolfe, dated April 18, 1915: "Many of the members of the community have dropped their all in the common pot and seeing the mismanagement of last year, the unbusiness-like trading of autos, truck and trees, view with alarm the future of the enterprise."[35]

Dissent developed not only over the lack of commitment to communal ownership, but also over the democratic management of community affairs. Because of the Articles of Incorporation under which the Llano del Rio Company was founded, management consisted of a Board of Directors composed of Job Harriman as president and several absentee directors like McCorkle. The board appointed a superintendent to run the day-to-day affairs of the colony. As noted in *The Western Comrade*: "Upon entering the colony members are assigned to a department subject to transfer at the direction of the superintendent to six departments: agriculture, building and engineering, commerce, industry, education, and finance."[36] In turn, these department heads formed a Board of Managers. Colonists who resisted assignments or what they construed as authoritarian or capricious work rules or sought more control over the Board of Managers and Directors soon developed into a dissenting faction known as the "Brush Gang" or who "Welfare League."[37]

Along with resistance to the management of Llano, members of the Brush Gang resented Harriman's leadership and the lack of commitment to what they regarded as socialist principles. One of the key players in the formation of the Brush Gang was Frank W. Miller, a former Oklahoma farmer and Sooner Socialist. Miller's notebook of his early months in Llano during the first part of 1915 records, in particular, his antagonism to Harriman. Calling Harriman "Czar-like," Miller notes Harriman's efforts to supersede elected colony leadership.[38] Harriman's situation may have been complicated by the fact that he was then in the midst of defending another client charged in the so-called conspiracy to bomb the *Los Angeles Times*. What is clear from both Miller's notebooks and his wife's letters to their daughter Mellie is their alienation from Harriman and his loyalists. One such letter from Josephine Miller makes reference to the "Fresno gang" (former SLPers connected with Harriman) and the "Harriman clique."[39]

Beyond specific loyalties to Harriman, Brush Gang members like Frank Miller believed that the economic and political organization of Llano worked against the realization of socialism. In a letter dated November 21, 1915, Miller wrote to his daughter that the "Directors have thrown aside all ideas of this being a 'Socialist Colony.' "[40] When the Statement and Purpose of the Welfare League was issued on December 3, 1915, signed by 78 Llano members, it called for the realization of "ethical, democratic, and cooperative principles of socialism" through direct control over company affairs, jury trials before the General Assembly, and secret ballots for all colony elections.[41] In response, one of Harriman's supporters, R. K.

Williams, wrote in *The Western Comrade*: "Newcomers arrived here filled with idealism and notions of a weird form of democracy that are utterly out of place in an institution dealing with . . . practicalities. It must be insisted that if this colony is to exist we must follow the well tried and wrought out formulas of corporations organized under capitalism. . . . We are not attempting an Utopian phantasmagoria."[42]

At the core of the debate between the Brush Gang and the Harriman supporters was the degree of democracy to be exercised, especially by the General Assembly. Arguing that to "take the power of discharge from the boards' hands would be a bid for anarchy and chaos" and that an "organized central control is absolutely necessary in the present stage of evolution towards Socialism," Williams underscored the need for a form of authoritarian socialism, or, at least, one that would curtail the radical democracy envisioned by the Welfare League.[43] Because the General Assembly was the one forum where all voices could be heard, organized opposition took advantage of it. In turn, those close to Harriman found such cantankerous dissent deliberately disruptive. Ernest Wooster noted later that "the lack of personal responsibility on the part of members, and the frequent lack of knowledge of the subjects discussed made it rather a hotbed of politics, vindictiveness, rivalries, suspicion, and discord, rather than a democratic assembly."[44] There were even some, like Williams, who believed that organized democratic dissent represented a deliberate effort by spies and provocateurs.[45]

There certainly was some reason to believe that external forces were out to wreck Llano. After the mid-1915 ouster of the Llano commission by Harriman supporters, the *Los Angeles Times* began a steady drumbeat of stories with such headlines as "Red Utopians Are Disgusted" and "New Wail from Reds' Utopia."[46] When McCorkle's financial arrangements were called into question in the summer of 1915, appeals were made by disgruntled colonists to the newly formed California State Commission of Corporations. After visits from the Deputy State Commissioner, a report was released which called Llano "an autocracy ruled by Job Harriman," noting that "the right to protest is practically denied the colonists under the penalty of dismissal."[47] In the aftermath of these attacks, Harriman felt justified in criticizing the Welfare League in a January 1916 stockholders meeting and taking the initiative to transfer all the Llano stock to a Nevada holding company. Several Brush Gang members were expelled from the colony and lost all their holdings in the legal move to Nevada.[48]

Even with these internal squabbles and external pressures, Llano was able to grow. By the summer of 1916, *The Western Comrade* (now moved into the colony's own print shop) listed a raft of industrial and agricultural activities from a paint shop to a lime kiln and a saw mill, from poultry yards to a rabbitry, and a fish hatchery. In the same issue R. K. Williams took the reader on "A Trip Over the Llano," noting the extensive alfalfa fields, fruit orchards, and dairy herds.[49] With all of this development, Llano was able to supply almost three-quarters of its provisions (driving for the rest the twenty miles or so to the nearest railroad depot town of Palmdale). With a population soon to increase to its maximum size in 1917 of one thousand, *The Western Comrade* clearly knew the answer to its rhetorical question: "Do you think Llano is thriving?"[50]

Of particular import to the Llano colonists and a measure of its well-being was the investment in its educational facilities. Education was, of course, an integral component of all utopian colonies, whether secular or religious, anarchist or socialist.[51] At Llano, two educational innovations, the Montessori and Industrial schools, were the backbone for socialization of young people into the experiment in practical socialism. As early as September 1915, one could read in the pages of *The Western Comrade* about how Llano's opening of a second California Montessori school would put it on the educational map, as well as reinforcing the insight of the progressive pedagogue Friedrich Froebel "that the child is a self-active, self-determining being."[52] Assuming the leadership for the Montessori school at Llano, Prudence Stokes Brown took charge of little ones, age 2½ to 6, first at a ranch and then at a schoolhouse and expounded on the Montessori method in the pages of *The Western Comrade*. Lauding the Montessori method as learning by "DOING" and "DISCOVERING," she oversaw a veritable minor industry at Llano.[53]

Even more integral to the educational and industrial development at Llano was the Industrial School or Kids' Colony. In this school children, under the guidance of George and Minnie Pickett, did practical work, including raising their own livestock and building their own facilities. As indicated in one of Llano's self-promotional publications, the boys at the Industrial School "have their managers of departments, make their own laws, try their own culprits, and acquire a sense of responsibility. . . . Boys who have seemed to be incorrigible have been transformed into loveable, tractable, good natured workers."[54] Girls would appear to have been made even more tractable workers by channeling them into the "domestic science department," thus reinforcing the gender division of labor which was particularly pronounced at Llano.[55]

Yet Llano attempted to create a cultural environment that incorporated all of the colonists into daily and special rituals. From the first full year of the colony's existence, May Day proved to be a time when the red banners were rolled out, the resident band struck up "The Red Flag," and the whole community marched, sang, and danced.[56] Establishing every kind of recreational club from the Women's Study Club to a "Live Wire Dramatic Club" to an Rod and Gun Club, Llano colonists were thoroughly engaged with the cultural life of their community.[57] Of special interest to all were the Thursday and Saturday night dances. One colonist waxed rhapsodic about these dances: "If Llano never offers or gives me more than the pleasure of attending these dances I shall feel repaid for all the effort I have made to become a member of this Colony."[58] Other recreational activities included a championship baseball team, a swimming pool, and tennis courts. In short, Llano provided an extensive cultural program for its members.

Although offering its members a wealth of activities to pursue, Llano did not escape either replicating the ideological hegemony in the dominant culture or enforcing strict Victorian codes of morality. A number of the weekend entertainment specials featured crude black-face minstrel shows.[59] Running throughout the minutes of the Llano Colony are notices of ordinances passed to exercise a measure of control over frowned-upon behavior. One ordinance was passed against the use of "smutty, obscene, or indecent language" where women and children congregate.[60] Several ordinances were promulgated dealing with the prohibition of liquor. Violating this prohibition, unless under a doctor's order, could result in the cancellation of the work contract and expulsion from the colony.[61] Llano thus wrestled with rules and regulations that made it seem little more than a mundane and mainstream WASP community, albeit with a slight socialist twist.

On the other hand, Llano colonists dreamed of a day when a new city would emerge from the growing colony. Noting that Llano del Rio on May Day 1916 was already a "city of hope, home of buoyant optimism," Ernest Wooster wrote about a "Vision City," built by socialist "pluck and energy."[62] Also mentioned in the same May issue of *The Western Comrade* was a reference to a Miss Austin as one of the designers of the future Llano.[63] In fact, Alice Constance Austin was to be the major force behind architectural plans for a socialist city, modeled after the Garden City visions of English utopian city-planner Ebenezer Howard and incorporating the feminist social and spatial designs of Charlotte Perkins Gilman.[64] From October 1916 to June 1917 Austin projected her vision of the socialist city in the pages of *The Western Comrade*. The general enthusiasm that surrounded her plans and the ultimate failure to realize the grandiose vision help explain both the utopian aspirations of Llano and its limitations.

Alice Constance Austin, a self-trained architect, had actually been employed as early as 1915 by Harriman to begin designing a socialist city. Revising an earlier plan submitted by Leonard Cooke that envisioned a city of up to ten thousand inhabitants, Austin's proposals soon became the focus of discussion in the expanding colony. "Nothing was more talked about among the hopeful colonists," notes one historian of Llano, "and nothing inspired more hope in the midst of adversity."[65] Such hope was reflected in an article in the October 1915 issue of *The Western Comrade*. "People now can realize that we intend to build a city," the writer exclaimed, "a model city in every way."[66] Of course, not all the colonists were convinced that this model was exactly what they had in mind for their place of residence. Referring to Austin's plan and the fact that she was not a stockholder, Josephine Miller noted that the individual homes allowed no place for a clothesline or woodshed. Her pronouncement on the housing arrangements left no doubt about her dissatisfaction: "I think it is perfectly hideous."[67]

Yet Austin's plans, rendered in models exhibited to Llano colonists and outlined in the pages of *The Western Comrade*, attempted to preserve the sanctity of the home within the larger socialist ideals of communal solidarity. The opening paragraph of her October 1916 article provides a key to understanding the balance she hoped to achieve through her adaptation of ideas in the architectural world and in the socialist discursive community. "The Socialist city should be beautiful, of course; it should be constructed on a definite plan, each feature having a vital relation to and complementing each other feature, thus illustrating in a concrete way the solidarity of the community; it should emphasize the fundamental principle of equal opportunity for all; and it should be the last word in the application of scientific discovery to the problems of every day life, putting every labor saving device at the service of every citizen."[68]

Austin's continual reference to labor-saving devices recalls the utopian visions informing both Bellamy's *Looking Backward* and the material feminists who inspired and followed Bellamy's ideas.[69] "Devices for minimizing the labor of housekeeping are an important part of the general conception of the Socialist city," she contended. "The frightfully wasteful process by which women throw away their time and strength and money in a continuous struggle to deal with a ridiculously haphazard equipment in the ordinary home is one of the great and useless extravagances of the present system." Envisioning centralized kitchens and laundries (paralleling Charlotte Perkins Gilman's own utopian propositions), Austin also managed to inscribe the use of electricity for "its thousand conveniences—lighting, heating, power for vacuum-cleaning and sewing machines, egg-beaters, irons, and who knows what devices the morrow may bring forth in this age of miracles."[70] Obviously, Austin believed that the socialist city would be on the cutting-edge of modern labor-saving devices.

Pursuing the notion of labor-saving devices, Austin wrote in another article in *The Western Comrade*: "It is a fundamental principle of the Socialist City to make the largest possible use of every mechanical means of saving labor. In Llano we expect to heat, light, and clean the city, cook, and run all our machinery, by electricity. In addition to these improvements which are being introduced everywhere, our city plan is based on a centralized underground delivery system, run by electricity, which will eliminate all surface transportation of parcels and commodities except such heavy and bulky articles as furniture and machinery." Although centralizing one form of transportation, Austin recognized that private automobiles would be the wave of the future, albeit envisioning them being "kept in community garages." She even proposed having a "race-course around the outside of the town . . . framed in foliage and supplied with permanent seating facilities."[71] In anticipating the significant and indeed compulsive role that the automobile would play in the future of Southern California, Austin seemed to be searching for a compromise between private and public uses of energy.

In her construction of the socialist city, she also committed herself to integrating work and leisure in an efficient manner while developing a variation of the greenbelt ideal that would find its way into New Deal city planning in the 1930s. Insisting that "garden cities are a great advance on former haphazard methods," Austin contended that "they have only been studied from the point of view of art and sanitation, not from efficiency."[72] Linking the idea of efficiency with situating industrial facilities in the socialist city, Austin incorporated factories into a vision of periphery and core that corresponded to the emergent planning sensibilities of socialists and nonsocialists alike. While her proposal to place an "outer circle" of factories on the rim of the socialist city reflected elements of Howard's Garden City, she insisted that the industrial occupations be available to all, even women and the infirm, in order to guarantee their productive involvement with the community.[73]

At the core of Austin's plans was the private house with its own garden. Built with a keen eye toward environmental conditions of the semi-arid region, Austin's private residences nonetheless had lots of shrubbery and flowers around them. Referring to the Mediterranean style then in vogue in Southern California, Austin hoped to make the home practical and beautiful.[74] Yet the home would also not be a prison for women. In Austin's feminist renderings she saw the home as "no longer . . . a Procrustean bed to which each feminine personality must be made to conform by whatever maiming or fatal spiritual or intellectual oppression, but a peaceful and beautiful environment in which she will have leisure to pursue her duties as wife and mother."[75] Inscribing motherhood into the home, Austin in effect neglected the very communal basis of child rearing that played a role already at Llano. On the other hand, recognizing the importance of home life to the Llano colonist, Austin hoped to remove the drudgery of the home. Reinforcing Austin's vision, a Llano colonist noted that "as the domestic drudgery is taken out of the home-life, the spiritual side of the home begins to develop in greater beauty. The mother loses the character of the cook, and becomes the comrade in harness with her husband."[76]

Whatever liberating possibilities were inscribed in Austin's utopian plans for the socialist city, the real limitations faced by the Llano colonists precluded realizing any of Austin's grandiose designs. As underscored by Dolores Hayden: "In Austin's proposals for a Socialist City one can find serious obstacles to realization: she planned large parks and gardens, knowing that the community did not have an adequate water supply, and she designed the extensive communal infrastructure knowing Llano lacked capital."[77] In actuality, while Austin was developing her models, a death-blow was being dealt to Llano in a lawsuit brought in July 1916 by local ranchers challenging Llano's water rights. On top of this, Llano's efforts to build a dam at Big Rock Creek were foiled when the California Commissioner of Corporations denied Llano's application with the stinging but prophetic rebuke: "Your people do not seem to have the necessary amount of experience and maybe the sums of money it will involve."[78] Nevertheless, Llano colonists and propagandists tried to keep the faith by asserting even as late as May 1917 that those "who contemplate joining us may rest assured as to the land and water problems."[79]

A problem, however, that the Llano colonists could not hide was one that plagued the especially fractious socialist movement—that of the effect of World War I and the United States involvement in the war. Although supporting the Socialist Party's antiwar position adopted at the April 1917 convention, Harriman and the Llano colonists were wary of the impact that conscription would have on the colony. The minutes of July 28, 1917, reflect a desire to "arrange for the exemption of men conscripted."[80] Llano's fear that the draft would drain the colony of its best and brightest was given voice in an article that appeared in *The Western Comrade* in September 1917. Cataloguing the important roles performed by those young men conscripted in the war effort, the article ended fatalistically with the comment that "in the face of the power of the government, we of Llano are helpless."[81]

Llano faced another crisis brought on by the war and that was the loss of labor. The minutes in the spring and summer of 1917 record scores of requests for permission to leave the colony. This loss of labor, in turn, prompted a group of women to sign a petition "to offer our assistance . . . to work in any Department where they can satisfactorily . . . replace the men." The board noted their "zeal" and informed the women that their "services would be most welcome during the season."[82] In effect, the less committed Llano men were being lured by the higher wages caused as a consequence of the war. Such a return to the outside world directly contradicted the claims of R. K. Williams in *The Western Comrade*: "Conditions are becoming so on the 'outside' that living is growing harder and harder and Llano offers about the only place of refuge and safety in the country."[83]

In fact, the refuge that Llano offered in California was about to undergo a final and fateful transformation. In the aftermath of the water and land rights difficulties, Harriman had begun to search out an alternative site for the colony. After months of looking around, Harriman found a location in a remote section of western Louisiana that he presented to the Llano colonists in the late summer of 1917. By fall of 1917 discussions had ensued about moving the whole operation to Louisiana. In November 1917, the front page of *The Western Comrade* headlined "Llano Invading Louisiana." Buried in the paper was notice that a "majority of Llano" would be transferred to Louisiana.[84] Although retaining a small contingent in California, this group suffered through the final financial machinations of McCorkle and additional legal maneuvering, eventually disbanding about the same time as *The Western Comrade* changed its name in May 1918 to the *Internationalist*, now located in Newllano, Louisiana.[85]

On the eve of his search for an alternate site and the entrance of the United States into the war, Job Harriman wrote about Llano as a "community of ideals." Averring that the "new system must be developed within the old," he maintained that Llano had "progressed from a 'utopian, chimerical idea' to a concrete practicality—from a dozen dreamers to a thousand determined doers." He then went on to pose a question that would concern him the rest of his life and trouble all of those pioneers who contemplated utopian experiments: "Can a new order of things be established in such a community out of which will grow a new social spirit?"[86] The year before his death in 1925, he wrote an introduction to a book on utopian communities written by his comrade and fellow Llano colonist Ernest Wooster. In it, Harriman asserted that the "ethical and spiritual quality . . . becomes of primary importance in community life."[87] It is the great tragedy of the Llano del Rio experiment in California that it never had the time or luxury to develop completely those very ethical and spiritual qualities that Harriman rightly saw as critical to building and sustaining utopian experiments.

On the other hand, the Llano del Rio experiment in California did manage to offer in a short time an alternative site for the construction of a socialist community, albeit not the "alternative future" posed by Mike Davis in his look back at Llano, or the oppositional socialist order yearned for by members of Llano's Brush Gang. While Llano was not even fully embraced by the very socialist and trade union movement that gave it its birth, it nonetheless endeavored to realize its own form of practical socialism and utopianism.[88] That Llano's socialist and utopian experiment was confounded by internal divisions and external pressures should not detract from the fact that it valiantly struggled to become a fully developed socialist city. That it failed is as much a commentary on the dilemmas of utopianism and radicalism in a reforming America as it is on the brief promise of an American socialism.

NOTES

1. Mike Davis, *City of Quartz: Excavating the Future of Los Angeles* (London: Verso, 1990), p. 3. The most complete accounts of the Llano del Rio colony can be found in Paul K. Conkin, *Two Paths to Utopia: The Hutterites and the Llano Colony* (Lincoln: University of Nebraska Press, 1964), pp. 103–85; Paul Greenstein, Nigey Lennon, and Lionel Rolfe, *Bread & Hyacinths: The Rise and Fall of Utopian Los Angeles* (Los Angeles: California Classics Books, 1992), pp. 85–128; Robert V. Hine, *California's Utopian Colonies* (San Marino, Calif.: Huntington Library, 1953), pp. 114–31; Paul Kagan, "Portrait of a California Utopia," *California Historical Quarterly* 51 (Summer 1972): 131–54; Yaacov Oved, *Two Hundred Years of American Communes* (New Brunswick, N.J.: Transaction Books, 1988), pp. 285–95; and Ernest S. Wooster, *Communities of the Past and Present* (Newllano, La.: Llano Colonist, 1924), pp. 117–27.

2. Davis, *City of Quartz*, p. 12.

3. Kevin Starr, *Inventing the Dream: California Through the Progressive Era* (New York: Oxford University Press, 1985), p. 46. For a portrait of the development of Southern California, see Carey McWilliams, *Southern California Country: An Island on the Land* (New York: Duell, Sloan and Pearce, 1946).

4. For a definition of framing, see Doug McAdam, John D. McCarthy, and Mayer N. Zald, eds., *Comparative Perspectives on Social Movements:*

Political Opportunities, Mobilizing Structures, and Cultural Framings (Cambridge: Cambridge University Press, 1996), p. 6. On the role of hegemony and counter-hegemony, see Raymond Williams, *Marxism and Literature* (Oxford: Oxford University Press, 1977), pp. 108–20.

5. On the claim of California's pre-eminence as a site of utopian colonies, see Hine, *California's Utopian Colonies*, pp. 6–7. On the difficulties for utopian experiments to separate from dominant hegemonic ideologies and institutions, see Carl J. Guarneri, "The Americanization of Utopia: Fourierism and the Dilemma of Utopian Dissent in the United States," *Utopian Studies* 5 (1994): 72–88.

6. For a critical evaluation of Haskell's socialism, see Bernard K. Johnpoll, *The Impossible Dream: The Rise and Demise of the American Left* (Westport, Conn.: Greenwood Press, 1981), pp. 180–204. For an overview of the Kaweah Co-operative Commonwealth, see Hine, *California's Utopian Colonies*, pp. 78–100; and Oved, *Two Hundred Years of American Communes*, pp. 233–46. On the anti-Chinese sentiments in California and the struggle of Asians to become accepted in America, see Alexander Saxton, *The Indispensable Enemy: Labor and the Anti-Chinese Movement in California* (Berkeley: University of California Press, 1971); and Ronald Takaki, *Strangers from a Different Shore: A History of Asian-Americans* (Boston: Little, Brown, 1989).

7. Starr, *Inventing the Dream*, p. 208.

8. Quoted in *ibid*. On Nationalism, populism, and early socialism in late nineteenth-century California, see Ralph Edward Shaffer, "Radicalism in California, 1869–1929," Ph.D. diss., University of California, Berkeley, 1962, pp. 74–126. On Nationalism making socialism "respectable," see Howard H. Quint, *The Forging of American Socialism: Origins of the Modern Movement* (Columbia: University of South Carolina Press, 1953), pp. 72–102. On the nature and development of the Nationalist movement throughout the United States, see Arthur Lipow, *Authoritarian Socialism in America: Edward Bellamy and the Nationalist Movement* (Berkeley: University of California Press, 1982).

9. Mari Jo Buhle, *Women and American Socialism, 1870–1920* (Urbana: University of Illinois Press, 1981), pp. 77–78, 119.

10. Quoted in Starr, *Inventing the Dream*, p. 213.

11. For the most complete biographical narrative of Harriman, covering his early life up to the founding of the Llano del Rio colony in 1914, see Greenstein et al., *Bread & Hyacinths*, pp. 17–25, 29–47, 62–84.

12. Quoted in Shaffer, "Radicalism in California," p. 130. On the Socialist Labor Party during this period, see Johnpoll, *The Impossible Dream*, pp. 249–72; and Quint, *The Forging of American Socialism*, pp. 142–74.

13. Greenstein et al., *Bread & Hyacinths*, pp. 32–35; and Hine, *California's Utopian Colonies*, pp. 115–16. On the birth of the Socialist Party from the SLP split and the short-lived Social Democracy, see Ira Kipnis, *The American Socialist Movement, 1897–1912* (New York: Columbia University Press, 1952), pp. 25–106; and Quint, *The Forging of American Socialism*, pp. 319–88.

14. On "constructive" or "step-at-a-time" socialism and its opposition to "impossibilism," see Kipnis, *The American Socialist Movement*, p. 154 and *passim*.

15. Robert Hyfler, *Prophets of the Left: American Socialist Thought in the Twentieth Century* (Westport, Conn.: Greenwood Press, 1984), p. 31. On the center-right of the Socialist Party in the first two decades of the twentieth century, see Kipnis, *The American Socialist Movement*, pp. 214–42.

16. Quoted in Greenstein et al., *Bread & Hyacinths*, p. 38. On Harriman's involvement with the Union Labor Party in Los Angeles and his consequent expulsion from the Socialist Party, see ibid., pp. 37–38; William M. Dick, *Labor and Socialism in America: The Gompers Era* (Port Washington, N.Y.: Kennikat Press, 1972), pp. 63–64; and Shaffer, "Radicalism in California," p. 157.

17. On Harriman's retreat to rural California, Arizona, and Colorado, see Greenstein et al., pp. 39–41. On Harriman's reminiscences of this period as it related to the labor-socialist fusion, see Wooster, *Communities of the Past and Present*, p. 118.

18. The story of the interconnections between the McNamara case and the mayoral campaign of Job Harriman is most completely discussed in Greenstein et al., *Bread & Hyacinths*, pp. 48–84; and Kipnis, *The American Socialist Movement*, pp. 348–57. For an inclusive, albeit highly charged, interpretation of the McNamara case, see Louis Adamic, *Dynamite: The Story of Class Violence in America*, rev. ed. (Gloucester, Mass.: Peter Smith, 1963), pp. 196–253.

19. Quoted in Greenstein et al., *Bread & Hyacinths*, p. 85.

20. Quoted in Wooster, *Communities of the Past and Present*, pp. 119–20.

21. Mellie Miller Calvert, "The Llano del Rio Cooperative Colony," manuscript, Llano del Rio Collection, Huntington Library, San Marino, California, p. 2.

22. The most complete description of McCorkle and his role at Llano can be found in Greenstein et al., *Bread & Hyacinths*, pp. 86–87, 120. For further criticism of McCorkle's financial duplicity, see Wooster, *Communities of the Past and Present*, pp. 127–28. For McCorkle's own side of his actions, see the excerpts from his autobiography in the uncatalogued files in the Llano Collection at the Huntington Library, San Marino, California.

23. Job Harriman, "The Gateway to Freedom," *Western Comrade* (June 1914): 6.

24. Ibid., p. 7.

25. *Western Comrade* (June 1914): 13.

26. Frank Wolfe, "Llano del Rio," *Western Comrade* (June 1914): 25.

27. Conkin, *Two Paths to Utopia*, p. 109; Davis, *City of Quartz*, p. 3; Greenstein et al. *Bread & Hyacinths*. The *Western Comrade* throughout this first year kept a running tab of the Llano's growth.

28. Quoted in Kagan, "Portrait of a California Utopia," p. 135. Further discussion of Eggleston's role as stock agent can be found in Hine, *California's Utopian Colonies*, p. 118.

29. Uncatalogued files, Llano del Rio Collection, Huntington Library, San Marino, California.

30. Kagan, "Portrait of a California Utopia," p. 134. On the relationship between commitment and utopian communities, see Rosabeth Moss Kanter, *Commitment and Community: Communes and Utopias in Sociological Perspective* (Cambridge, Mass.: Harvard University Press, 1977), esp. pp. 64–74.

31. *Western Comrade* (April 1916): 2.

32. On the racist beliefs informing the attitudes of white Southern Californians, see Starr, *Inventing the Dream*, pp. 89–92 and *passim*. On the position of the Socialist Party toward African-Americans and other minorities, especially Asians, see Sally M. Miller, *Race, Ethnicity, and Gender in Early Twentieth-Century American Socialism* (New York: Garland Publishing, 1996), pp. 33–44, 153–240.

33. Wooster, *Communities of the Past and Present*, p. 119.

34. See, for example, the "Declaration of Principles" in *Western Comrade* (August/September 1916): 3. Also, in the minutes of the General Assembly for April 30, 1915, there is a unanimous vote recorded for the following resolution: "The rights of the community shall be paramount over those of any individual" (Uncatalogued files, Llano del Rio Collection, Huntington Library, San Marino, California).

35. Uncatalogued files, Llano del Rio Collection, Huntington Library, San Marino, California.

36. *Western Comrade* (January/February 1915): 24.

37. The management organization of Llano and the development of the dissenting "Brush Gang" can be found in the following: Greenstein et al., *Bread & Hyacinths*, pp. 98–108; Hine, *California's Utopian Colonies*, pp. 122–24; and Oved, *Two Hundred Years of American Communes*, pp. 291–93.

38. Miller notebooks, pp. 4, 8, uncatalogued files, Llano del Rio Collection, Huntington Library, San Marino, California.

39. Josephine Miller to Millie Miller Calvert, September 4, 1915. Llano del Rio, uncatalogued files, Huntington Library, San Marino, California.

40. Uncatalogued files, Llano del Rio Collection, Huntington Library, San Marino, California.

41. Ibid. Further discussion of the Welfare League manifesto can be found in Greenstein et al., *Bread & Hyacinths*, p. 105.

42. *Western Comrade* (December 1915): 20.

43. Ibid., p. 21.

44. Wooster, *Communities of the Past and the Present*, p. 123.

45. R. K. Williams, *Western Comrade* (December 1915): 21. For a later charge that "the Llano project was invested with an army of stool pigeons, informers, and agents provocateurs," see McWilliams, *Southern California Country*, p. 286.

46. Greenstein et al., *Bread & Hyacinths*, p. 101–2.

47. *Los Angeles Record*, 8 January 1916, n.p. For other elements of this highly critical report, see Greenstein et al., *Bread & Hyacinths*, p. 102.

48. Josephine Miller letters of February 8 and 23, 1916, and Mellie Miller Calvert manuscript, p. 63. Uncatalogued files, Llano del Rio Collection, Huntington Library, San Marino, California. Further discussion of the Brush Gang demise can be found in Greenstein et al., *Bread & Hyacinths*, pp. 107–8.

49. *Western Comrade* (June/July 1916): 10–11, 22.

50. Ibid., p. 22.

51. Oved, *Two Hundred Years of American Communes*, pp. 393–402. On the role of education for socialists during this period, see Kenneth Teitelbaum, *Schooling for "Good Rebels": Socialist Education for Children in the United States, 1900–1920* (Philadelphia: Temple University Press, 1993). On anarchist educational endeavors during this time, see Paul Avrich, *The Modern School Movement: Anarchism and Education in the United States* (Princeton: Princeton University Press, 1980).

52. "Our Wonderful School," *Western Comrade* (September 1915): 21.

53. "Montessori—What It Achieves," *Western Comrade* (August 1917): 13.

54. Cited in Greenstein et al., *Bread & Hyacinths*, p. 114.

55. "What Llano Women Do," *Western Comrade* (June/July 1916): 24, 30. An earlier article offered advice to women coming to reside at Llano, including the following: "Don't forget the cookstove" "(How We Live at Llano," *Western Comrade* [October 1915]: 21).

56. *Western Comrade* (May 1915): 15, 18.

57. *Western Comrade* (May 1915): 16; (August 1915): 24; and (February 1917): 9.

58. R. K. Williams, "Llano—A Social Success," *Western Comrade* (February 1917): 8.

59. *Western Comrade* (April 1915): 18; and *Western Comrade* (December 1916): 18. One of Josephine Miller's letters referred to a minstrel show where the "girls did not blacken up" (Miller letter, October 3, 1915, uncatalogued files, Llano del Rio Collection, Huntington Library, San Marino, California). On the intricate relationship between minstrel shows and white working class audiences, see Eric Lott, *Love and Theft: Blackface Minstrelsy and the American Working Class* (New York: Oxford University Press, 1993).

60. May 7, 1915, minutes, uncatalogued files, Llano del Rio Collection, Huntington Library, San Marino, California.

61. April 30, 1915, minutes and June 21, 1917, minutes, uncatalogued files, Llano del Rio Collection, Huntington Library, San Marino, California.

62. Ernest Wooster, "What Two Years Have Wrought," *Western Comrade* (May 1916): 18.

63. R. K. Williams, "Co-operation at Llano," *Western Comrade* (May 1916): 20.

64. The most complete presentation of the role of Alice Constance Austin at Llano can be found in Dolores Hayden, *Seven American Utopias: The Architecture of Communitarian Socialism, 1790–1975* (Cambridge: MIT Press, 1976), pp. 288–317. On the role of Ebenezer Howard's utopian

urban planning, see Stanley Buder, *Visionaries and Planners: The Garden City Movement and the Modern Community* (New York: Oxford University Press, 1990). On Charlotte Perkins Gilman's social and spatial feminist designs, see Polly Wynn Allen, *Building Domestic Liberty: Charlotte Perkins Gilman's Architectural Feminism* (Amherst: University of Massachusetts Press, 1988).

65. Conkin, *Two Paths to Utopia*, p. 110. Also, see Hayden, *Seven American Utopias*, p. 300.

66. *Western Comrade* (October 1915): 19.

67. Josephine Miller letter, September 11, 1915, uncatalogued files, Llano del Rio Collection, Huntington Library, San Marino, California. For a brief overview of the positive and negative responses of Llano colonists to Austin's plans, see Hayden, *Seven American Utopias*, p. 308.

68. A. Constance Austin, "Building a Socialist City," *Western Comrade* (October 1916): 17. On the "City Beautiful" ideal as the reigning concept in American architecture, see Buder, *Visionaries and Planners*, p. 157.

69. For a discussion of the connections between Bellamy and the material feminists, see Dolores Hayden, *The Grand Domestic Revolution* (Cambridge: MIT Press, 1981), pp. 135–37 and *passim*.

70. A. Constance Austin, "The Socialist City," *Western Comrade* (June 1917): 14.

71. Ibid (January 1917): 26.

72. Ibid. (February 1917): 19.

73. Ibid. (April 1917): 25. On Howard's influence on Austin, see Hayden, *Seven American Utopias*, pp. 300–301. On the Garden City ideal and greenbelt communities in the United States, see Buder, *Visionaries and Planners*, pp. 157–80. On the cult of efficiency during the Progressive Era, see Samuel Haber, *Efficiency and Uplift: Scientific Management in the Progressive Era* (Chicago: University of Chicago Press, 1964).

74. Austin, "Building a Socialist City," *Western Comrade* (October 1916): 17, 26–27.

75. Austin, "Socialist City," *Western Comrade* (June 1917): 26.

76. Dr. John Dequer, "Our Homes," *Western Comrade* (January 1917): 27. On Austin's feminist housing designs, see Hayden, *Seven American Utopias*, p. 301.

77. Hayden, *Seven American Utopias*, p. 308.

78. Greenstein et al., *Bread & Hyacinths*, pp. 116–17.

79. Frank E. Wolfe, "Three Years of Achievement," *Western Comrade* (May 1917): 9.

80. July 28, 1917, minutes, uncatalogued files, Llano del Rio Collection, Huntington Library, San Marino, California. On the Socialist Party's fractious position on World War I, see James Weinstein, *The Decline of Socialism in America, 1912–1925* (New York: Monthly Review Press, 1967), pp. 119–76.

81. Myrtle Manana (Ernest Wooster), "Conscription—What It Means to Llano," *Western Comrade* (September 1917): n.p. Also see Greenstein et al., *Bread & Hyacinths*, pp. 118–19.

82. May 17, 1917, minutes, uncatalogued files, Llano del Rio Collection, Huntington Library, San Marino, California.

83. R. K. Williams, "Llano—Community of Progress," *Western Comrade* (July 1917): 6. On the labor drain at Llano and the attraction of the wartime boom economy, see Greenstein, et al., *Bread & Hyacinths*, p. 118; and Hine, *California's Utopian Colonies*, p. 173.

84. *Western Comrade* (November 1917): 6. The minutes of September 1, October 1, and November 1 are filled with the plans to move to Louisiana. Uncatalogued files, Llano del Rio Collection, Huntington Library, San Marino, California.

85. The story of the Louisiana transfer and Newllano can be found in its greatest detail in Conkin, *Two Paths to Utopia*, pp. 113–85; and Oved, *Two Hundred Years of American Communes*, pp. 295–308.

86. Job Harriman, "Llano—Community of Ideals," *Western Comrade* (March 1917): 8.

87. "Introduction," Wooster, *Communities of the Past and Present*, p. viii.

88. See Walter Millsap's bitter reflections on the failure of the socialist and trade union movement to support Llano del Rio. Cited in Oved, *Two Hundred Years of American Communes*, p. 461.

Conclusion: The Dilemmas of Utopianism and Radicalism in a Reforming America

"The American is most characteristically a reformer," argues cultural historian Warren Susman; and, while one may agree with Susman about "the persistence of reform," one must also acknowledge that the definition of what constitutes an American and the conditions under which the American engages in reform are, themselves, under constant reformulation.[1] It is precisely within the temporal context of that reformulation that multiple struggles over norms and values take place. To the extent that the goals of the reformer constitute a critique of the dominant order and a radicalization of certain common ideals such as liberty and equality, the struggle for the realization of those ideals becomes invested with utopianism. Utopianism, therefore, achieves a historical resonance at those exact moments when agents engaged in a willed transformation of reality seek to redress the imbalance between what is lacking and what they desire.[2]

As this book has attempted to demonstrate, the historical resonance of utopianism and radicalism in the literary expressions, political/cultural projects, and communal experiments of the period 1888–1918 was contingent upon residual and emergent patterns of thought and social practice. At times the residual and emergent patterns of thought and social practice offered alternative or oppositional formations that challenged the hegemonic order. At other points, those residual and emergent patterns of thought and social practice replicated elements of the hegemonic order. So, for example, as much as Job Harriman and the Llano colonists touted their innumerable examples of noncommercial culture available at Llano, the residues of white supremacism and male chauvinism were also evident throughout their cultural activities.[3] Thus, one dilemma of utopianism and radicalism in this period was over whether and how residual and emergent patterns of thought and practice would conform to or challenge the hegemonic order.

Against the backdrop of the economic crises of industrial capitalism and the loss of faith in the verities of republicanism in the late nineteenth century, utopian projects in politics, communal experiments, and literary utopias sought to revitalize American republicanism. Believing in progress while preserving their visions of the past, radicals and reformers like Edward Bellamy, Charlotte Perkins Gilman, Julius Wayland, and Norman Lermond spoke to different constituencies with utopian longings. While the medium was, at times, different, the message was the same: America and its inhabitants could only be redeemed by realizing the ideals of equality and harmony. Unfortunately, often embedded in the message was a presumption of racial exclusivity that compromised the egalitarian thrust of such residual republicanism.[4]

Another component of the residual trajectory of utopianism and radicalism in the late nineteenth and early twentieth century was evangelical Protestantism. Beyond the ideology of the social gospel, evangelical Protestantism was often deployed to arouse moral outrage whether in the writings of African-Americans like Sutton Griggs and Pauline Hopkins or of old-stock Americans like Bellamy, Gilman, Wayland, and Frances Willard. In the emergence of socialism and the women's movement at the turn of the century, the evangelical appeals were rampant. In a letter to the *Appeal to Reason*, one Oklahoma woman wrote: "I see in Socialism the possibility of the literal practice of the Golden Rule." Another woman from a small town in Indiana wrote that Socialism "is the only true religion, according to the teachings of the New Testament."[5] Of course, such residual evangelical Protestant sensibilities could work to alienate those who did not share the same Christian assumptions and, in turn, make difficult, if not impossible, the mobilization of sentiments for an oppositional politics.

Another factor in the dilemma of building continuity in oppositional and alternative cultural and political projects was the clash between residual and emergent values. For example, Charlotte Perkins Gilman's Victorian and Gilded Age socialist feminism was at odds with the modern and Progressive anarcho-feminism of

Emma Goldman. While both stressed women's autonomy, Gilman's feminism could not accommodate the message of sexual emancipation articulated by Emma Goldman. On the other hand, Goldman's emphasis on sexual emancipation could be subsumed under the emergence of the changing morality of modern feminism.[6] Thus, even when emergent values seemed to promise a radical realization of utopian desires, those desires could be channeled into a de-radicalized alternative or mainstream social practice, posing in the process the dilemma of hegemonic reformulation.

Another dilemma that invested utopianism and radicalism with dialectical tensions in this period was the articulation of discursive strategies, especially in the construction of what sociologists David Snow and Robert Benford call "master frames."[7] Such master frames provide aggrieved groups with a mobilizing focus for challenging the social order. In the late nineteenth and the early twentieth century, with the massive influx of immigrants and the realignment of the political economy, there emerged a master frame under a contested discourse on citizenship. To the extent that citizenship reinforced an ideology of exclusion, whether of immigrants or African-Americans, and normalization, as seen in the mainstream historical pageantry movement, such discursive strategy lent itself to stabilization of the dominant hegemonic order.[8] On the other hand, the appeals by African-American writers and activists like Griggs, Hopkins, and W.E.B. Du Bois for being granted political citizenship propelled their protest literature and activity, informing such literature and activity, at times, with utopian and radical discourse.

Yet that struggle for political citizenship for African-Americans was fraught with peril not only because of the coercive rule of Jim Crow but also with the potential coopting features of political citizenship. Nowhere was this more evident than in Du Bois's eventual endorsement of the United States involvement in World War I. Encouraging African-Americans to enlist, Du Bois argued: "Let us, while this war lasts, forget our special grievances and close our ranks shoulder to shoulder with our white fellow citizens and the allied nations that are fighting for democracy."[9] Expecting this imagined citizenship to transcend and transform racism, Du Bois and countless black soldiers were betrayed by the persistence of white supremacy inside and outside the military. While African-Americans during this time did fight for political citizenship in both on-stage and off-stage arenas, gaining that citizenship would wait for a longer time than Du Bois expected.[10]

For others, especially marginalized and radicalized workers during this period, political citizenship was little more than a ruse. An article in the IWW newspaper, the *Industrial Worker*, claimed: "The 'right' to citizenship is as useful to the worker as a phonograph to a deaf man. Modern industry makes the toiler a wanderer. Property and residential qualifications deprive him of the 'sacred expression of sovereign citizenship'—the vote."[11] On the other hand, women, like Gilman and countless others, mobilized around achieving political citizenship through suffrage protests and political organization. However, to some, namely Emma Goldman, suffrage was a "delusion and a snare" because having women vote and electing women to office was hardly a guarantee for true liberty and equality.[12] In effect, while political citizenship might offer a master frame for mobilization, the utopian and radical thrust of such political citizenship remained, at best, contingent realities.

Beyond political citizenship what motivated utopianism and radicalism, underscoring in the process a further discursive dilemma, was the desire for social citizenship. Such social citizenship was an integral component of attaining economic security and social justice. Evident throughout the utopian projections highlighted in the previous chapters, social citizenship ran the gamut from Bellamy's ideas of "cradle-to-grave" security to Hopkins's pleas and the IWW's demands for simple recognition as fellow human beings entitled to dignity. Moreover, the construction of communal experiments, especially at Ruskin, Equality, and Llano del Rio, embodied efforts to realize social citizenship in practice. More than "enclaves of difference," these utopian colonies were enclaves of social citizenship.[13]

While social citizenship afforded radicals a discursive strategy to frame both political ideas and social practices, there were ways in which such social citizenship was confined by the hegemonic struggle. Constant debate during this period over who was an American signaled that citizenship had meanings beyond who could participate in the political process. Conflicts over immigrant absorption bothered not only conservative nativists but also, as we have seen, radicals like Charlotte Perkins Gilman.[14] Even within what appeared to be a compelling radical aspiration, the very utopian longing could be domesticated by the movement to Americanize those working class immigrants who had previously been despised and excluded. Although such Americanization strategies employed the tactics of de-radicalizing such constituencies, immigrant workers still found ways to redefine that Americanism at certain points to realize alternative or even oppositional political goals.[15]

Ultimately, these discursive dilemmas over citizenship and the expansion of the definition of Americanism merged with the larger strategic realignment that marked the political, social, and economic transformations from the Gilded Age through the Progressive Era to the end of World War I. That realignment centered on three

strategic fields where norms and values were undergoing reformulation during this thirty-year period (and, indeed, beyond into the
1930s): (1) corporate power and the role of industrial workers and
middle class consumers; (2) the role of women, African-Americans,
and immigrants in social and political life; and (3) the role of the
state in determining the welfare of people within and outside the
United States.[16] As has been demonstrated in the previous chapters,
the utopianism and radicalism of this period could not escape
contending with these strategic fields. Although generating a variety
of alternative and oppositional political and cultural formations, the
question remains why it proved so difficult to sustain those formations.

On one level that question is part of the ongoing debate about the
lack of a continuous socialist tradition in the United States. Without
becoming bogged down in that debate, identifiable factors such as
economic prosperity, political cooptation, ethnic/racial competition, and individual mobility certainly weighed against building
such socialism. On the other hand, Eric Foner's critique of ahisto-
rically assuming these factors is directly pertinent to understanding
the contested strategic fields from 1888 to 1918. Moreover, as he
cogently contends: "Perhaps, because mass politics, mass culture,
and mass consumption came to America before it did to Europe,
American socialists were the first to face the dilemma of how to
define socialist politics in a capitalist democracy."[17] Certainly, such
mass culture and consumption rechanneled utopian longings into
privatized and highly segmented households, away from collective
oppositional politics. Yet, even within those households, a culture
of resistance could still be fashioned and kept alive.[18]

Nevertheless, the ability to realize the utopian and radical ideals
articulated in the political formations of the period, whether socialist, anarchist, syndicalist, feminist, or black nationalist, had to
contend with the developing role of the state in alternating between
incorporating reforms and repressing radicals. Progressives in California, for example, managed to "de-socialize" Llano del Rio's attempt as an oppositional site by adopting policies for
state-sponsored land settlements.[19] The adoption by the admini-
strations of Theodore Roosevelt and, more particularly, Woodrow
Wilson of ameliorative reforms around antitrust and child-labor law,
and other legislative acts, did attempt to respond to radical ideas
and movements, especially aiming to undercut the influence of
socialism. Such enacted reforms underscore historian Alan
Dawley's insight that "Progressivism *contained* socialism, in both
senses of the word" (author's emphasis).[20]

Yet, if Progressivism was successful in containing socialism through legislation, it also did so by mobilizing utopian hopes. This was particularly prominent in Wilson's pledge to "make the world safe for democracy." While enlisting the enthusiasm of even many radicals, both the propaganda and administrative arms of the wartime government boosted a "consecration" of the state. When antiwar radicals attempted to dissent from that consecration, they quickly and effectively could be labeled as heretical traitors.[21] Principally hard-hit by wartime repression were the Wobblies and the Socialist Party, especially in the aftermath of the June 1917 passage of the Espionage Act. James Weinstein estimates that over fifteen hundred socialist locals were destroyed by wartime repression, mostly in the midwest and southwest where socialism had built an oppositional politics and alternative culture.[22] Moreover, once the wartime crusade against radicals was put in motion, it generated a momentum that carried it into the postwar hysteria around a "red scare."[23]

Beyond this intensive and extensive repression, the forces of opposition were badly splintered in the post–World War I period as a consequence of events both external and internal. The external event was the Russian Revolution. For many radicals the Russian Revolution transformed what had been a utopian longing for a good place outside of history into a historical site for that good place. Unfortunately, in slavishly hitching a radical wagon to the Soviet star, the left was split asunder and rendered for a time transfixed in its utopian orientation.[24] Internally, although the period from 1916 to 1919 saw an increase in labor militancy resulting in the explosive strikes of 1919, those strikes, after a brief flickering as in the Seattle general strike, imploded, leading to increased fragmentation by ethnicity and race.[25] On top of this came the bitter and bloody race riots of 1919. Together, these events were of such magnitude as to mark 1919, in the words of historian Mari Jo Buhle, "the close of a distinct era in the history of American radicalism."[26]

If the dilemmas facing utopianism and radicalism were brought to a screeching halt in 1919, the roots of those dilemmas and the legacies of utopianism and radicalism were not contained in one year or even the thirty-year period under investigation. One deeply rooted dilemma that confronted utopianism and radicalism from the nineteenth century through World War I was an incurable optimism. Fueled by the sense of inevitable progress, one could find again and again such sentiments as the following that appeared in the *Western Comrade*: "[Socialism] is an irresistible spirit and there is not likely to come out of capitalism any immovable object to halt its progress."[27] Labeling this condition "mechanistic optimism," Gabriel

Kolko suggests that this "led socialists to slight the negative consequences of action or inaction in relation to desired goals, and to try
to fit every major event of political and economic development into
a pattern of inevitable progression that justified optimism."[28] (Perhaps another explanation for the critical reception given London's
The Iron Heel by numerous socialists was its lack of mechanistic
optimism.)

On the other hand, while the mechanistic optimism of much of
the radicalism during the period 1888–1918 drained that radicalism
of its critical capacities to mount and sustain an oppositional
politics and culture, the desire to bring about a willed transformation marked the utopian aspirations of this period with an urgency
for its time and beyond. Writing in 1903 in the midst of the terrible
travails of segregation, lynching, and disfranchisement, W.E.B. Du
Bois prophesied: "Some day the Awakening will come, when the
pent-up vigor of ten million souls shall sweep irresistibly toward the
Goal, out of the Valley of the Shadow of Death, where all that makes
life worth living—Liberty, Justice, and Right—is marked 'For White
People Only.' "[29] Fourteen years later, in an American courtroom
facing a conspiracy charge against the wartime conscription act,
Emma Goldman defended herself by embracing "the kind of patriotism which loves America with open eyes." Spelling out that love,
she concluded by saying that "we [Goldman and her coconspirator
Alexander Berkman] love the dreamers and the philosophers and
the thinkers who are giving America liberty."[30] Without those dreamers like Goldman, Du Bois, and the others—both noted and un-
noted—scattered throughout this period from 1888 to 1918, without
their radical and utopian aspirations, the cherished ideals of liberty
and equality and the vaunted reforms that have enlarged, although
not completed, American democracy would be lacking. That a lack
yet remains suggests that utopianism and radicalism may again
play a significant role in a reforming America, as they did from 1888
to 1918, and as they were to do in the 1930s and 1960s.[31]

NOTES

1. Warren I. Susman, "The Persistence of Reform," in Susman, *Culture as History: The Transformation of American Society in the Twentieth
Century* (New York: Basic Books, 1984), pp. 86–97.

2. Comparable definitions of utopianism can be found in Barbara
Goodwin and Keith Taylor, *The Politics of Utopia: A Study in Theory and
Practice* (New York: St. Martin's Press, 1982), p. 138; and Ruth Levitas,
The Concept of Utopia (Syracuse: Syracuse University Press, 1990), p. 182.

3. See, for example, Harriman's praise for the noncommercialism of
"amusements" at Llano in Harriman, "Llano—Community of Ideals," *West-*

ern Comrade (March 1917): 9. On dominant, residual, and emergent patterns of culture and social practices, see Raymond Williams, *Marxism and Literature* (Oxford: Oxford University Press, 1977), pp. 121–27.

4. Nick Salvatore, "Some Thoughts on Class and Citizenship in America in the Late Nineteenth Century," in *In the Shadow of the Statue of Liberty: Immigrants, Workers, and Citizens in the American Republic, 1880–1920*, ed. Marianne Debouzy (Urbana: University of Illinois Press, 1992), esp. pp. 223–24.

5. Quoted in Mari Jo Buhle, *Women and American Socialism, 1870–1920* (Urbana: University of Illinois Press, 1981), p. 116. On the deep and persistent connections between the evangelical sensibility and moral reform, see Susman, "The Persistence of Reform," pp. 88–91.

6. On Gilman's Gilded Age socialist and feminist sensibilities, see Mark Pittenger, *American Socialists and Evolutionary Thought, 1870–1920* (Madison: University of Wisconsin Press, 1993), p. 87. On Goldman's modern message of woman's emancipation, see Marian J. Morton, *Emma Goldman and the American Left: "Nowhere at Home"* (New York: Twayne, 1992), pp. 59–80. On the values and developments of modern feminism and the "new woman," see Nancy Cott, *The Grounding of Modern Feminism* (New Haven: Yale University Press, 1987), pp. 13–50.

7. David A. Snow and Robert D. Benford, "Master Frames and the Cycle of Protest," *Frontiers in Social Movement Theory*, ed. Aldon D. Morris and Carol McClurg Mueller (New Haven: Yale University Press, 1992), pp. 133–55.

8. On anti-immigrant attitudes among the working class and its conservative function, see Catherine Collomp, "Unions, Civics, and National Identity: Organized Labor's Reaction to Immigration, 1881–1897," in Debouzy, *In the Shadow of the Statue of Liberty*, pp. 229–55. On the historical pageantry of this period, see David Glassberg, *American Historical Pageantry: The Uses of Tradition in the Early Twentieth Century* (Chapel Hill: University of North Carolina Press, 1990).

9. Quoted in David Levering Lewis, *W.E.B. Du Bois: Biography of a Race, 1868–1919* (New York: Henry Holt, 1993), p. 556.

10. For a debate about the intentions of Du Bois and the repercussions of his "close ranks" strategy, see William Jordan, " 'The Damnable Dilemma': African-American Accommodation and Protest During World War I," *Journal of American History* 81 (March 1995): 1562–83; and Mark Ellis, "W.E.B. Du Bois and the Formation of Black Opinion in World War I: A Commentary on 'The Damnable Dilemma,' " *Journal of American History* 81 (March 1995): 1584–90. On black soldiers and struggles for citizenship during this time, see Steven A. Reich, "Soldiers of Democracy: Black Texans and the Fight for Citizenship, 1917–1921," *Journal of American History* 82 (March 1996): 1478–1504.

11. *Industrial Worker*, May 13, 1916, p. 2.

12. Quoted in Morton, *Emma Goldman and the American Left*, p. 64. On women's suffrage during this period, see Sara Hunter Graham, *Woman Suffrage and the New Democracy* (New Haven: Yale University Press,

1996); and Aileen Kraditor, *Ideas of the Woman Suffrage Movement, 1890–1920* (New York: Columbia University Press, 1965).

13. For an application of Robert Weibe's idea of "enclave of difference" to late nineteenth- and early twentieth-century utopian colonies, see Robert S. Fogarty, *All Things New: American Communes and Utopian Movements, 1860–1914* (Chicago: University of Chicago Press, 1990), pp. 4–5. On T. H. Marshall's concept of social citizenship, see Michael Mann, *States, War and Capitalism: Studies in Political Sociology* (New York: Basil Blackwell, 1988), p. 188.

14. The seminal study of the conflict between nativists and immigrants can be found in John Higham, *Strangers in the Land: Patterns of American Nativism, 1860–1925* (New York: Atheneum, 1963). On Gilman's anti-immigrant attitudes, see Carol Farley Kessler, *Charlotte Perkins Gilman: Her Progress Toward Utopia* (Syracuse: Syracuse University Press, 1995), pp. 76–77 and *passim.*

15. On Americanization and its contested terrain, see James R. Barrett, "Americanization from the Bottom Up: Immigration and the Remaking of the Working Class in the United States, 1880–1930," *Journal of American History* 79 (December 1992): 996–1020; and Gary Gerstle, *Working-Class Americanism: The Politics of Labor in a Textile City, 1914–1960* (New York: Cambridge University Press, 1989).

16. Alan Dawley, *Struggles for Justice: Social Responsibility and the Liberal State* (Cambridge, Mass.: Belknap Press of Harvard University Press, 1991), p. 64.

17. Eric Foner, "Why Is There No Socialism in the United States," *History Workshop* 17 (Spring 1984); 57–80. For one accounting of the factors militating against socialism in America, see James T. Kloppenberg, *Uncertain Victory: Social Democracy and Progressivism in European and American Thought, 1870–1920* (New York: Oxford University Press, 1986), p. 206.

18. On the insidious role of consumer culture, see Stuart Ewen, *Captains of Consciousness: Advertising and the Social Roots of the Consumer Culture* (New York: McGraw-Hill, 1976). For a more nuanced reading of the private world of working class men and women and the creation of cultures of resistance, see Ardis Cameron, *Radicals of the Worst Sort: Laboring Women in Lawrence Massachusetts, 1860–1912* (Urbana: University of Illinois Press, 1993); and Lizabeth Cohen, *Making a New Deal: Industrial Workers in Chicago, 1919–1939* (Cambridge: Cambridge University Press, 1990).

19. Kevin Starr, *Inventing the Dream: California Through the Progressive Era* (New York: Oxford University Press, 1985), pp. 169–70; on reform and California Progressivism, see pp. 199–282.

20. Dawley, *Struggles for Justice*, p. 137. On ameliorative reforms and the undercutting of socialism, see James Weinstein, *The Decline of Socialism in America, 1912–1925* (New York: Monthly Review Press, 1967), pp. 103–5. For additional insights into the political meaning of Progressivism, see Richard L. McCormick, *The Party Period and Public Policy: American Politics from the Age of Jackson to the Progressive Era* (New York: Oxford

University Press, 1986), pp. 263–356; and Martin Sklar, *The United States as a Developing Country* (New York: Cambridge University Press, 1992), pp. 37–77.

21. Walter Karp, *The Politics of War* (New York: Harper and Row, 1979), p. 223. For the impact of World War I on American society and dissenters, see David M. Kennedy, *Over Here: The First World War and American Society* (New York: Oxford University Press, 1980); and H. C. Peterson and Gilbert C. Fite, *Opponents of War, 1917–18* (Seattle: University of Washington Press, 1968).

22. Weinstein, *The Decline of Socialism in America*, pp. 119–76, 182. On political repression of the IWW, see Melvyn Dubofsky, *We Shall Be All: A History of the IWW* (New York: Quadrangle, 1973); William Preston, Jr., *Aliens and Dissenters: Federal Suppression of Radicals, 1903–1933* (New York: Harper Torchbooks, 1966), pp. 88–151; and Francis Shor, "The IWW and Oppositional Politics in World War I: Pushing the System Beyond Its Limits," *Radical History Review* 64 (Winter 1996): 74–94.

23. Robert Murray, *Red Scare: A Study in National Hysteria, 1919–1920* (New York: McGraw-Hill, 1955).

24. On the split and disintegration of the left in the United States, see Weinstein, *The Decline of Socialism in America*, pp. 177–257.

25. On the strikes of this period, see Jeremy Brecher, *Strike* (San Francisco: Straight Arrow Press, 1972), pp. 101–43. On the implosion, subsequent fragmentation, and meaning of 1919, especially in Chicago, see Cohen, *Making a New Deal*, pp. 11–52.

26. Mari Jo Buhle, *Women and American Socialism*, p. 318. On the race riots of 1919, see William Tuttle, *Race Riot: Chicago in the Red Summer of 1919* (New York: Atheneum, 1970).

27. *Western Comrade* (June 1913): 93.

28. Gabriel Kolko, "The Decline of American Radicalism in the Twentieth Century," *For A New America: Essays in History and Politics from "Studies on the Left," 1959–1967*, ed. James Weinstein and David W. Eakins (New York: Vintage, 1970), p. 198. Also, Kolko notes that "the failure of American radicalism was due, at least between 1917 and 1920, to the failure of American politics to operate according to the conventionally accepted but rarely practiced ideal theories of democratic political processes" (ibid., p. 207).

29. W.E.B. Du Bois, *The Souls of Black Folk* (Greenwich, Conn.: Fawcett Premier, 1961), p. 151.

30. Quoted in Richard Drinnon, *Rebel in Paradise: A Biography of Emma Goldman* (New York: Bantam, 1973), pp. 240–41.

31. Francis Shor, "Utopianism," *The Encyclopedia of the American Left*, ed. Mari Jo Buhle, Paul Buhle, and Dan Georgakas (New York: Garland, 1990), pp. 810–11.

Selected Bibliography

PRIMARY SOURCES

Archival Sources

Industrial Workers of the World Collection, Walter Reuther Archives, Wayne State University, Detroit, Michigan

Llano del Rio Collection, Huntington Library, San Marino, California

Jack London Collection, Huntington Library, San Marino, California

Newspapers and Magazines

American (Nashville)

The American Fabian

Appeal to Reason

Arena

Chicago Dial

Chicago Socialist

Coming Nation

Discontent

Duluth Herald

Industrial Freedom

Industrial Solidarity

Industrial Worker

International Socialist Review

Johnstown Democrat

Los Angeles Record

Manchester Union

Mother Earth

Nashville Banner

Philadelphia Telegram

Post-Express (Rochester)

Religious Telescope

San Francisco Chronicle

The Socialist (Seattle)

Solidarity

Tacoma News

Wall Street Journal

The Western Comrade

Wilshire's Magazine

The Worker

Published Materials, Books, and Pamphlets

Bellamy, Edward. *Equality.* New York: D. Appleton, 1897.

_____ . *Looking Backward 2000–1887.* Ed. and intro. Cecelia Tichi. New York: Penguin, 1984.

Broome, Isaac. *The Last Days of the Ruskin Cooperative Association.* Chicago: Charles H. Kerr, 1902.

Cooper, Anna Julia. *A Voice from the South.* New York: Oxford University Press, 1988.

Du Bois, W.E.B. *Creative Writings of W.E.B. Du Bois: A Pageant, Poems, Short Stories, and Playlets.* Ed. and comp. Herbert Aptheker. White Plains, N. Y.: Kraus-Thompson Organization, 1985.

_____ . Pamphlets and Leaflets by W.E.B. Du Bois. Ed. and comp. Herbert Aptheker. White Plains, N.Y.: Kraus-Thompson Organization, 1986.

_____ . *The Souls of Black Folk.* Greenwich, Conn.: Fawcett Premier, 1961.

Fiske, John. *Outlines of Cosmic Philosophy.* Boston: Houghton Mifflin, 1892.

Gilman, Charlotte Perkins. *The Living of Charlotte Perkins Gilman: An Autobiography.* New York: D. Appleton-Century, 1935.

_____ . *Women and Economics.* Ed. Carl Degler. New York: Harper Torchbooks, 1966.

———. "A Woman's Utopia." *The Times Magazine*, January, February, and March 1907.

Goldman, Emma. *Living My Life*, Vols. 1 & II. New York: Dover Publications, 1970.

———. *Red Emma Speaks*. Ed. Alix Kates Shulman. New York: Schocken, 1983.

Gramsci, Antonio. *Selections from the Prison Notebooks*. Trans. and ed. Quintin Hoare and Geoffrey Nowell Smith. New York: International Publishers, 1971.

Griggs, Sutton E. *Imperium in Imperio*. Miami: Mnemosyne, 1969.

Hapgood, Hutchins. *A Victorian in the Modern World*. New York: Harcourt, Brace, 1939.

Hopkins, Pauline E. *Contending Forces*. Carbondale: Southern Illinois Press, 1978.

———. "Of One Blood," in *The Magazine Novels of Pauline Hopkins*. New York: Oxford University Press, 1988, pp. 441–621.

Kornbluh, Joyce L., ed. *Rebel Voices: An IWW Anthology*. Ann Arbor: University of Michigan Press, 1972.

London, Jack. *The Complete Short Stories of Jack London*, Vol. II. Ed. Earle Labor, Robert C. Leitz, and Milo Shephard, Stanford: Stanford University Press, 1993.

———. *The Iron Heel*. Westport, Conn.: Lawrence Hill, 1980.

———. *The Letters of Jack London*, Vol II. Ed. Earle Labor, Robert C. Leitz, and Milo Shephard. Stanford: Stanford University Press, 1988.

———. *The Science Fiction of Jack London*. Ed. Richard Gid Powers. Boston: Gregg Press, 1975.

———. *War of the Classes*. New York: Grossett and Dunlap, 1905.

Luhan, Mable Dodge. *Movers and Shakers*. Albuquerque: University of New Mexico Press, 1985.

Pomeroy, Eltweed. "A Sketch of the Socialist Colony in Tennessee." *The American Fabian*. (April 3, 1897): 1.

Songs of the Workers. 34th ed. Chicago: IWW, 1974.

Wayland, J. A. *Leaves of Life: A Story of Twenty Years of Socialist Agitation*. Girard, Kan.: Appeal to Reason, 1912.

Wooster, Ernest S. *Communities of the Past and Present*. Newllano, La.: Llano Colonist, 1924.

SECONDARY SOURCES

Aaron, Daniel. *Men of Good Hope: A Story of American Progressivism*. New York: Oxford University Press, 1961.

Ackelsberg, Martha A. *Free Women of Spain: Anarchism and the Struggle for the Emancipation of Women*. Bloomington: Indiana University Press, 1991.

Adamic, Louis. *Dynamite: The Story of Class Violence in America*. Rev. ed. Gloucester, Mass.: Peter Smith, 1963.

Adamson, Walter L. *Hegemony and Revolution: A Study of Antonio Gramsci's Political and Social Theory*. Berkeley: University of California Press, 1980.

Adorno, Theodor W. "The Sociology of Knowledge and Its Consciousness," in *The Essential Frankfurt School Reader*, ed. Andrew Arato and Elkie Gebhardt. New York: Urizen Books, 1978, pp. 452–65.

Allen, Polly Wynn. *Building Domestic Liberty: Charlotte Perkins Gilman's Architectural Feminism*. Amherst: University of Massachusetts Press, 1988.

Ammons, Elizabeth. *Conflicting Stories: American Women Writers at the Turn into the Twentieth Century*. New York: Oxford University Press, 1991.

Appiah, Kwame Anthony. *In My Father's House: Africa in the Philosophy of Culture*. New York: Oxford University Press, 1992.

Auerbach, Jonathan. " 'The Nation Organized': Utopian Impotence in Edward Bellamy's *Looking Backward*." *American Literary History* 6 (Spring 1994): 24–47.

Avrich, Paul. *An American Anarchist: The Life of Voltairine de Cleyre*. Princeton: Princeton University Press, 1978.

———. *Anarchist Voices: An Oral History of Anarchism in America*. Princeton: Princeton University Press, 1995.

———. *The Haymarket Tragedy*. Princeton: Princeton University Press, 1984.

———. *The Modern School Movement: Anarchism and Education in the United States*. Princeton: Princeton University Press, 1980.

Ayers, Edward L. *The Promise of the New South: Life After Reconstruction*. New York: Oxford University Press, 1992.

Bacchi, Carol Lee. *Liberation Deferred? The Ideas of the English-Canadian Suffragists, 1877–1918*. Toronto: University of Toronto Press, 1983.

Badger, Reid. *The Great American Fair: The World's Columbian Exposition and American Culture*. Chicago: University of Chicago Press, 1979.

Baker, Keith Michael. "On the Problems of the Ideological Origins of the French Revolution," in *Modern European Intellectual History: Reappraisals and New Perspectives*, ed. Dominick LaCapra and Steven L. Caplan. Ithaca, N.Y.: Cornell University Press, 1982, pp. 197–219.

Baldelli, Giovanni. *Social Anarchism*. Chicago: Aldine, 1971.

Barkun, Michael. "Communal Societies and Cyclical Phenomena." *Communal Societies* 4 (1984): 35–48.

Barltrop, Robert. *Jack London: The Man, the Writer, the Rebel*. London: Pluto Press, 1976.

Barrett, James R. "Americanization from the Bottom Up: Immigration and the Remaking of the Working Class in the United States, 1880–1930." *The Journal of American History* 79 (December 1992): 996–1020.

Bauman, Zygmunt. *Socialism: The Active Utopia*. New York: Holmes and Meier, 1976.

Beauchamp, Gorman. "Jack London's Utopia Dystopia and Dystopia Utopia," in *America as Utopia*, ed. Kenneth M. Roemer. New York: Burt Franklin, 1981, pp. 91–107.

Bederman, Gail. *Manliness & Civilization: A Cultural History of Gender and Race in the United States, 1880–1917*. Chicago: University of Chicago Press, 1995.

Benhabib, Seyla. *Critique, Norm, and Utopia: A Study of the Foundations of Critical Theory*. New York: Columbia University Press, 1986.

Bennett, Tony. "Text, Readings, Reading Formations," in *Modern Literary Theory: A Reader*, ed. Philip Rice and Patricia Waugh. London: Edward Arnold, 1989, pp. 206–20.

––––––. "Texts in History: The Determination of Readings and Their Texts," in *Post-Structuralism and the Question of History*, ed. Derek Attridge, Geoff Bennington, and Robert Young. Cambridge: Cambridge University Press, 1987, pp. 63–81.

Berman, Marshall. *All That Is Solid Melts into Air: The Experience of Modernity*. New York: Simon and Schuster, 1982.

Berry, Brian J. L. *America's Utopian Experiments: Communal Havens from Long-Wave Crisis*. Hanover, N.H.: University Press of New England, 1992.

Bloch, Ernst. *The Principle of Hope*. Vol. I. Trans. Neville Plaice, Stephen Plaice, and Paul Knight. Cambridge: MIT Press, 1986.

Bordin, Ruth. *Women and Temperance: The Quest for Power and Liberty, 1873–1900*. Philadelphia: Temple University Press, 1981.

––––––. *Frances Willard: A Biography*. Chapel Hill: University of North Carolina Press, 1986.

Bowman, Sylvia E. *Edward Bellamy*. Boston: Twayne, 1986.

––––––. *Edward Bellamy Abroad. An American Prophet's Influences*. Boston: Twayne, 1962.

––––––. *The Year 2000: A Critical Biography of Edward Bellamy*. New York: Bookman, 1958.

Brecher, Jeremy. *Strike*. San Francisco: Straight Arrow Press, 1972.

Brittan, Arthur. *Masculinity and Power*. New York: Basil Blackwell, 1989.

Bruce, Dickson D., Jr. *Black American Writing from the Nadir: The Evolution of a Literary Tradition, 1877–1915*. Baton Rouge: Louisiana State University Press, 1989.

Brundage, W. Fitzhugh. *A Socialist Utopia in the New South: The Ruskin Colonies in Tennessee and Georgia, 1894–1901*. Urbana: University of Illinois Press, 1996.

Buber, Martin. *Paths in Utopia*. Trans. R.F.C. Hull. Boston: Beacon Press, 1966.

Buci-Glucksmann, Christine. *Gramsci and the State*. Trans. David Fernback. London: Lawrence and Wishart, 1980.

Buder, Stanley. *Visionaries and Planners: The Garden City Movement and the Modern Community*. New York: Oxford University Press, 1990.

Buhle, Mari Jo. *Women and American Socialism, 1870–1920*. Urbana: University of Illinois Press, 1981.

Buhle, Paul. *Marxism in the United States: Remapping the History of the American Left*. London: Verso, 1987.

Byerman, Keith E. *Seizing the Word: History, Art, and Self in the Work of W.E.B. Du Bois*. Athens: University of Georgia Press, 1994.

Cameron, Ardis. *Radicals of the Worst Sort: Laboring Women in Lawrence, Massachusetts, 1860–1912*. Urbana: University of Illinois Press, 1993.

Cantor, Milton. *The Divided Left: American Radicalism, 1900–1975*. New York: Hill & Wang, 1978.

Capra, Fritjof. *The Tao of Physics*. Berkeley: Shambhala, 1975

————. *The Turning Point: Science, Society, and the Rising Culture*. London: Fontana, 1983.

Carby, Hazel V. *Reconstructing Womanhood: The Emergence of the Afro-American Woman Novelist*. New York: Oxford University Press, 1987.

Carlson, Peter. *Roughneck: The Life and Times of Big Bill Haywood*. New York: W. W. Norton, 1983.

Chew, Geoffrey F. *S-Matrix Theory of Strong Interactions*. New York: W. A. Benjamin, 1962.

Clark, John P. "What Is Anarchism," in *Anarchism*, ed. J. Roland Pennock and John W. Chapman. New York: New York University Press, 1978, pp. 3–28.

Clecak, Peter. *America's Quest for the Ideal Self*. New York: Oxford University Press, 1983.

Cogan, Frances B. *All-American Girl: The Ideal of Real Womanhood in Mid-Nineteenth-Century America*. Athens: University of Georgia Press, 1989.

Cohen, Lizabeth. *Making a New Deal: Industrial Workers in Chicago, 1919–1939*. Cambridge: Cambridge University Press, 1990.

Collomp, Catherine. "Unions, Civics, and National Identity: Organized Labor's Reaction to Immigration, 1881–1897," in *In the Shadow of the Statue of Liberty: Immigrants, Workers, and Citizens in the American Republic,. 1880–1920*, ed. Marianne Debouzy. Urbana: University of Illinois Press, 1992, pp. 229–55.

Conkin, Paul K. *Two Paths to Utopia: The Hutterites and the Llano Colony*. Lincoln: University of Nebraska Press, 1964.

Conn, Peter. *The Divided Mind: Ideology and Imagination in America, 1898–1917*. Cambridge: Cambridge University Press, 1983.

Connell, R. W. *Gender and Power: Society, the Person and Sexual Politics*. Cambridge, Mass.: Polity Press, 1987.

Cotkin, George. *Reluctant Modernism: American Thought and Culture, 1880–1900*. New York: Twayne, 1992.

Cott, Nancy. *The Grounding of Modern Feminism*. New Haven: Yale University Press, 1987.

Crunden, Robert M. *Ministers of Reform: The Progressives' Achievement in American Civilization, 1889–1920*. New York: Basic Books, 1982.

Davis, Mike. *City of Quartz: Excavating the Future of Los Angeles*. London: Verso, 1990.

———. *Prisoners of the American Dream: Politics and Economy in the History of the US Working Class.* London: Verso, 1990.

Dawley, Alan. *Struggles for Justice: Social Responsibility and the Liberal State.* Cambridge, Mass.: Belknap Press of Harvard University Press, 1991.

Degler, Carl. "Introduction," in Charlotte Perkins Gilman, *Women and Economics.* New York: Harper Torchbooks, 1966, pp. vi–xxxv.

DeLeon, David. *The American as Anarchist: Reflections on Indigenous Radicalism.* Baltimore: Johns Hopkins University Press, 1978.

Dick, William M. *Labor and Socialism in America: The Gompers Era.* Port Washington, N.Y.: Kennikat Press, 1972.

Donald, James, and Stuart Hall, eds. *Politics and Ideology: A Reader.* Philadelphia: Open University Press, 1986.

Drinnon, Richard. *Rebel in Paradise: A Biography of Emma Goldman.* New York: Bantam, 1973.

Dubofsky, Melvyn. *We Shall Be All: A History of the Industrial Workers of the World.* New York: Quadrangle, 1973.

DuBois, Ellen Carol. *Feminism and Suffrage: The Emergence of an Independent Women's Movement in America, 1848–1869.* Ithaca, N.Y.: Cornell University Press, 1978.

Eagleton, Terry. "Ideology, Fiction, Narrative," *Social Text* 2 (Summer 1979): 62–80.

———. "Ideology and Scholarship," in *Historical Studies and Literary Criticism,* ed. Jerome J. McGann. Madison: University of Wisconsin Press, 1985, pp. 114–25

Egerton, John. *Visions of Utopia: Nashoba, Rugby, and the "New Communities" in Tennessee's Past.* Knoxville: University of Tennessee Press, 1977.

Ehrenreich, Barbara, and Deidre English. *For Her Own Good.* New York: Anchor Doubleday, 1979.

Elder, Arlene A. *The "Hindered Hand": Cultural Implications of Early African-American Fiction.* Westport, Conn.: Greenwood Press, 1978.

Ellis, Mark. "W.E.B. Du Bois and the Formation of Black Opinion in World War I: A Commentary on 'The Damnable Dilemma,' " *Journal of American History* 81 (March 1995): 1584–90.

Epstein, Barbara Leslie. *The Politics of Domesticity: Women, Evangelism, and Temperance in Nineteenth Century America.* Middletown: Wesleyan University Press, 1981.

Erasmus, Charles. *In Search of the Common Good.* New York: Free Press, 1977.

Evans, Richard J. *The Feminists: Women's Emancipation Movements in Europe, America, and Australasia, 1840–1920.* London: Croom Helm, 1977.

Ewen, Stuart. *Captains of Consciousness: Advertising and the Social Roots of the Consumer Culture.* New York: McGraw-Hill, 1976.

Femia, Joseph. *Gramsci's Political Thought: Hegemony, Consciousness, and the Revolutionary Process.* Oxford: Clarendon Press, 1981.

Fenn, Richard K. *The Spirit of Revolt: Anarchism and the Cult of Authority.*
    Totowa, N.J.: Rowman and Littlefield, 1986.

Filene, Peter G. *Him/Her/Self: Sex Roles in Modern America.* 2d edition.
    Baltimore: Johns Hopkins University Press, 1986.

Fine, Sidney. *Laissez Faire and the General Welfare State.* Ann Arbor:
    University of Michigan Press, 1964.

Fogarty, Robert S. *All Things New: American Communes and Utopian
    Movements, 1860–1914.* Chicago: University of Chicago Press,
    1990.

————— , ed. *American Utopianism.* Itasca, Ill.: E. F. Peacock, 1972.

Foner, Eric. "Why Is There No Socialism in the United States," *History
    Workshop* 17 (Spring 1984): 57–80.

Foner, Philip S. *The Case of Joe Hill.* New York: International Publishers,
    1965.

Foucault, Michel. *The History of Sexuality,* Volume I—*An Introduction.*
    Trans. Robert Harley. New York: Pantheon, 1978.

————— . "The Subject of Power," in *Michel Foucault: Beyond Structuralism
    and Hermeneutics,* ed Hubert L. Dreyfus and Paul Rabinow. Lon-
    don: Harvester Press, 1982, pp. 208–26.

Fredrickson, George M. *The Black Image in the White Mind: The Debate on
    Afro-American Character and Destiny, 1817–1914.* Middletown,
    Conn.: Wesleyan University Press, 1987.

Freeden, Michael. *The New Liberalism: An Ideology of Social Reform.* Ox-
    ford: Clarendon, 1978.

Fried, Albert. *Socialism in America: From the Shakers to the Third Interna-
    tional.* Garden City, N.Y.: Doubleday, 1970.

Frow, John. *Marxism and Literary History.* Oxford: Basil Blackwell, 1986.

Gaines, Kevin. "Black Americans' Racial Uplift Ideology as 'Civilizing Mis-
    sion': Pauline E. Hopkins on Race and Imperialism," in *Cultures of
    United States Imperialism,* ed. Amy Kaplan and Donald E. Pease.
    Durham, N.C.: Duke University Press, 1993, pp. 433–55.

Gardiner, Michael. "Bakhtin's Carnival: Utopia as Critique," *Utopian Stud-
    ies* 3 (1992): 21–49.

Gerstle, Gary. *Working-Class Americanism: The Politics of Labor in a Textile
    City, 1914-1960* (New York: Cambridge University Press, 1989).

Giddens, Anthony. *Central Problems in Social Theory: Action, Structure,
    and Contradiction.* London: Macmillan 1979.

Gilbert, James. *Designing the Industrial State: The Intellectual Pursuit of
    Collectivism in America, 1880–1940.* Chicago: Quadrangle Books,
    1972.

Glassberg, David. *American Historical Pageantry: The Uses of Tradition in
    the Early Twentieth Century.* Chapel Hill: University of North
    Carolina Press, 1990.

Golin, Steve. *The Fragile Bridge: Paterson Silk Strike, 1913.* Philadelphia:
    Temple University Press, 1988.

Goodwin, Barbara, and Keith Taylor. *The Politics of Utopia: A Study in
    Theory and Practice.* New York: St. Martin's Press, 1982.

Gordon, Milton. *Assimilation in America*. New York: Oxford University Press, 1964.

Graham, Sara Hunter. *Woman Suffrage and the New Democracy*. New Haven: Yale University Press, 1996.

Green, James R. *Grass-Roots Socialism: Radical Movements in the Southwest, 1895–1943*. Baton Rouge: Louisiana State University Press, 1978.

———. *The World of the Worker: Labor in Twentieth Century America*. New York: Hill and Wang, 1980.

Green, Martin. *New York 1913: The Armory Show and the Paterson Strike Pageant*. New York: Charles Scribner's, 1988.

Greenstein, Paul, Nigey Lennon, and Lionel Rolfe. *Bread & Hyacinths: The Rise and Fall of Utopian Los Angeles*. Los Angeles: California Classics Books, 1992.

Guarneri, Carl J. "The Americanization of Utopia: Fourierism and the Dilemma of Utopian Dissent in the United States," *Utopian Studies* 5 (1994): 72–88.

Guerin, Daniel. *Anarchism: From Theory to Practice*. Trans. Mary Klopper. New York: Monthly Review Press, 1970.

Haaland, Bonnie. *Emma Goldman: Sexuality and the Impurity of the State*. Montreal: Black Rose, 1993.

Haber, Samuel. *Efficiency and Uplift: Scientific Management in the Progressive Era*. Chicago: University of Chicago Press, 1964.

Harpham, Geoffrey. "Jack London and the Tradition of Superman Socialism." *American Studies* 16 (Spring 1975): 23–33.

Hayden, Dolores. *The Grand Domestic Revolution*. Cambridge: MIT Press, 1981.

———. *Seven American Utopias: The Architecture of Communitarian Socialism, 1790–1975*. Cambridge: MIT Press, 1976.

Hearn, Francis. *Domination, Legitimation and Resistance: The Incorporation of the Nineteenth Century English Working Class*. Westport, Conn.: Greenwood Press, 1978.

Hearn, Jeff. *Men in the Public Eye: The Construction and Deconstruction of Public Men and Public Patriarchies*. London: Routledge, 1992.

Hedrick, Joan. *Solitary Comrade: Jack London and His Work*. Chapel Hill: University of North Carolina Press, 1982.

Henning, E. M. "Archaeology, Deconstruction and Intellectual History," in *Modern European Intellectual History: Reappraisals and New Perspectives*, ed. Dominick LaCapra and Steven L. Caplan. Ithaca: Cornell University Press, 1982, pp. 153–96

Higginbotham, Evelyn Brooks. "African-American Women's History and the Metalanguage of Race." *Signs* 17 (Winter 1992): 251–74.

Higham, John. "The Reorientation of American Culture in the 1890's," in *The Origins of Modern Consciousness*, ed. John Weiss. Detroit: Wayne State University Press, 1965, pp. 25–48.

———. *Strangers in the Land: Patterns of American Nativism 1860–1925*. New York: Atheneum, 1963.

Hill, Mary A. *Charlotte Perkins Gilman: The Making of a Radical Feminist, 1860–1896*. Philadelphia: Temple University Press, 1980.

Hine, Robert V. *California's Utopian Colonies*. San Marino, Calif.: Huntington Library, 1953.

Hobsbawm, E. J. *The Age of Empire, 1875-1914*. New York: Vintage, 1989.

Holub, Robert C. *Reception Theory: A Critical Introduction*. London: Methuen, 1984.

Homberger, Eric. *American Writers and Radical Politics, 1900–1939: Equivocal Commitments*. London: Macmillan, 1986.

Howard, June. *Form and History in American Literary Naturalism*. Chapel Hill: University of North Carolina Press, 1985.

Hyfler, Robert. *Prophets of the Left: American Socialist Thought in the Twentieth Century*. Westport, Conn.: Greenwood Press, 1984.

Jaher, Frederic C. *Doubters and Dissenters: Cataclysmic Thought in America, 1885–1918*. New York: Free Press of Glencoe, 1964.

Jameson, Fredric. *The Political Unconscious: Narrative as a Socially Symbolic Act*. Ithaca: Cornell University Press, 1981.

Johnpoll, Bernard K. *The Impossible Dream: The Rise and Demise of the American Left*. Westport, Conn.: Greenwood Press, 1981.

Johnson, Yvonne Belanger. "The Ruskin Colony: A Paradox in the Communitarian Movement." Ph.D. diss., University of Oklahoma, 1992.

Johnston, Carolyn. *Jack London—An American Radical?* Westport, Conn.: Greenwood Press, 1984.

Jordan, William. " 'The Damnable Dilemma': African-American Accommodation and Protest During World War I." *Journal of American History* 81 (March 1995): 1562–83.

Kagan, Paul. "Portrait of a California Utopia." *California History Quarterly* 51 (Summer 1972): 131–54.

Kanter, Rosabeth Moss. *Commitment and Community: Communes and Utopias in Sociological Perspective*. Cambridge, Mass.: Harvard University Press, 1977.

Karp, Walter. *The Politics of War*. New York: Harper and Row, 1979.

Kasson, John F. *Civilizing the Machine: Technology and Republican Values in America, 1776–1900*. New York: Penguin, 1976.

Kegal, Charles H. "Ruskin's St. George in America." *American Quarterly* 9 (Winter 1957): 412–20.

Kelley, Robin D. G. " 'We Are Not What We Seem': Rethinking Black Working-Class Opposition in the Jim Crow South." *Journal of American History* 80 (June 1993): 75–112.

Kennedy, David M. *Over Here: The First World War and American Society*. New York: Oxford University Press, 1980.

Kessler, Carol Farley. *Charlotte Perkins Gilman: Her Progress Toward Utopia with Selected Writings*. Syracuse: Syracuse University Press, 1995.

———. "Consider Her Ways: The Cultural Work of Charlotte Perkins Gilman's Pragmatopian Stories, 1908–1913," in *Utopian and Science Fiction by Women: Worlds of Difference*, ed. Jane L. Donawerth and Carol A Kolmerten. Syracuse: Syracuse University Press, 1994, pp. 126–36.

Kimmel, Michael S. "The Contemporary 'Crisis' of Masculinity in Historical Perspective," in *The Making of Masculinities: The New Men's Studies*, ed. H. Brod. Boston: Allen and Unwin, 1987, pp. 121–53.

King, Richard. *The Party of Eros: Radical Social Thought and the Realm of Freedom*. Chapel Hill: University of North Carolina Press, 1972.

Kipnis, Ira *The American Socialist Movement, 1897–1912*. New York: Columbia University Press, 1952.

Kirkpatrick, Frank G. " 'Begin Again!': The Cutting Social Edge of Charlotte Perkins Gilman's Gentle Religious Optimism," in *Critical Essays on Charlotte Perkins Gilman*, ed. Joanne B. Karpinski. New York: G. K. Hall, 1992 pp. 129–43.

Kiser, Edgar, and Kriss A. Drass. "Changes in the Core of the World System and the Production of Utopian Literature in Great Britain and the United States, 1883–1975," *American Sociological Review* 52 (April 1987): 286–93.

Kloppenberg, James T. *Uncertain Victory: Social Democracy and Progressivism in European and American Thought, 1870–1920*. New York: Oxford University Press, 1986.

Kolko, Gabriel. "The Decline of American Radicalism in the Twentieth Century," in *For A New America: Essays in History and Politics from "Studies on the Left," 1959–1967*, ed. James Weinstein and David W. Eakins. New York: Vintage, 1970, pp. 197–220.

———. *The Triumph of Conservatism*. Chicago: Quadrangle Books, 1963.

Kolmerten, Carol A. "Texts and Contexts: American Women Envision Utopia, 1890–1920," in *Utopian and Science Fiction by Women: Worlds of Difference*, ed. Jane L. Donawerth and Carol A. Kolmerten. Syracuse: Syracuse University Press, 1994, pp. 107–25.

Kraditor, Aileen. *Ideas of the Woman Suffrage Movement, 1890–1920*. New York: Columbia University Press, 1965.

———. *The Radical Persuasion, 1890–1917*. Baton Rouge: Louisiana State University Press, 1981.

Kumar, Krishan. *Utopia and Anti-Utopia in Modern Times*. New York: Basil Blackwell, 1987.

LaCapra, Dominick. "Rethinking Intellectual History and Reading Texts," in *Modern European Intellectual History: Reappraisals and New Perspectives*, ed. Dominick LaCapra and Steven L. Caplan. Ithaca: Cornell University Press, 1982, pp. 47–85.

———. *Rethinking Intellectual History: Texts, Contexts, Language*. Ithaca: Cornell University Press, 1983.

Laclau, Ernesto, and Chantal Mouffe. *Hegemony and Socialist Strategy: Towards a Radical Democratic Politics*. Trans. Winston Moore and Paul Cammack. London: Verso, 1985.

LaFeber, Walter. *The New Empire: An Interpretation of American Expansion, 1860–1898*. Ithaca: Cornell University Press, 1963.

Lancaster, Jane. " 'I could easily have been an acrobat': Charlotte Perkins Gilman and the Providence Ladies' Sanitary Gymnasium 1881–1884." *ATQ* 8 (March 1994): 33–52.

Lane, Ann J. *To Herland and Beyond: The Life and Work of Charlotte Perkins Gilman.* New York: Pantheon, 1990.

Lasch, Christopher. *The New Radicalism in America, 1889–1963: The Intellectual as Social Type.* New York: Vintage, 1967.

Lasky, Melvin J. *Utopia and Revolution.* Chicago: University of Chicago Press, 1976.

Laslett, John H. M., and Seymour Martin Lipset, eds. *Failure of a Dream: Essays in the History of American Socialism.* Rev. ed. Berkeley: University of California Press, 1984.

Leach, William. "Looking Forward Together: Feminists and Edward Bellamy." *democracy* 2 (January 1982): 120–34.

———. *True Love and Perfect Union: The Feminist Reform of Sex and Society.* London: Routledge and Kegan Paul, 1981.

Lears, T. J. Jackson. "The Concept of Cultural Hegemony: Problems and Possibilities." *American Historical Review* 90 (June 1985): 567–93.

———. *No Place of Grace: Antimodernism and the Transformation of American Culture, 1880–1920.* New York: Pantheon, 1981.

Levine, Phillippa. *Victorian Feminism, 1850–1900.* London: Hutchinson, 1987.

Levitas, Ruth. *The Concept of Utopia.* Syracuse: Syracuse University Press, 1990.

———. " 'Who Holds the Hose?' Domestic Labour in the Work of Bellamy, Gilman and Morris." *Utopian Studies* 6 (1995): 65–84.

LeWarne, Charles Pierce. *Utopias on Puget Sound, 1885-1915.* Seattle: University of Washington Press, 1975.

Lewis, David Levering. *W.E.B. Du Bois: Biography of a Race, 1868–1919.* New York: Henry Holt, 1993.

Lipow, Arthur. *Authoritarian Socialism in America: Edward Bellamy and the Nationalist Movement.* Berkeley: University of California Press, 1982.

Logan, Rayford W. *The Betrayal of the Negro: From Rutherford B. Hayes to Woodrow Wilson.* New York: Collier-Macmillan, 1972.

London, Joan. *Jack London and His Times: An Unconventional Biography.* Seattle: University of Washington Press, 1968.

Lott, Eric. *Love and Theft: Blackface Minstrelsy and the American Working Class.* New York: Oxford University Press, 1993.

Macnair, Everett W. *Edward Bellamy and the Nationalist Movement, 1889–1894.* Milwaukee: Fitzgerald, 1957.

Magner, Lois N. "Darwinism and the Woman Question: The Evolving Views of Charlotte Perkins Gilman," in *Critical Essays on Charlotte Perkins Gilman,* ed. Joanne B. Karpinski. New York: G. K. Hall, 1992, pp. 115–28.

Mann, Arthur. *Yankee Reformers in the Urban Age.* New York: Harper Torchbooks, 1966.

Mann, Michael. *States, War and Capitalism: Studies in Political Sociology.* New York: Basil Blackwell, 1988.

Mannheim, Karl. *Ideology and Utopia.* Trans. Louis Wirth and Edward Shils. New York: Harvest, 1936.

Manuel, Frank E. "Towards a Psychological History of Utopias," in *Utopias and Utopian Thought,* ed. Frank E. Manuel. Boston: Houghton Mifflin, 1965, pp. 69–98.

Manuel, Frank E., and Fritzie P. Manuel. *Utopian Thought in the Western World.* Cambridge, Mass.: Belknap Press of Harvard University Press, 1979.

Marcuse, Herbert. *Eros and Civilization.* New York: Vintage, 1962.

――――. *One Dimensional Man.* Boston: Beacon Press, 1968.

Marsh, Margaret S. *Anarchist Women, 1870–1920.* Philadelphia: Temple University Press, 1981.

Martin, James J. *Men Against the State: The Expositors of Individualist Anarchism in America, 1827–1908.* DeKalb, Ill.: Adrian Allen, 1953.

Martin, Tony. *Race First: The Ideology and Organizational Struggles of Marcus Garvey and the Universal Negro Improvement Association.* Westport, Conn.: Greenwood Press, 1976.

McAdam, Doug, John D. McCarthy, and Mayer N. Zald, ed. *Comparative Perspectives on Social Movements: Political Opportunities, Mobilizing Structures, and Cultural Framings.* Cambridge: Cambridge University Press, 1996.

McCormick, Richard L. *The Party Period and Public Policy: American Politics from the Age of Jackson to the Progressive Era.* New York: Oxford University Press, 1986.

McKinley, Blaine. "Anarchist Jeremiads: American Anarchists and American History." *Journal of American Culture* 6 (Summer 1983): 75–84.

――――. " 'The Quagmires of Necessity': American Anarchists and Dilemmas of Vocation." *American Quarterly* 34 (Winter 1982): 503–23.

――――. " 'A Religion of the New Time': Anarchist Memorials to the Haymarket Martyrs, 1888–1917." *Labor History* 28 (Summer 1987): 386–400.

McWilliams, Carey. *Southern California Country: An Island on the Land.* New York: Duell, Sloan and Pearce, 1946.

Meisner, Maurice. *Marxism, Maoism, and Utopianism.* Madison: University of Wisconsin Press, 1982.

Miller, Sally M. *Race, Ethnicity, and Gender in Early Twentieth-Century American Socialism.* New York: Garland, 1996.

Mort, Frank. "Purity, Feminism, and the State: Sexuality and Moral Politics, 1880–1914," in *Crises in the British State, 1880–1930,* ed. Mary Langan and Bill Schwarz. London: Hutchison, 1985, pp. 209–25.

Morton, Marian J. *Emma Goldman and the American Left: "Nowhere at Home."* New York: Twayne, 1992.

Moses, Wilson Jeremiah. *The Golden Age of Black Nationalism, 1850–1925.* New York: Oxford University Press, 1978.

Mouffe, Chantal, ed. *Gramsci and Marxist Theory.* London: Routledge and Kegan Paul, 1979.

Moylan, Tom. *Demand the Impossible: Science Fiction and the Utopian Imagination.* New York: Methuen, 1986.

Murray, Robert. *Red Scare: A Study in National Hysteria, 1919–1920.* New York: McGraw-Hill, 1955.

Oestreicher, Richard J. *Solidarity and Fragmentation: Working People and Class Consciousness in Detroit, 1872–1900.* Urbana: University of Illinois Press, 1986.

Otten, Thomas J. "Pauline Hopkins and the Hidden Self of Race." *ELH* 59 (Spring 1992): 227–56.

Oved, Yaacov. *Two Hundred Years of American Communes.* New Brunswick, N.J.: Transaction Books, 1988.

Painter, Nell Irvin. *Standing at Armageddon: The United States, 1877–1919.* New York: W. W. Norton, 1987.

Parrington, Vernon Louis, Jr. *American Dreams: A Study of American Utopias.* Providence: Brown University Press, 1947.

Patai, Daphne, ed. *Looking Backward, 1988–1888: Essays on Edward Bellamy.* Amherst: University of Massachusetts Press, 1988.

———. "Introduction: The Double Vision of Edward Bellamy," in *Looking, Backward*, pp. 3–20.

Patterson, Martha. " 'Survival of the Best Fitted': Selling the American New Woman as Gibson Girl, 1895-1910," *ATQ* 9 (June 1995): 73–85.

Peterson, H. C., and Gilbert C. Fite. *Opponents of War, 1917–1918.* Seattle: University of Washington Press, 1964.

Peyser, Thomas Galt. "Reproducing Utopia: Charlotte Perkins Gilman and *Herland.*" *Studies in American Fiction* 20 (Spring 1992): 1–16.

Pfaelzer, Jean. "The Impact of Political Theory on Narrative Structures," in *America as Utopia*, ed. Kenneth M. Roemer. New York: Burt Franklin, 1981, pp. 117–32.

———. *The Utopian Novel in America, 1886–1896: The Politics of Form.* Pittsburgh: University of Pittsburgh Press, 1984.

Pittenger, Mark. *American Socialists and Evolutionary Thought, 1870–1920.* Madison: University of Wisconsin Press, 1993.

Plattel, Martin G. *Utopian and Critical Thinking.* Pittsburgh: Duquesne University Press, 1972.

Portrelli, Alessandro. "Jack London's Missing Revolution: Notes on *The Iron Heel.*" *Science Fiction Studies* 27 (July 1982): 180–94.

Powers, Richard Gid, ed. "Introduction," in *The Science Fiction of Jack London.* Boston: Gregg Press, 1975, pp. vii-xxiv.

Preston, William, Jr. *Aliens and Dissenters: Federal Suppression of Radicals, 1903–1933.* New York: Harper Torchbooks, 1966.

Quint, Howard H. *The Forging of American Socialism: Origins of the Modern Movement.* Columbia: University of South Carolina Press, 1953.

Ramirez, Bruno. *When Workers Fight: The Politics of Industrial Relations in the Progressive Era, 1898–1916*. Westport, Conn.: Greenwood Press, 1978.

Reich, Steven A. "Soldiers of Democracy: Black Texans and the Fight for Citizenship, 1917–1921." *Journal of American History* 82 (March 1996): 1478–1504.

Reichert, William O. *Partisans of Freedom: A Study of American Anarchism*. Bowling Green, Ohio: Bowling Green University Press, 1976.

Ricoeur, Paul. *Lectures on Ideology and Utopia*. Ed. G. Taylor. New York: Columbia University Press, 1986.

Rideout, Walter B. *The Radical Novel in the United States, 1900–1954*. New York: Hill and Wang, 1966.

Roemer, Kenneth M. "Getting 'Nowhere' Beyond Stasis: A Critique, a Method, and a Case," in *Looking Backward, 1988–1888: Essays on Edward Bellamy*, ed. Daphne Patai. Amherst: University of Massachusetts Press, 1988, pp. 126–46.

_____ . *The Obsolete Necessity: America in Utopian Writings, 1888–1900*. Kent, Ohio: Kent State University Press, 1976.

_____ , ed. *American as Utopia*. New York: Burt Franklin, 1981.

Rooney, Charles J., Jr. *Dreams and Visions: A Study of American Utopias, 1865–1917*. Westport, Conn.: Greenwood Press, 1985.

Rosemont, Franklin. "Bellamy's Radicalism Reclaimed," in *Looking Backward, 1988–1888: Essays on Edward Bellamy*, ed. Daphne Patai. Amherst: University of Massachusetts Press, 1988, pp. 147–209.

Rosenberg, Rosalind. *Beyond Separate Spheres: Intellectual Roots of Modern Feminism*. New Haven: Yale University Press, 1982.

Rosenstone, Robert A. *Romantic Revolutionary: A Biography of John Reed*. New York: Knopf, 1975.

Rosenzweig, Roy. *Eight Hours for What We Will: Workers and Leisure in an Industrial City, 1870–1920*. Cambridge: Cambridge University Press, 1983.

Ruppert, Peter. *Reader in a Strange Land: The Activity of Reading Literary Utopias*. Athens: University of Georgia Press, 1986.

Salamini, Leonardo. *The Sociology of Political Praxis: An Introduction to Gramsci's Theory*. London: Routledge and Kegan Paul, 1981.

Salerno, Salvatore. *Red November/Black November: Culture and Community in the Industrial Workers of the World*. Albany: State University of New York Press, 1989.

Salvatore, Nick. "Some Thoughts on Class and Citizenship in America in the Late Nineteenth Century," in *In the Shadow of the Statue of Liberty: Immigrants, Workers, and Citizens in the American Republic, 1880–1920*, ed. Marianne Debouzy. Urbana: University of Illinois Press, 1992, pp. 213–28.

_____ . *Eugene V. Debs: Citizen and Socialist*. Urbana: University of Illinois Press, 1982

Sargent, Lyman Tower. "The Three Faces of Utopianism Revisited." *Utopian Studies* 5 (1994): 1–37.

Saxton, Alexander. *The Indispensable Enemy: Labor and the Anti-Chinese Movement in California.* Berkeley: University of California Press, 1971.

Schaefer, Axel Rolf. "The Intellectual Dilemma of Socialist Communitarian Thought: The Communal Settlements of Equality and Burley in Washington." *Communal Societies* 10 (1990): 24–38.

Scharnhorst, Gary. *Charlotte Perkins Gilman.* Boston: Twayne, 1985.

Schottler, Peter. "Historians and Discourse Analysis." *History Workshop* 27 (Spring 1989): 37–65.

Scott, James C. *Domination and the Arts of Resistance.* New Haven: Yale University Press, 1990.

Scott, Joan Wallach. *Gender and the Politics of History.* New York: Columbia University Press, 1988.

Segal, Howard P. *Technological Utopianism in American Culture.* Chicago: University of Chicago Press, 1985.

Seretan, Glen L. *Daniel De Leon: The Odyssey of an American Marxist.* Cambridge, Mass.: Harvard University Press, 1979.

Shaffer, Ralph Edward. "Radicalism in California 1869–1929." Ph.D. diss., University of California, Berkeley 1962.

Shor, Frances. "Contradictions in the Emergence of American Socialism and the Utopian Ruskin Colony of Tennessee." *Journal of American Culture* 12 (Winter 1989): 21–27.

———. "Cultural Identity and Americanization: The Life History of a Jewish Anarchist." *biography* 9 (Fall 1986): 324–46.

———. "The Iron Heel's Marginal(ized) Utopia." *Extrapolation* 35 (Fall 1994): 211–29.

———. "The IWW and Oppositional Politics in WWI: Pushing the System Beyond Its Limits." *Radical History Review* 64 (Winter 1996): 74–94.

———. "Masculine Power and Virile Syndicalism: A Gendered Analysis of the IWW in Australia." *Labour History* 63 (November 1992): 83–99.

———. "Utopianism," in *The Encyclopedia of the American Left*, ed. Mari Jo Buhle, Paul Buhle, and Dan Georgakas. New York: Garland, 1990, pp. 810–11.

Shore, Elliott. *Talkin' Socialism: J. A. Wayland and the Role of the Press in American Radicalism, 1890–1912.* Lawrence: University Press of Kansas, 1988.

Shurter, Robert L. *The Utopian Novel in America, 1865–1900.* New York: AMS Press, 1973.

Sinclair, Andrew. *Jack: A Biography of Jack London.* London: Weidenfeld and Nicolson, 1978.

Sklar, Martin. *The United States as a Developing Country.* New York: Cambridge University Press, 1992.

Slotkin, Richard. *Gunfighter Nation: The Myth of the Frontier in Twentieth Century America.* New York: Harper Perennial, 1992.

Smith-Rosenberg, Carroll. *Disorderly Conduct: Visions of Gender in Victorian America.* New York: Oxford University Press, 1986.

Snow, David A., and Robert D. Benford. "Master Frames and the Cycle of Protest," in *Frontiers in Social Movement Theory*, ed. Aldon D. Morris and Carol McClurg Mueller. New Haven: Yale University Press, 1992, pp. 133–55.

Sonn, Richard D. *Anarchism.* New York: Twayne, 1992.

Sorrin, Gerald. *The Prophetic Minority: American Jewish Immigrant Radicals, 1880–1920.* Bloomington: Indiana University Press, 1985.

Spann, Edward K. *Brotherly Tomorrows: Movements for a Cooperative Society in America, 1820–1920.* New York: Columbia University Press, 1989.

Starr, Kevin. *Inventing the Dream: California Through the Progressive Era.* New York: Oxford University Press, 1985.

Stasz, Clarice. *American Dreamers: Charmian and Jack London.* New York: St. Martin's Press, 1988.

———. "Androgyny in the Novels of Jack London." *Western American Literature* 11 (May 1976): 121–33.

Stearns, Peter N. *Be a Man!: Males in Modern Society.* New York: Holmes and Meier, 1990.

Stein, Paul. "Jack London's *The Iron Heel*: Art as Manifesto." *Studies in American Fiction* 6 (Spring 1978): 77–92.

Stites, Richard. *Revolutionary Dreams: Utopian Vision and the Experimental Life in the Russian Revolution.* New York: Oxford University Press, 1989.

Strauss, Sylvia. "Gender, Class, and Race in Utopia," in *Looking Backward, 1988–1888: Essays on Edward Bellamy,* ed. Dapne Patai. Amherst: University of Massachusetts Press, 1988, pp. 68–90.

Suleiman, Susan R. "Introduction," in *The Reader in the Text: Essays on Audiences and Interpretation.* ed. Susan R. Suileiman and Inge Crossman. Princeton: Princeton University Press, 1980.

Sundquist, Eric. *To Wake the Nations: Race in the Making of American Literature.* Cambridge, Mass.: The Belknap Press of Harvard University Press, 1993.

Susman, Warren I. "The Persistence of Reform," in *Culture as History: The Transformation of American Society in the Twentieth Century,* ed. Warren I. Susman. New York: Basic Books, 1984, pp. 86–97.

Suvin, Darko. *Metamorphoses of Science Fiction: On the Poetics and History of a Literary Genre.* New Haven: Yale University Press, 1979.

Takaki, Ronald T. *Iron Cages: Race and Culture in Nineteenth-Century America.* Seattle: University of Washington Press, 1982.

———. *Strangers from a Different Shore: A History of Asian-Americans.* Boston: Little, Brown, 1989.

Talmon, Yonina. *Family and Community in the Kibbutz.* Cambridge, Mass: Harvard University Press, 1972.

Tax, Meredith. *The Rising of the Women: Feminist Solidarity and Class Conflict, 1880–1917* New York: Monthly Review Press, 1980.

Teitelbaum, Kenneth. *Schooling for "Good Rebels": Socialist Education for Children in the United States, 1900–1920.* Philadelphia: Temple University Press, 1993.

Thomas, John L. *Alternative America: Henry George, Edward Bellamy, Henry Demarest Lloyd and the Adversary Tradition.* Cambridge, Mass.: Belknap Press of Harvard University Press, 1983.

Thompson, Kenneth. *Beliefs and Ideology.* Chichester, England,: Ellis Horwood, 1986.

Tillich, Paul. "Critique and Justification of Utopia," in *Utopias and Utopian Thought,* ed. Frank E. Manuel. Boston: Houghton Mifflin, 1965, pp. 296–309.

Trachtenberg, Alan. *The Incorporation of America: Culture and Politics in the Gilded Age.* New York: Hill and Wang, 1982.

Turner, Frederick. *Beyond Geography: The Western Spirit Against the Wilderness.* New York Viking, 1980.

Turner, Victor. *The Anthropology of Performance.* New York: PAJ Publications, 1986.

——— . *Dramas, Fields, and Metaphors: Symbolic Interaction in Human Society.* Ithaca, N.Y.: Cornell University Press, 1974.

Tuttle, William. *Race Riot: Chicago in the Red Summer of 1919.* New York: Atheneum, 1970.

Tuveson, Ernest L. *Redeemer Nation: The Idea of America's Millennial Role.* Chicago: University of Chicago Press, 1968.

Tyler Robert L. *Rebels of the Woods: The IWW in the Pacific Northwest.* Eugene: University of Oregon Press, 1967.

Van Deburg, William L. *New Day in Babylon: The Black Power Movement and American Culture 1965–1975.* Chicago: University of Chicago Press, 1992.

Veysey, Laurence. *The Communal Experience: Anarchist and Mystical Communities in Twentieth Century America.* Chicago: University of Chicago Press, 1973.

Walker, Robert H. *Reform in America: The Continuing Frontier.* Lexington: University Press of Kentucky, 1985.

Watson, Carole McAlpine. *Prologue: The Novels of Black American Women, 1891–1965.* Westport, Conn.: Greenwood Press, 1985.

Watson, Charles N., Jr. *The Novels of Jack London: A Reappraisal.* Madison: University of Wisconsin Press, 1983.

Weinstein, James. *The Decline of Socialism in America, 1912–1925.* New York: Monthly Review Press, 1967.

Wertheim, Arthur Frank. *The New York Little Renaissance: Iconoclasm, Modernism, and Nationalism in American Culture, 1908–1917.* New York: New York University Press, 1976.

Wexler, Alice. *Emma Goldman: An Intimate Life.* New York: Pantheon Books, 1984.

White, Hayden. *The Content of the Form: Narrative Discourse and Historical Representation.* Baltimore: Johns Hopkins University Press, 1987.

White, R. C., and C. H. Hopkins. *The Social Gospel: Religion and Reform in Changing America.* Philadelphia: Temple University Press, 1976.

White, Ronald C., Jr. *Liberty and Justice for All: Racial Reform and the Social Gospel.* New York: Harper and Row, 1990.

Widmer, Kingsley. "Thinking About Libertarian Good Places: Some Notes on Anarchism and Utopia." *Social Anarchism* 3 (1983): 3–14.

Wiebe, Robert H. *The Search for Order, 1877–1920.* New York: Hill and Wang, 1967.

Williams, Gwyn A. "The Concept of 'Egemonia' in the Thought of Antonio Gramsci: Some Notes and Interpretation." *Journal of the History of Ideas* 21 (October–December 1960): 586–99.

Williams, Raymond. *Marxism and Literature.* Oxford: Oxford University Press, 1977.

Williamson, Joel. *The Crucible of Race: Black-White Relations in the American South Since Emancipation.* New York: Oxford University Press, 1984.

_____ . *A Rage for Order: Black-White Relations in the American South Since Emancipation.* New York: Oxford University Press, 1986.

Winkler, Barbara Scott. "Victorian Daughters: The Lives and Feminism of Charlotte Perkins Gilman and Olive Schreiner," in *Critical Essays on Charlotte Perkins Gilman,.* ed. Joanne B. Karpinski. New York: G. K. Hall, 1992, pp. 173–83.

Winters, Donald E., Jr. *The Soul of the Wobblies: The IWW, Religion, and American Culture in the Progressive Era, 1905–1917.* Westport, Conn.: Greenwood Press, 1985.

Woloch, Nancy. *Women and the American Experience,* 2d ed. New York: McGraw-Hill, 1994.

Woodcock, George. *Anarchism: A History of Libertarian Ideas and Movements.* Cleveland: Meridian, 1970.

Index

About the Author

FRANCIS ROBERT SHOR is Associate Professor in the Interdisciplinary Studies Program at Wayne State University.

ISBN 0-313-30379-7

90000>

EAN

9 780313 303791

HARDCOVER BAR CODE